(Continued)

Young Children Continue to Reinvent Arithmetic
— 3rd Grade —

IMPLICATIONS OF PIAGET'S THEORY

Constance Kamii
with Sally Jones Livingston

TEACHERS
COLLEGE
PRESS

Teachers College, Columbia University
New York and London

Published by Teachers College Press, 1234 Amsterdam Avenue
New York, NY 10027

Copyright © 1994 by Teachers College, Columbia University

Figure 6.3 from *Look Into the Facts: Multiplication and Division,* by Carol A. Thornton & Cathy Noxon is reprinted by permission of the publisher, Creative Publications, Inc, of Palo Alto, California. Copyright © 1977 by Carol A. Thornton & Cathy Noxon.

Quotations from "The Development of Children's Place-Value Numeration Concepts in Grades Two through Five" by Sharon H. Ross, a paper presented at the annual meeting of the American Educational Research Association, San Francisco, in April 1986, are reprinted by permission of the author. ERIC Documentary Reproduction Service No. ED 273 482.

Algorithms from "Summing It All Up: Pre-1900 Algorithms" by Eleanor S. Pearson, an article appearing in *Arithmetic Teacher, 33* (March, 1986), are reprinted by permission of the publisher, National Council of Teachers of Mathematics, Reston, Virginia.

Figures 9.1 and 9.3 are adapted from Figures 6.2 and 6.3 of the chapter "Thinking Strategies: Teaching Arithmetic through Problem Solving" by Paul Cobb and Graceann Merkel in *New Directions for Elementary School Mathematics* (1989 NCTM Yearbook), edited by Paul R. Trafton and are adapted and reprinted by permission of the publisher, National Council of Teachers of Mathematics, Reston, Virginia.

Quotations from Jean Piaget, *The Moral Judgment of the Child,* translated by Marjorie Gabain. New York: The Free Press 1965. Reprinted with permission of the publisher.

Quotations from Jean Piaget, *The Psychology of Intelligence* (1963) are reprinted by permission of the publisher. Paterson, NJ: Littlefield, Adams, & Co.

Quotations from *La Formation des Raisonnements Récurrentiels* by P. Gréco, B. Inhelder, B. Matalon, and J. Piaget, Copyright © 1963 by P. Gréco et al., are translated and reprinted by permission of the publisher, Presses Universitaire de France, Paris, France.

Quotations from *A Survey of Mathematics: Elementary Concepts and Their Historical Development,* by Vivian Shaw Groza, Copyright © 1968 by Vivian Shaw Groza, are reprinted by permission of the author, and of the publisher, Holt, Rinehart, and Winston, Inc., Fort Worth, Texas.

Excerpts of historical mathematical methods of different ethnic-geographic groups are adapted from *History of Mathematics, Vol II,* by David Eugene Smith, Copyright © 1925, by D. E. Smith, published by Ginn and Company. Used by permission of Silver Burdett Ginn, Inc.

Library of Congress Cataloging-in-Publication Data

Kamii, Constance.
    Young children continue to reinvent arithmetic—3rd grade : implications of Piaget's theory / Constance Kamii ; with Sally Jones Livingston.
    p.   cm.
    Includes bibliographical references and index.
    ISBN 0-8077-3324-5.—ISBN 0-8077-3323-7 (pbk.)
    1. Arithmetic—Study and teaching (Elementary)   2. Number concept—Study and teaching (Elementary)   3. Piaget, Jean, 1896–   I. Jones Livingston, Sally.   II. Title.
QA135.5K1855   1994
372.7'2044—dc20   93-43026

Printed on acid-free paper   **168576**

Manufactured in the United States of America

98 97 96 95 94   8 7 6 5 4 3 2 1

AAY-2161

Contents

Introduction

The term *construct* was seldom heard when *Young Children Continue to Reinvent Arithmetic, 2nd Grade* (Kamii, 1989a) was written, but it has suddenly become popular in recent years. This quick acceptance is both good news and bad news. The good news is that this is evidence of a new openness to change. However, the bad news is that many people are saying "construct" without understanding that constructivism is a theory about how knowledge is elaborated both by the human species over many centuries and by each child.

We believe that the constructivism of Jean Piaget explains the nature of logico-mathematical knowledge better than any other theory. It scientifically describes the origin of logico-mathematical knowledge in infancy as can be seen in *The Origins of Intelligence in Children* (Piaget, 1936/1952), *The Construction of Reality in the Child* (Piaget, 1937/1954), and *Play, Dreams, and Imitation in Childhood* (Piaget, 1945/1962). These books were the true beginning of the psychological part of Piaget's theory, but Piaget never departed from his main epistemological aim of explaining humanity's construction of knowledge in general that led him to a particular view of the history of science. His 60 years of research is documented in countless books and has been replicated all over the world. Although the details about ages and sequence have been questioned, constructivism remains the most coherent account of how knowledge, especially logico-mathematical knowledge, develops in children.

Piaget's constructivism emphasizes that logico-mathematical reasoning is necessary in many domains of knowledge besides logic and mathematics. More important, it denies that logico-mathematical knowledge can simply be transmitted to the child like a neatly packaged parcel; it holds that this knowledge has to be constructed by children themselves—but obviously in interaction with and with the help of educators and others in their environment. In this sense, constructivism goes against traditional educational practice.

Going from an epistemological and psychological theory to a theory of education in mathematics demands various arduous steps, since it is not possible to "apply" Piaget's theory directly to education. Over the years, I (CK) have progressed toward such a theory about education, and this book is the result of much thinking and discussion with teachers, especially Sally Livingston at Hall-Kent Elementary School near Birmingham, Alabama. The book is also the result of experimentation and observation of what children actually *do* in dealing with mathematical problems. By interpreting children's thinking in terms of deep, constructivist principles, Sally and I combined the perspectives of a teacher and a researcher in conceptualizing goals and activities for children.

I hope the reader will find in this book what I intended to convey—a scientific approach to a nascent theory of math education that combines meticulous observation of what children actually *do* in solving math problems with a theoretical interpretation of their thinking. As Piaget stated about his own work, meticulous observation combined with a search for deep, general principles is what led him to his theory about knowledge. He considered this combination to be the basis of all truly scientific endeavors.

This book follows three earlier volumes about kindergarten and the first two grades entitled, respectively, *Number in Preschool and Kindergarten* (Kamii, 1982), *Young Children Reinvent Arithmetic* (Kamii, 1985), and *Young Children Continue to Reinvent Arithmetic, 2nd Grade* (Kamii, 1989a). A videotape entitled *Double-Column Addition: A Teacher Uses Piaget's Theory* (Kamii, 1989b) accompanies the book on second grade. *Multiplication of Two-Digit Numbers* (Kamii, 1990a) and *Multidigit Division* (Kamii, 1990b) are two other videotapes about arithmetic in second and third grade.

The present volume is the result of collaboration with Sally Livingston since 1987 and is divided into four parts. The first part gives the theoretical foundations about the nature of logico-mathematical knowledge, the process of construction that can be seen in the history of computational techniques, evidence about the harmful effects of conventional algorithms, and the importance of social interaction in Piaget's theory.

Part II, which is about goals and objectives for third-grade arithmetic, is important because a theory that revolutionizes our understanding of how human beings acquire knowledge drastically changes what we think schools should try to do. Educators have long been trying to transmit knowledge to children from the outside. What reform needs is a focus inside the child to maximize the process of construction from within.

Part III describes classroom activities and consists of chapters on problem solving, group games, and other activities. The principles of teaching are given in Part IV in answer to such frequently asked questions as: How do you approach multidigit multiplication? What do you say to children when you work with them individually? How do you assess children's thinking in problem solving?

The last chapter is about the evaluation of constructivist teaching, and we hope it will be read by administrators, parents, and the public. Standardized achievement tests "measure" only the extent to which children have mastered superficial, narrow, and behavioristic objectives. The only thing that counts in this psychometric tradition is the correctness of the answers. Chapter 13 documents what we found out by probing below the surface of correct answers. By posing a variety of questions, we documented that children who had had three years of constructivist math could reason far better than traditionally instructed children.

Although specific names of children are mentioned in this book, these are all pseudonyms used to protect the students' privacy. While many sections are written with "I (CK)" or "I (SL)" to make the reader's comprehension easier, the opinions expressed are shared by both of us with conviction.

At a time when many principals and teachers feel caught between the desire for reform and "accountability" as defined by achievement test scores, it behooves us to note the role of autonomy in other reform movements. Martin Luther King would not have accomplished anything merely by obeying the old laws discriminating against African-Americans. Likewise, the American Revolution was not won by people obedient to British laws. We hope that the idea of autonomy, which was the aim of education for Piaget (as discussed in Chapter 5), will inspire more teachers and principals to lead the public toward true education reform. The time has come for educators to lead education on the basis of a new scientific theory, rather than allowing ourselves to be mandated into one "quick fix" after another.

Constance Kamii

Acknowledgments

The person without whom this book could not have been written is Donald Eugene (Gene) Burgess, principal of Hall-Kent Elementary School in Homewood, Alabama, until his retirement in 1990. It was very difficult in 1984 to find a public school willing to try what had never been done before—basing mathematics education on Piaget's theory. Gene Burgess was informed enough and autonomous enough to commit mathematics instruction in his school to constructivism. Jack Allison, the principal who succeeded him, has also been very supportive, and we very much appreciate his enthusiasm.

From the standpoint of Piaget's theory, the person who has guided and encouraged the senior author since 1965 is Hermina Sinclair. She observed in our classrooms, read the manuscript of this book, and generously offered her unusual insights and suggestions.

Faye Clark helped collect many of the data reported in Chapters 3 and 13 and critically read the manuscript of this book while she was a graduate assistant at the University of Alabama at Birmingham. We are grateful to her for her dedication and readiness always to help in countless other ways.

Two teachers especially helped us in thinking through the problems involved in children's invention of multidigit multiplication. They are Ann Dominick and Philip Westbrook of Shades Cahaba Elementary School in Homewood, Alabama. Their willingness to read Chapters 10 and 12 critically, to discuss our questions, to let us observe in their classrooms, and to let us interview their children clarified and enriched our ideas about what we were doing with our third graders.

We also express appreciation to Cheryl Ingram, a fourth-grade teacher at Hall-Kent School. After 10 years of teaching algorithms, Cheryl decided not to teach them any more. Without her willingness to change and to let us observe almost daily in her classroom, we would not have known how hard it is to undo the damage caused by algorithms.

Special thanks go to two third-grade teachers who let their classes serve as a comparison group. In order to evaluate our program, we needed to compare our children's performance with that of other third graders who had had three years of traditional instruction. The two teachers knew that serving as a comparison group was a thankless task but were most generous in helping us with data collection. If we had not promised to keep them and their school anonymous, we would publicly address our deep appreciation to them.

Mel Knight, of the University of Alabama at Birmingham, helped us enormously in a unique way. Without his assistance, we would not have had the videotape used in writing Chapter 11 and the tapes widely distributed by Teachers College Press (Kamii, 1989b, 1990a, 1990b). Since our research was conducted without external funding, his offer to videotape gratuitously was most welcome.

Finally, we are grateful to the teachers of the Constructivist Math Network, a group of 18 teachers in the Birmingham area who became so convinced of the desirability of constructivist teaching that they organized themselves to inform teachers in Alabama and other states. They have been conducting an annual constructivist math conference every summer since 1991, and their names are given below. We thank them for voluntarily replicating our research and confirming our conclusions. They were autonomous enough to abandon the textbook, and continue to teach in ways that are better for children than the textbook and workbook approach. Their support encourages our scientific efforts and gives us faith in the future of reform. The Constructivist Math Network consists of: Leasha Abercrombie, Teresa Ballard, Toni Brown, Cora Causey, Ann Dominick, Alicia Fox, Cheryl Ingram, Linda Joseph, Lynn Kirkland, Linda Klopack, Angela Lewis, Sally Jones Livingston, Leigh Martin, Tami Puchta, Vasha Rosenblum, Lori St. Clair, Madeline Thompson, and Philip Westbrook.

Young Children Continue to Reinvent Arithmetic
— 3rd Grade —

IMPLICATIONS OF PIAGET'S THEORY

Part I

THEORETICAL
FOUNDATIONS

CHAPTER 1

The Nature of Logico-Mathematical Knowledge

Why do we want children to reinvent arithmetic when we can simply tell or show them how to add, subtract, multiply, and divide? Our answer to this question is presented in the first three chapters of this book. In the present chapter, we discuss the nature of logico-mathematical knowledge to show that children acquire it by *constructing* (making) it from the inside, in interaction with the environment, not by *internalizing* it from the outside through social transmission.

We begin by clarifying how children acquire concepts of small numbers. We then describe what children do in Piaget's class-inclusion task to explain the hierarchical thinking involved in the construction of number concepts as well as of the base-ten system. The chapter ends with a task requiring multiplicative thinking showing that children construct multiplication, too, through their own mental actions.

THE ORIGIN OF NUMBER CONCEPTS

The best way to explain how children acquire number concepts is with a task devised by Inhelder and Piaget (1963). Two identical glasses and 30 to 50 wooden beads (or chips, beans, or other objects) are used in a simplified version of this task. The child is given one of the glasses, and the researcher takes the other glass. The adult then asks the child to drop a bead into his glass each time she drops one into hers. After about five beads have been dropped into each glass with one-to-one correspondence, the adult says, "Let's stop now, and you watch what I am going to do." The researcher then drops one bead into her glass and says to the child, "Let's get going again." Each person drops about five more beads into his or her glass with one-to-one correspondence, until the adult says, "Let's stop."

The following is what has happened so far:

Adult: $1 + 1 + 1 + 1 + 1 + 1 + 1 + 1 + 1 + 1 + 1$
Child: $1 + 1 + 1 + 1 + 1 \quad\quad + 1 + 1 + 1 + 1 + 1$

The adult then asks, "Do you and I have the same number (or amount), or do *you* have more, or do *I* have more?"

Four-year-olds usually reply that the two glasses have the same amount. When the interviewer goes on to ask, "How do you know we have the same amount?" the children explain, "Because I can see that we both have the same (amount)." Some 4-year-olds, however, reply that *they* have more, and when we ask them how they know that they have more, their explanation consists of only one word: "Because."

The adult continues and asks, "Do you remember how we dropped the beads?" and 4-year-olds usually give all the empirical, or observable, facts correctly: "Then you told me to stop, and you put one in your glass. Only *you* put one in your glass, and I watched 'cause you told me to wait. Then we got going again." In other words, 4-year-olds remember all the empirical facts correctly and base their judgment of equality on the empirical appearance of the two quantities.

By age 5 or 6, however, most children deduce logically that the experimenter has one more. When we ask these children how they know that the adult has one more, they invoke exactly the same empirical facts as the 4-year-olds.

If a child says that the adult's glass has one more bead, the researcher poses the next question: "If we continued to drop beads all day (or all night) in the same way (with one-to-one correspondence), do you think you and I will have the same number at the end, or will *you* have more, or will *I* have more?" Five- and 6-year-olds divide themselves into two groups at this point. Some answer in the way that adults would, that there will *always* be one more in the researcher's glass. The others make empirical statements, such as "I don't know because we haven't done it yet" or "You don't have enough beads to keep going all day."

The preceding task is one of the countless Piagetian experiments that demonstrate the difference between empirical knowledge and logico-mathematical knowledge. The difference can best be clarified by reviewing the distinction Piaget (1950a, 1950b, 1950c, 1967/1971) made among three kinds of knowledge according to their ultimate sources and modes of structuring: physical, logico-mathematical, and social (conventional) knowledge.

Three Kinds of Knowledge

Physical knowledge is knowledge of objects in external reality. The color and weight of a bead are examples of physical properties that are *in* objects in external reality and can be known empirically by observation. The knowledge that a bead will fall into the glass when we let go of it is also an example of physical knowledge.

Logico-mathematical knowledge, on the other hand, consists of *relationships* created by each individual. For instance, when we are presented with a red bead and a blue one and think that they are "different," this difference is an example of logico-mathematical knowledge. The beads are indeed observable, but the *difference* between them is not. The difference is a *relationship* created mentally by each individual who puts the two objects into this relationship. The difference is neither *in* the red bead nor *in* the blue one, and if a person did not put the objects into this relationship, the difference would not exist for him or her.

Other examples of relationships the individual can create between the same beads are "similar," "the same in weight," and "two." It is just as correct to say that the red and blue beads are similar as it is to say that they are different. The relationship an individual puts the objects into is up to that individual. From one point of view the two beads are different, and from another point of view they are similar. If the individual wants to compare the weight of the two beads, he or she is likely to say that the objects are "the same" (in weight). If, on the other hand, the individual wants to think about the objects numerically, he or she will say that there are "two." The two beads are observable, but the "two-ness" is not. Number is a relationship created mentally by each individual.°

Physical knowledge is thus empirical knowledge that has its source partly in objects. (Our reason for saying "partly" is clarified in the next paragraph.) Logico-mathematical knowledge, on the other hand, is not empirical knowledge, as its source is in each individual's mind. Relationships must be created by each individual because relationships such as "different," "same," and "two" do not exist in the observable, external world. Children go on to elaborate their logico-mathematical knowledge by making more complex relationships with the simple relationships they created before.

Our reason for saying that the source of physical knowledge is only *partly* in objects is that a logico-mathematical framework is necessary even to "read" the color of an object off reality. To notice a red chip as being red, for example, we have to have a classificatory framework that enables us to think about colors. We also have to categorize "red" in opposition to "all the other colors." Physical and logico-mathematical knowledge are thus inextricably related in the psychological reality of the young child. The relationship "different" could not be made

---

°We hasten to say that "two" is not a good number to choose to illustrate the logico-mathematical nature of number because it is a perceptual number. Piaget referred to small numbers up to four or five as "perceptual numbers" because small collections of objects, such as "oo" and "ooo," can easily be distinguished at a glance, perceptually. When seven or more objects (ooooooo and ooooooo, for example) are presented, however, it is impossible to distinguish them by perception alone.

The number "two" can also be a logico-mathematical number for an adult who has constructed the system of logico-mathematical numbers. We chose the number "two" in this example in spite of the problem of perceptual numbers because, with two beads, we could illustrate other simple relationships such as "different," "similar," and "the same in weight."

if all the objects in the world were identical. It would also be impossible to "read" the physical properties of objects if we did not have a logico-mathematical framework.

The ultimate source of *social knowledge,* the third kind of knowledge, is conventions worked out by people. Examples of social knowledge are the fact that Halloween is October 31, that a tree is called "tree," and that tables were not made to stand on. The main characteristic of social knowledge is that it is largely arbitrary in nature. The fact that a tree is called "tree" is an example of the arbitrariness of social knowledge. In another language, the same object is called by another name, since there is no physical or logical relationship between an object and its name. It follows that, for the child's acquisition of social knowledge, input from people is indispensable. This kind of knowledge must be transmitted from one person or generation to the next.

Just as a logico-mathematical framework is necessary for the construction of physical knowledge, children cannot build social knowledge without a logico-mathematical framework. For example, we could not understand the statement about Halloween without categorizing "Halloween" in opposition to "all the other days of the year."

One-to-One Correspondence and the Three Kinds of Knowledge

To return to the task with beads and glasses, the knowledge that the beads stay in the glasses as separate entities (rather than becoming one continuous quantity like drops of water) is an example of empirical, physical knowledge. On the other hand, words such as *more* and *one, two, three,* and *four,* which children often use, belong to social knowledge. However, the numerical thinking underlying these words belongs to logico-mathematical knowledge.

The distinction among the three kinds of knowledge is essential to explain why most 4-year-olds say that the two glasses have the same quantity. When children cannot yet make the logico-mathematical relationships of number in their heads, all they can get from the experiment is physical, empirical knowledge. This is why 4-year-olds can remember the empirical fact of having dropped all the beads except one with one-to-one correspondence. This one-to-one correspondence, however, is only an observable happening for 4-year-olds, and they judge the quantity of beads by what they can see. This is why they say that the two glasses have the same amount and justify this judgment by saying, "I can *see* that they have the same amount."

By age 5 or 6, however, most children have become able to make the logico-mathematical relationship of one-to-one correspondence and can deduce from the same empirical facts that the experimenter has one more bead. The system of numerical relationships takes many years to construct, however, and the child who has number concepts up to 10 or 15 does not necessarily have concepts of

50, 100, or more. This is why many 5- and 6-year-olds who can judge that the experimenter has one more bead fall back on empirical knowledge when asked what would happen if the one-to-one correspondence were continued a long time. Later, when they have constructed a larger system of numbers, they become able to deduce that there will *always* be one more in the experimenter's glass, no matter how many beads are dropped with one-to-one correspondence.

The main mechanism that children use to construct relationships is abstraction. Piaget described the kinds of abstraction children engage in when they construct number concepts. The following discussion of abstraction is an elaboration of Piaget's theory of number.

Abstraction

There are two kinds of abstraction according to Piaget (1967/1971). One is empirical (or simple) abstraction, and the other is constructive (or reflecting) abstraction.

In *empirical* abstraction, the child focuses on a certain property of the object and ignores the others. For example, when children abstract the color of a bead, they focus on its color and ignore the other properties such as the weight and the material of which the bead is made.

Constructive abstraction, by contrast, involves the child's making relationships between and among objects. Relationships, as stated earlier, do not have an existence in external reality. The similarity or difference between two beads exists only in the minds of those who create it mentally.

The reader may have noted that empirical abstraction is involved in the child's acquisition of physical knowledge, while constructive abstraction is involved in the acquisition of logico-mathematical knowledge. (Piaget went on to say, however, that, in the psychological reality of the child, one kind of abstraction cannot take place without the other. For example, the child could not construct the relationship "different" if all the objects in the world were identical.)

Traditional math educators often say that a number is a property of a set and that children acquire number concepts by (empirically) abstracting this property from sets of objects. This is a serious misconception. This misconception can perhaps be corrected when we further understand that number concepts are made by each child through the synthesis of two kinds of relationships— order and hierarchical inclusion (Gréco, Grize, Papert, & Piaget, 1960).

Order. All teachers of young children have seen the common tendency among 4-year-olds to count objects while skipping some and counting others more than once. When given eight objects, for example, a child who can recite "One, two, three, four . . ." correctly up to thirty may end up claiming that there are thirty by counting the same objects over and over. This behavior shows that the child

FIGURE 1.1 The relationships of order (a) and hierarchical inclusion (c).

(a)

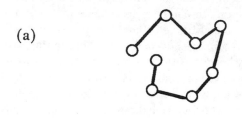

"Eight"

(b)

"Eight"

(c)

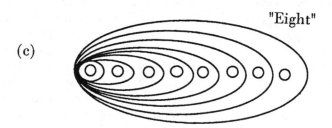

does not feel the logical necessity of putting the objects into an ordered relationship to make sure he or she does not skip any or count the same one(s) more than once.

The only way we can be sure of not overlooking any or counting the same object(s) more than once is by putting them in a relationship of order. However, we do not have to move the objects or put them in a line to order them. What is important is that we order the objects *mentally,* as shown with a randomly arranged set in Figure 1.1a.

Hierarchical Inclusion. If the child puts the objects into a relationship of order, he or she does not necessarily quantify the collection. For example, after
counting eight objects ordered in a line as shown in Figure 1.1b, 4-year-olds
usually say that there are eight. If we then ask them to show eight, they sometimes point to the last one (the eighth object as indicated in Figure 1.1b). This
behavior demonstrates that, for this child, the words *one, two, three,* and so on
are names of individual elements in a series, like *January, February,* and *March.*
When asked how many there are, therefore, the child says what amounts to
August. For this child, *eight* stands for the last element in the series, not for the
entire group.

To quantify the collection numerically, the child must put the objects into a
relationship of hierarchical inclusion. This relationship, shown in Figure 1.1c,
means that the child mentally includes "one" in "two," "two" in "three," "three"
in "four," and so on. When presented with eight objects, the child can quantify
the collection numerically only if he or she can put all the objects into a single
relationship, thus synthesizing order and hierarchical inclusion.

Young children's reactions to the class-inclusion task help us understand how
difficult it is to construct the hierarchical structure. We therefore now turn to
this task.

CLASS INCLUSION

In the class-inclusion task (Inhelder & Piaget, 1959/1964), the child is presented with several objects, such as six tulips and two roses of the same size
made of plastic. He or she is asked, "What do you see?" so that the examiner
can use words from the child's vocabulary. The child is then asked to show "*all*
the flowers," "*all* the tulips," and "*all* the roses" with the words he or she used
(such as "the red flowers"). Only after ascertaining the child's understanding of
these words does the adult ask the following class-inclusion question: "Are there
more tulips or more flowers?"

Four-year-olds typically answer "More tulips," whereupon the adult asks
"Than what?" Four-year-olds' answer is "Than roses." In other words, the question the examiner asks is "Are there more tulips or more flowers?" but the question young children "hear" is "Are there more tulips or more roses?"

Young children hear a question that is different from the one the adult asked
because once they mentally cut the whole (flowers) into two parts (tulips and
roses), the only thing they can think about is the two parts. For them, at that
moment, the whole no longer exists. They can think about the whole, but not
when they are thinking about the parts. In order to compare the whole with a
part, the child has to perform two opposite mental actions *simultaneously—*

cutting the whole into two parts and putting the parts back together into a whole. This is precisely what 4-year-olds cannot do.

By 7 to 8 years of age, however, most children's thought becomes mobile enough to be reversible. Reversibility refers to the ability to perform opposite mental actions *simultaneously*—in this case, separating the whole into two parts and reuniting the parts into a whole. In physical, material action, it is not possible to do two opposite things simultaneously. In our heads, however, this is possible when thought has become reversible. Only when he or she can mentally reunite the parts can a child "see" that there are more flowers than tulips.

Piaget thus explained the making of a hierarchical structure by the increasing mobility of children's thought. When children put all kinds of contents into all kinds of relationships, their thought becomes more mobile. One of the results of this increasing mobility is the ability to make class-inclusion relationships. Another is the construction of the structure of number shown in Figure 1.1c.

The class-inclusion task demonstrates how different logico-mathematical knowledge is from empirical knowledge. Four-year-olds can think about all the flowers or about the tulips and roses successively, but they cannot think about all the flowers at the same time that they are thinking about tulips or roses. The *simultaneous* coordination of relationships is the essence of logico-mathematical knowledge.

The class-inclusion task also demonstrates that language is not the source of logico-mathematical knowledge. The proof is that the examiner ascertains the child's knowledge of words before asking the crucial question about class inclusion. Language is a useful tool in logical reasoning, but it is not the source of logico-mathematical knowledge.

The class-inclusion task was discussed partly to explain how difficult hierarchical inclusion is in children's construction of number concepts. The concept "eight," for example, is an eight-story structure, and the child has to include one in two, two in three, three in four, and so on, all the way to eight, *simultaneously*. The class-inclusion task was discussed also to show how difficult it is for children to construct the base-ten system. Below is a discussion of the hierarchical structure involved in this system.

THE BASE-TEN SYSTEM

The system of ones, which we have been discussing so far, is represented in Figure 1.2a. When most first graders say "one hundred twelve," they are thinking about one hundred twelve *ones* as indicated by this figure. Note that the circles in Figure 1.2a stand not for objects in the external world but for number concepts that exist *in children's heads*.

Figure 1.2 The difference between the system only of ones (a and d) and hierarchical systems with higher-order ones (b and c).

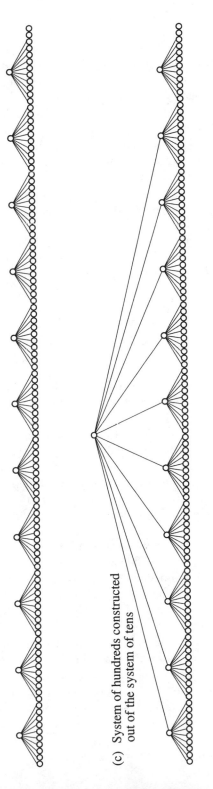

(a) System of ones

(b) System of tens constructed out of the system of ones

(c) System of hundreds constructed out of the system of tens

(d) Partitioning the system of ones (base-ten blocks)

Figure 1.2b shows that the child has constructed a system of tens *out of the system of ones*. He or she does this by creating one unit of ten out of 10 ones and then coordinating relationships of order and hierarchical inclusion with the new, higher-order units. As Figure 1.2b indicates, the child can now think about one ten and ten ones at the same time, and can, therefore, think about eleven tens and two ones, as well as about one hundred twelve ones, *simultaneously*.

Figure 1.2c shows that the child has begun to construct a system of hundreds *out of the systems of ones and of tens*. The new unit at this level is a unit of one hundred. The child can now think about one hundred, one ten, and two ones, as well as about eleven tens and two ones, and about one hundred twelve ones, *simultaneously*.

This hierarchical conceptualization is very different from the assumptions on which traditional teaching is based (see Figure 1.2d). According to this traditional way of teaching with base-ten blocks and/or straws with rubberbands around them, "tens" are only ones that are partitioned into groups of ten.

In the hierarchical conception, the child does not lose the system of ones when he or she constructs the system of tens. Likewise, the child does not lose the systems of tens and of ones when he or she constructs the system of hundreds. According to Piaget's theory, in the logico-mathematical realm, previously constructed structures remain intact and unchanged when a higher-order structure is constructed. Instead of disappearing, the previously constructed structure becomes integrated in the higher-order structure that is constructed later.

The traditional way of teaching with base-ten blocks and/or straws bunched together with rubberbands is unfortunate for another reason. It assumes that ideas such as "one ten" and "one hundred" can be acquired by empirical abstraction from objects in the external world. Logico-mathematical knowledge is constructed by constructive (reflecting) abstraction on previously constructed relationships. "One ten" is a construction *out of the system of ones* that is in the child's head.

The following two experiments by Ross (1986, 1990) demonstrate how we can tell whether or not a child has constructed both the system of tens *and* the system of ones that function *simultaneously*. [The second study (Ross, 1990) confirmed the earlier findings with even more convincing evidence, but only the 1986 data are reported below in the interest of brevity.]

The subjects in Ross's study consisted of 60 children, 15 each in grades 2 through 5. Her sampling was unusual in that she randomly selected children from 33 classrooms "from the grade level enrollment lists of five elementary schools in Butte County, California. . . . The schools were selected to represent urban and rural communities, public and private funding, and diversity with respect to the mathematics textbook series used, school size, and social class"

TABLE 1.1 Building 52 with base-ten blocks (by number of children; $n = 15$ for each grade)

	Level of performance		
Grade	1	2	3
2	5	1	9
3	0	3	12
4	1	1	13
5	0	1	14
Total	6	6	48

(Ross, 1986, p. 3). In individual interviews, she used base-ten blocks in one task and lima beans in the other.

Ross's Experiment Using Base-Ten Blocks

In the first part of the task, Ross studied children's strategies for making 52. She presented each child with base-ten blocks representing ones (1 cm × 1 cm × 1 cm), tens (1 cm × 1 cm × 10 cm), and hundreds (1 cm × 10 cm × 10 cm) and asked him or her to build 52 with the blocks. She provided the child with only 40 unit-blocks (1 cm × 1 cm × 1 cm) so that it would be impossible to make 52 without using some of the ten-blocks (1 cm × 1 cm × 10 cm). If the child did not understand the task, various restatements were offered, such as "so they will count up to 52." After the child indicated that he or she was finished, the interviewer asked, "How do you know that is 52?"

The data about the performance of the children by grade are summarized in Table 1.1. Ross identified the following three levels of performance:

Level 1: The child was unsuccessful in making 52.
Level 2: The child was successful, but usually began by attempting to use only the unit-blocks. After discovering that the quantity available was insufficient, he or she eventually solved the problem by using some of the ten-blocks.
Level 3: The child quickly chose five ten-blocks and two unit-blocks to represent 52.

It can be observed in Table 1.1 that this task was easy for most of the children except for those in second grade. The second part of the task proved to be much harder.

In the second part of the task, the children who succeeded in producing a

TABLE 1.2 Building 52 with base-ten blocks
in two ways (by number of children; $n=15$ for
each grade)

	Level of performance			
Grade	0	1	2	3
2	4	5	4	2
3	0	2	5	8
4	0	1	5	9
5	0	0	4	11
Total	4	8	18	30

representation of 52 were asked if they could find another way to represent 52. The three levels of performance Ross identified were the following, which are summarized in Table 1.2 (Level 0 is obviously an even lower level of performance than level 1 in this table):

Level 1: The child was unsuccessful.

Level 2: The child first attempted to use only unit-blocks. Upon discovering that there were not enough unit-blocks, he or she eventually succeeded with or without a prompt from the interviewer (such as "Could you use some of these blocks?").

Level 3: The child quickly produced a different representation. Some traded a ten-block for ten unit-blocks, and others counted up from 40 (40, 41, 42, . . .).

It can be seen in Table 1.2 that only half of all the children were at level 3. As can be seen in the column for level 3, this task turned out to be difficult not only for second and third graders but also for fourth graders. Only 2 (13%), 8 (53%), and 9 (60%) of the children in grades 2, 3, and 4, respectively, demonstrated the *simultaneous* functioning of two systems (the system of ones *and* the system of tens). The children at level 2 approached the task with the system of ones only.

For those who feel that some of the children may not have been familiar with base-ten blocks, we present findings from another task devised by Ross.

Ross's Experiment Using Lima Beans

In individual interviews, Ross presented each of the same children with 48 lima beans and nine 1-ounce plastic cups. She first asked the child to put 10

TABLE 1.3 Counting 48 Beans (by number of children; $n=15$ for each grade)

Grade	Level of performance		
	1	2	3
2	2	4	9
3	0	4	11
4	1	1	13
5	0	0	15
Total	3	9	48

beans into each cup. When there were four cups, each containing 10 beans, and 8 loose beans, she asked the child how many beans there were altogether. If necessary, she prompted the child to include the loose beans as well as those in the cups. Whatever the child answered, she always asked how he or she knew that there were that many beans. Ross identified the following three levels of performance, which are summarized in Table 1.3:

Level 1: The child was unable to give a reasonable number. (Small counting errors were ignored, as Ross's focus was on counting strategies.)

Level 2: The child depended heavily on counting by ones rather than using any of the more efficient methods characteristic of level 3.

Level 3: The child used an efficient method such as counting by tens and mentally adding or counting-on the remaining 8 beans. Some children used multiplication either explicitly ("Four times ten is forty") or implicitly ("Four tens is forty").

The significant point to note in Table 1.3 is that in grades 2 and 3, only 9 (60%) and 11 (73%) children, respectively, counted by tens. When children do not have confidence in their system of tens, they use their system of ones even after empirically making groups of ten.

After completing the preceding part of the task, Ross spilled one of the four cups of beans onto the table, so that there would be ten beans in each of three cups and 18 loose beans. The child was then asked, "Do you think there are now more beans or fewer than there were before?" After the child responded, Ross asked, "How do you know?" The data about the following three levels are summarized in Table 1.4:

Level 1: The child was convinced that the quantity changed either to more or to less when one cup of beans was spilled.

TABLE 1.4 Conservation with 48 beans (by number of children; $n=15$ for each grade)

Grade	Level of performance		
	1	2	3
2	6	4	5
3	3	1	11
4	1	3	11
5	0	1	14
Total	10	9	41

Level 2: The child initially gave a nonconserving answer but went on to count the beans and concluded that the number remained the same.

Level 3: The child replied, without counting the beans, that the number remained the same.

The difficulty the children evidenced, even in grade 4, is surprising. Only 11 children in grades 3 and 4 (73%) conserved the numerical quantity and said there were still as many beans as before. "One ten" is not necessarily the same thing as "ten ones" even for children in grades 3 and 4.

For adults, who have already constructed the system of tens out of the system of ones, it is easy to think of a ten-block or a cupful of beans as "one ten" *and* "ten ones" *simultaneously.* For children who have not constructed these systems (illustrated in Figure 1.3), however, it is impossible to think about the objects simultaneously as tens *and* as ones. Figure 1.3 shows that both the system of tens and the system of ones consist of the synthesis of the two kinds of relationships discussed earlier—order and hierarchical inclusion. The system of tens is at a higher level of abstraction, however, since a unit of ten must be constructed and then put into relationships of order and hierarchical inclusion. Only when children have constructed all these complex relationships can they perform at level 3 in Ross's tasks with ease and certitude.

FIGURE 1.3 The relationships of order and hierarchical inclusion simultaneously made at two levels of abstraction.

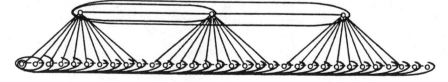

Third-grade arithmetic includes multiplication. We conclude this chapter with a discussion of a task demonstrating that multiplicative thinking, too, is constructed by children from within.

MULTIPLICATIVE THINKING

Inhelder and Piaget (1963) devised a task similar to the one described at the beginning of this chapter. In this task, however, children were asked to drop beads into the two glasses with two-to-one correspondence. The glasses were covered with boxes placed upside down over them so that the child could not see the beads in them. The beads were dropped through slits made in the bottom of the upside-down boxes.

After a child dropped beads with two-to-one correspondence a few times (with two dropped into A and one into B each time), the researcher asked the child how many were in glass A if there were two in B, three in B, four in B, and so forth. After thus dropping beads with two-to-one correspondence 10 to 20 times, the child was asked how many more A had than B. Whether or not the child said that A had the double of B, the researcher went on to uncover A and to ask the child to divide the contents of A into two groups, A1 and A2, with one-to-one correspondence. When the child had done this task, the final questions about A1 and A2 concerned (1) whether or not A1 and A2 were equal and (2) whether or not each was equal to the number in B. The last two questions about the equality or inequality of A1 and B, and of A2 and B, permitted the interviewer to assess the child's multiplicative thinking without asking for precise, numerical answers.

The findings from this study are summarized below in two parts. The first part deals with children's numerical answers about the number in A when there were three, four, five, and so forth in B. These questions in the first part have the disadvantage of getting at children's thinking through precise, numerical answers. The second part involving the division of A into two equal parts allows us to know about children's thinking in qualitative terms, such as "the same," "double," and "half" rather than in precise, numerical terms.

With respect to the first part of the study, Inhelder and Piaget (1963) categorized children's responses into three levels. At the first level, the child thought that the difference between A and B was 1 or 2 beads. Below are two examples. (All the examples have been translated into English and edited for clarity.)

MAS (5;3) Are there more in one or not?—*Yes, in this one* (A).—(MAS continues 6 times with two-to-one correspondence.) Does one have more?—*Yes, this one* (A).—Many more?—*No, one more.*—Why?—*Because we put 2 here and 1 here.*—Are you sure?—*Yes.* (p. 76)

DEL (5;3) . . . *This one (A) will have more.*—Why?—*Because we put two and one.* (She continues 7 times.)—And now, how many are there in this one (B)? (removing the cover over B and leaving glass A hidden)—(She counts the beads in B.) *Seven.*—And here (A)?—*Two more.*—Why?—*We put two and one.* (We continue).—And now, how many do we need to put in here (B) to make the two the same?—*Two.*—A little girl told me: We have to put many more to make them the same. Who is right, she or you?—*Me.* (p. 76)

These examples about the first level are instructive. The children knew that the first action of dropping two into A and one into B produced a difference of one (or two). However, they did not put this difference into relationship with the number of times the two-to-one correspondence was repeated. They therefore thought of the difference only after one or two actions.

At the second level, the children believed that the difference was more than one or two as we can see in the next example, BRU. Other children like FER began by thinking about the difference multiplicatively when the number in B was small but ended up thinking additively.

BRU (5;11) . . . *Always more here* (A).—Do you know how many more?—*No, I don't know but it's more.*—One more?—*Oh, no! the first time, yes, but now there are more than one.*—When there are 4 here (B), how many do you think are in here (A)?—*5 or 6. Oh, no, more than that.*—When there was 1 here (B), there were 2 there (A). When there were 2 here (B), there were how many there (A)?—*3, I think, 3 or 4.*—And when there are many here (B), like 10?—*More than 10.*—11?—*More?*—How many do you think?—*12, no, I think more, 14.*—Could there be 20?—*I don't think so. That would be too much.* (pp. 77–78)

FER (6;0) . . . *One here, two there.*—(Second time).—*Two here, three, no, four there, it's two and two more.*—(Third time).—*More there* (A).—How many do you have (in B)?—*Three.*—And me (A)?—*Six.*—And when there are 6 in B?—*Nine* (in A).—Why?—*Three more again.*—And when there are 10 in B?—*Thirteen, no, 4 more than that.* (p. 78)

Since the third level is easy to imagine, only one example is given below.

GRAF (6;11) . . . counts 4 in B.—And in A?—*Eight.*—(Fifth time). And now, how many in A?—*Ten.*—And in B?—*Five.*—And if there were 6 in B, how many in A?—*Twelve.*—And ten in B?—*Twenty* (in A)—. . . . When A is full, up to where will B be filled?—*Half.* (p. 79)

In the second part of the task, after the child divided A into two subgroups, A1 and A2, with one-to-one correspondence, he or she was asked whether A1 = A2, and whether or not A1 = B and A2 = B. The children who were at level

2 in the first part of the task divided themselves into two groups on this part of the task where division was involved: One group thought that A1 > B because A1 came from A, which was a larger collection than B. The other, more advanced group reacted in various intermediary ways such as (1) saying that A1 = A2 = B without any justification, (2) logically explaining why A1 = A2 = B for small numbers but not for larger numbers, and (3) beginning to generalize these relationships for larger numbers but after much hesitation. Below is an example of (2):

> TOP (5;9) (A is divided into A1 and A2.) Do A1 and A2 and B have the same amount?—*Yes.*—How do you know?—*Because I put in one, one, one.*   And if we continued?—*It will be the same thing.*—How does that happen?—*We put one (in B) and two (in A), and then divided (A), so that makes the same thing.*—And if we continued many, many times?—*There (B), there will be less.*—Why?—*Or else more.* (p. 84)

This child reminds us of the 5-year-olds in the one-to-one correspondence task who knew that one glass had one more than the other but could not anticipate the outcome of continuing the one-to-one correspondence all day. Just as children construct small numbers up to about 10 or 15 first, they become able to put small collections into multiplicative relationships before becoming able to generalize these relationships to larger groups.

Children at level 3 in the first part of the task could deduce that if there were 6 in B, there had to be 12 in A, and that if there were 10 in B, there had to be 20 in A. In the second part of the task, however, these children divided themselves into two groups. The less advanced group responded in ways similar to TOP. The more advanced children, however, generalized the multiplicative relationship to larger numbers with certitude and a logical explanation. Below is an example of this level, which is attained around 7;6 to 8;0.

> ROU (7;4). *Me, I did two, you, one, and then we divided them.*—So?—*It's all the same number* (in A1, A2, and B).—And if we continued with a whole lot of beads?—*It's always the same thing.*—Are you sure?—*Yes.*—But can you know in advance without doing it?—*Yes.*—And you're absolutely sure?—*Yes.* (p. 85)

CONCLUSION

To return to the question posed at the beginning of this chapter, why we want children to reinvent arithmetic, our answer is that logico-mathematical knowledge is the kind of knowledge that children *can* and *must* construct from within. The base-ten system and algorithms have long been taught as if arithmetic were social and/or physical knowledge. We can now see that if some children understand the base-ten system and algorithms, it is because they have already constructed the logico-mathematical knowledge necessary for this understanding.

The teaching of algorithms is not only unnecessary but also harmful, as we will see in Chapter 3. When we understand that children have to do their own thinking, we stop hindering it and try, instead, to facilitate the constructive process. The process of construction from one level to the next can also be seen in the next chapter about the history of computational techniques.

CHAPTER 2

The History of Computational Techniques

As a scientist trained in biology, Piaget believed that the way to study the nature of human knowledge was not through speculation and debate as philosophers had done for centuries but through scientific investigation. He also believed that if we want to understand human knowledge, we have to study its origin and evolution in history (Piaget, 1967, 1976; Piaget & Garcia, 1983/1989). However, facts about the prehistoric sociogenesis and subsequent development of human knowledge were scant or no longer available. He therefore decided to complement this scant information with facts about the way today's children construct knowledge. He reasoned that if today's knowledge was created over centuries through a process of construction, there might be parallels between the way children build knowledge today and the way humanity built it in the past.

For example, once children construct the system of whole numbers, this structure does not change even after they learn fractional and negative numbers. However, their understanding of whole numbers changes when whole numbers become part of a larger system that includes fractional and negative numbers. Likewise, in history, the structure of so-called natural numbers did not change after the invention of rational and irrational numbers. Knowing these parallels between the individual's construction of number concepts and humanity's construction of the same concepts helps us enormously in understanding the nature of logico-mathematical knowledge and of number concepts.

We agreed with Piaget that children have to go through a constructive process similar to our ancestors', at least in part, if they are to understand today's mathematics. We therefore examined the history of computation techniques to find out if there were parallels between the procedures invented by children and those invented by humanity in the past.

We indeed found many parallels and sketch some of them in this chapter. Our purpose is to point out the undesirability of trying to transmit to children, in readymade form, the results of centuries of construction by adult mathematicians. We also want to highlight the conventional nature of today's algorithms and to emphasize the difference between social (conventional) knowledge and logico-mathematical knowledge.

As revealed in the following statement by Groza (1968), today's algorithms

FIGURE 2.1 Various ways of using objects to represent 4,365.

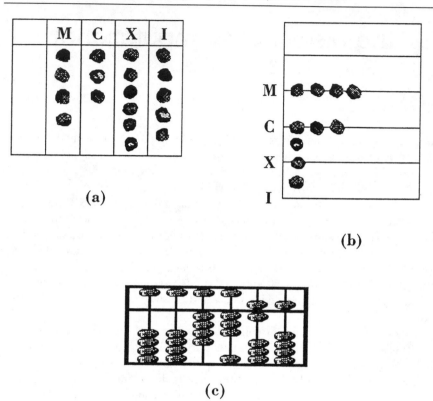

(a)

(b)

(c)

are a very late achievement in human history: "It was not until 1600 that our modern Hindu-Arabic decimal system of numeration became generally accepted as the standard system of computations, replacing the use of Roman numerals" (p. 211). Until this surprisingly late date, most of our ancestors performed their computations with objects such as pebbles and counters, and with abacuses. Following is a sketch of how these objects were used before they were replaced by writing.

THE USE OF OBJECTS

The Roman calculation board shown in Figure 2.1a consisted of a frame with parallel columns. The first column, on the right, was for ones, the second for tens, and so on, and pebbles or counters were placed in each column as shown in this figure to represent, for example, 4,365.

A variety of boards, tablets, and abacuses have been invented, but the basic principle of representing the base-ten system remained the same for centuries. Figure 2.1b shows 4,365 with a horizontal system that used the space above the lines to represent fives—five ones, five tens, and so on. "Four thousands" is thus represented with four pebbles on the line for the thousands. "Six tens" is shown with one pebble above the tens line, to represent five tens, and one on the tens line. This use of five as an intermediate higher-order unit made it easy to recognize five, six, seven, eight, and nine at a glance. (While five as a higher-order unit and 5 + 1, 5 + 2, and so on can be recognized immediately at a glance, six ones, seven ones, and eight ones require counting.)

By putting 10 beads on a cord or a stick, our ancestors made the kind of abacuses that can still be seen today in many classrooms. The abacus had disappeared from Europe by 1700 but is still being used in Asia. The most modern abacus being used in Japan today is shown in Figure 2.1c. Each of the beads above the horizontal divider stands for a five, and each one below it stands for a one. Figure 2.1c shows 4,365 represented by raising four ones in the thousands column, raising three ones in the hundreds column, lowering a five and raising a one in the tens column, and lowering a five in the ones column.

It is important to note that when our ancestors used the abacus, they used writing to record only the *results* of the calculations carried out with the abacus. Groza (1968) stated:

> Around 1100 the general public used Roman numerals and an abacus. Businessmen sat before a line abacus or counting table or "counter" (from which we obtain our present word *counter* as used in stores). Lines were ruled on the table [as shown in Figure 2.1b] to indicate the powers of 10 and loose counters were placed on these lines or between them and then moved as the calculations were performed. (p. 212)

In Japan today, addition and subtraction are performed on the abacus by beginning with the highest-order unit and proceeding to the right, toward the ones. Instead of "carrying" and "borrowing," the abacus is used in the following ways. Note how the column to the left representing the next power of ten is used.

In the following problem, for example,

$$\begin{array}{r} 1,234 \\ +\ \ 999 \\ \hline \end{array}$$

900 is added first and then 90 and then 9. Figure 2.2a shows how calculation begins by entering 1,234 first—by raising one bead in the thousands place, two beads in the hundreds place, three beads in the tens place, and four beads in the ones place. To add 900, 100 is subtracted (lowered) first, and 1,000 is then

FIGURE 2.2 The computation of 1,234 + 999 using a Japanese abacus.

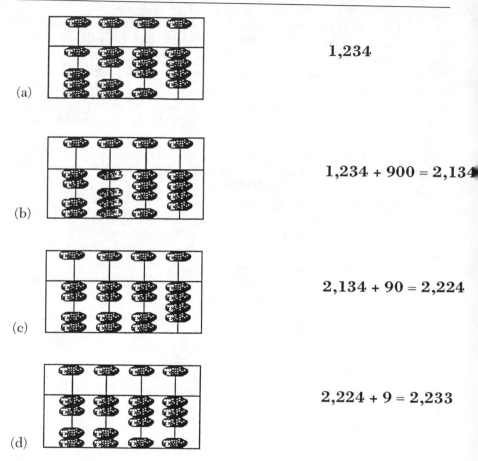

(a) 1,234

(b) 1,234 + 900 = 2,134

(c) 2,134 + 90 = 2,224

(d) 2,224 + 9 = 2,233

added (raised), as shown in Figure 2.2b. To add 90 (see Figure 2.2c), 10 is subtracted (lowered) first and 100 is then added (raised). Finally, 9 is added by subtracting (lowering) 1 and adding (raising) 10 as shown in Figure 2.2d.

Subtraction such as the following problem

$$\begin{array}{r} 1,234 \\ -\ \ 999 \\ \hline \end{array}$$

is carried out in a similar manner by subtracting 900, 90, and then 9. After entering 1,234, as shown in Figure 2.3a, 900 is subtracted by subtracting (lowering) 1,000 and adding (raising) 100 (see Figure 2.3b). The next step is to subtract 90 by subtracting (lowering) 100 and adding (raising) 10 (see Figure

FIGURE 2.3 The computation of 1,234 − 999 using a Japanese abacus.

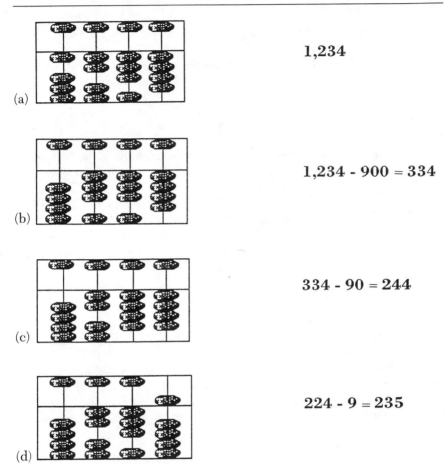

(a)   1,234

(b)   1,234 - 900 = 334

(c)   334 - 90 = 244

(d)   224 - 9 = 235

2.3c). Finally, 9 is subtracted by subtracting (lowering) 10 and adding 1 (by lowering the five bead and four ones) as shown in Figure 2.3d.

Compared to writing, physical actions on pebbles and beads are much more directly related to mental actions (thinking). In fact, the mental actions are directly represented by these physical actions. For example, pushing two beads up to add two is a direct representation of the mental action, but writing "+ 2" is not. The use of an abacus is also closely related to mental actions in another way: The person using an abacus has to know whether the place value is ones, tens, hundreds, and so on. In a written algorithm, by contrast, once the columns have been aligned, every column can be treated as ones.

THE USE OF WRITING

While the general public were using counters and abacuses, a literate minority were perfecting computational procedures that used writing. Much of this history has been lost, but a variety of procedures have been preserved. We give some examples, limiting ourselves to addition and multiplication.

Addition

To illustrate the constructive process our ancestors underwent, five major procedures for addition are described below using the same problem of adding 278 and 356.

According to Groza (1968, p. 215), the following method is attributed to Bhaskara, a twelfth-century Indian mathematician. This method used dots to represent zeros. The column to the right in parentheses is a version reported by Smith (1925, p. 91) that used only spaces and placement without utilizing any dots.

Sum of the units	$8 + 6 =$	14	(14)
Sum of the tens	$7 + 5 =$	12•	(12)
Sum of the hundreds	$2 + 3 =$	5••	(5)
Sum of the sums		634	(634)

Groza (1968) states that the Hindus probably began their addition at the right and proceeded to the left, as can be seen above. However, with Arabic and European influences a Hindu Scratch Method developed that went from left to right, and the sum was written at the top in steps. An example is shown below.

$$
\begin{array}{ccc}
 & 6 & 63 \\
5 & \cancel{6}2 & \cancel{6}\cancel{2}4 \\
\cancel{2}78 \longrightarrow & \cancel{2}\cancel{7}8 \longrightarrow & \cancel{2}\cancel{7}\cancel{8} \\
\cancel{3}56 & \cancel{3}\cancel{5}6 & \cancel{3}\cancel{5}\cancel{6}
\end{array}
$$

When this computation was done on a "dust" board, the digits were erased as they were used instead of being scratched out. The successive steps of the same procedure resulted in progressively less writing, as can be seen below:

$$
\begin{array}{cccc}
278 \longrightarrow & 578 \longrightarrow & 628 \longrightarrow & 634 \\
356 & 56 & 6 &
\end{array}
$$

According to Smith (1925), the Hindus sometimes wrote the sum at the bottom from left to right before popularizing a right-to-left procedure. The following example begins to resemble today's conventional algorithm:

$$278$$
$$+356$$
$$\cancel{5\cancel{2}}4$$
$$63$$

Finally, in a collection of algorithms from American textbooks copyrighted prior to 1900, Pearson (1986) included the following two methods:

278	
+356	
5	(for 200 + 300)
12	(for 70 + 50)
14	(for 8 + 6)
634	

	2	7	8
+	3	5	6
	5	12	14
	6	3	4

Smith (1925) gave the following account of "carrying," which is helpful for understanding the lateness of its invention:

> The expression "to carry" . . . probably dates from the time when a counter was actually carried on the line abacus to the space or line above, but it was not common in English works until the 17th century. Thus, we have Recorde (c. 1542) using "keepe in mynde," Baker (1568) saying "keepe the other in your minde," and Digges (1572) employing the same phraseology and also saying "keeping in memorie," and "keeping repose in memorie." The later popularity of the word "carry" in English is largely due to Hodder (3rd ed., 1664). (p. 93)

A general statement can be made about all the preceding procedures: They are less efficient than today's conventional algorithm. They do, however, allow a person to externalize his or her reasoning step by step. They also highlight the conventional nature of algorithms. We get the same result (logico-mathematical knowledge) whether we work from left to right or in the opposite direction, and whether we write the answer at the top or at the bottom.

The children at Hall-Kent School who are encouraged to invent their own procedures also work from left to right. We agree with Madell's (1985) statement that if children are allowed to do their own thinking, they *universally* invent left-to-right procedures. The reason is that when we think about 278, for example, we think "200, 70, and 8" and not "8, 70, and 200." Since arithmetic was invented by human beings in the past, it is not surprising that today's children invent the same procedures.

Multiplication

Duplation, or the method of doubling, was probably being used by the Egyptians by about 1650 B.C. (Smith, 1925). To calculate 15 × 17, for example, the following procedure of doubling each preceding multiplier and product was used:

1	17	(for 1 × 17)
2	34	(for 2 × 17)
4	68	(for 4 × 17)
8	136	(for 8× 17)
16	272	(for 16 × 17)
1	17	(to subtract 1 × 17)
	255	

Since (16 × 17) is (1 × 17) more than (15 × 17), 17 was subtracted from the result of 16 × 17 .

Smith (1925) describes another method involving doubling that is still found today among Russian peasants. This method involves halving the other number. To multiply 58 by 32, for example, the smaller number is halved successively, and the other is doubled as shown below:

32	16	8	4	2	1
58	116	232	464	928	1,856

This method works because if we halve 32, we can simply double 58 and get the same product. Likewise, if we halve 16, we can double 116 and get the same product. By continuing to halve the top number until we reach 1, and by continuing to double the bottom number, we can get the final result, which is 1 × 1,856 in this example.

This method becomes a bit more complicated when the smaller number is odd, as in 33 × 58. When the number at the top is odd, the remainder is ignored after halving the top number, and only the whole number is recorded, as can be seen below. At the end, the numbers below each of the odd numbers are added to the number under 1.

33	16	8	4	2	1
58	116	232	464	928	1,856

$$\begin{array}{l} 1{,}856 \text{ (the number under 1)} \\ \underline{\quad 58} \text{ (the number under 33)} \\ 1{,}914 \end{array}$$

It is necessary to add 58 to 1856 at the end because by ignoring 1 in halving 33, we changed 33× 58 to 32 × 58. Since we thus ignored 1 × 58, we have to add it at the end to include it in the final answer.

Smith (1925) states that the first serious work in methods of multiplication goes back to Bhaskara, the twelfth-century Indian mathematician, although a few earlier sources have been found. The influence of Bhaskara and the Hindus passed to Italy in the fourteenth and fifteenth centuries through China and Arabia, and one of Bhaskara's methods was to partition the multiplier additively, as can be seen in the following example:

$$32 \times 58 = (8 + 8 + 8 + 8) \times 58$$
$$= 464 + 464 + 464 + 464 = 1,856$$

A similar method for the same problem was to decompose the multiplier into factors and to multiply 58 by 8 and then by 4 .

A different method of partitioning was to base it on digits. In the following way of multiplying 135 by 12, for example, only 135 was partitioned into 100, 30, and 5, and calculation proceeded from left to right:

$$
\begin{array}{ll}
135 & \\
\underline{12} & \\
12 & (\text{for } 12 \times 100 = 1{,}200) \\
36 & (\text{for } 12 \times 30 = 360) \\
\underline{60} & (\text{for } 12 \times 5 = 60) \\
1620 &
\end{array}
$$

The same problem was also solved by partitioning only 12 into 10 and 2 as follows:

$$
\begin{array}{ll}
135 & \\
\underline{12} & \\
1350 & (\text{for } 10 \times 135 = 1{,}350) \\
\underline{270} & (\text{for } 2 \times 135 = 270) \\
1620 &
\end{array}
$$

In the Hindu Scratch Method, the order of work was likewise from left to right, but the final answer appeared at the top. The example in Figure 2.4 shows the following steps given by Groza (1968, p. 222) for the multiplication of 54 by 37:

Step 1: 30 × 50 = 1500. Record 15.
Step 2: 30 × 4 = 120, and 1500 + 120 = 1620. Record 62.
Step 3: Shift 54 for the multiplication by 7. 7 × 50 = 350, and 1,620 + 350 = 1,970. Record 97.
Step 4: 7 × 4 = 28, and 1970 + 28 = 1,998. Record 98. The result is 1,998.

Although today's algorithm was generally accepted by the fifteenth century in Europe, the relative position of the digits was unsettled for a long time. In

FIGURE 2.4 The Hindu Scratch Method of computing 37 × 54.

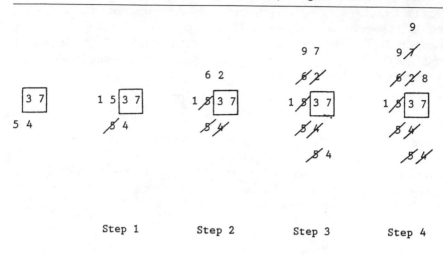

Step 1   Step 2   Step 3   Step 4

Figure 2.5, for example, the multiplier of 45 appears above the multiplicand, 34. This arrangement was found in a manuscript in Paris around 1424 (Smith, 1925).

The final example we give is the lattice method from a book published in Italy in 1478. This method, illustrated in Figure 2.6, used a rectangle ruled into cells by vertical, horizontal, and diagonal lines. To do 934 × 314, for example, 934 was written at the top outside the rectangle and 314 was written vertically to the right of each row. Each cell was then filled by multiplying the corresponding factors as if they were 1s and by separating the result into 10s and 1s by the diagonal line. For instance, the cell at the top left-hand corner was filled by computing 9 × 3 and recording 27 above and below the diagonal line. All the other cells were filled in a similar manner.

The final answer was obtained by adding the numbers diagonally, beginning with the 6 at the lower right-hand corner. The sum for this diagonal is 6, which appears below the bottom right-hand cell. The 7 to its left was obtained by adding 4, 1, and 2 diagonally. The 2 to its left came from 2 + 0 + 3 + 1 + 6 (10 was carried to the next diagonal after recording the 2). The next sum of 3 was the result of adding the 1 (which was carried) to 1 + 9 + 0 + 9 + 3 = 22. The 2 that was carried was then added to 0 + 7 + 0, and the sum of 9 was recorded above the 3. Since the last diagonal contained only a 2, the total appearing above the 9 was 2.

The final answer of 293,276 was read down and to the right below the rectangle. This procedure worked because the product in each cell, beginning with the top row, stood for the following values that totaled 293,276:

FIGURE 2.5 A method of computing 45 × 34 by writing the multiplier above the multiplicand.

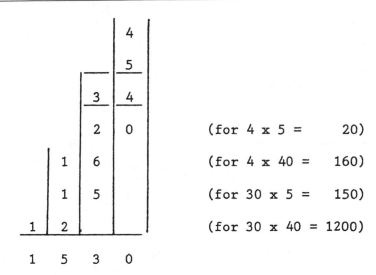

(for 4 x 5 = 20)

(for 4 x 40 = 160)

(for 30 x 5 = 150)

(for 30 x 40 = 1200)

FIGURE 2.6 The lattice method of computing 934 × 314.

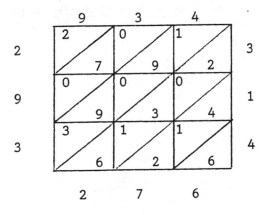

9 × 3:	900 × 300 =	270,000
3 × 3:	30 × 300 =	9,000
4 × 3:	4 × 300 =	1,200
9 × 1:	900 × 10 =	9,000
3 × 1:	30 × 10 =	300
4 × 1:	4 × 10 =	40
9 × 4:	900 × 4 =	3,600
3 × 4:	30 × 4 =	120
4 × 4:	4 × 4 =	16
		293,276

While the written procedure in this lattice method looks very different from today's algorithm, the logic of multiplying each digit of the multiplicand by each digit of the multiplier and of adding all the results at the end is exactly the same.

CONCLUSION

We return to the question posed at the beginning of Chapter 1: Why do we want children to reinvent arithmetic? Today's algorithms are the results of centuries of construction by adult mathematicians. By trying to transmit in ready-made form the results of centuries of reflection by adults, we deprive children of opportunities to do their own thinking. Children today invent the same kinds of procedures our ancestors did and need to go through a similar process of construction to become able to understand adults' algorithms.

Children's first methods are admittedly inefficient. However, if they are free to do their own thinking, they invent increasingly efficient procedures just as our ancestors did. By trying to bypass the constructive process, we prevent them from making sense of arithmetic. The harmful effects of teaching algorithms are described next in the following chapter.

CHAPTER 3

The Harmful Effects of Algorithms

In Chapters 1 and 2 we have demonstrated that children should reinvent arithmetic because (1) logico-mathematical knowledge is the kind of knowledge that each child *can* and *must* construct from within, through his or her own thinking, and (2) children have to go through a constructive process similar to our ancestors' if they are to understand today's algorithms. Our third rationale for saying that children have to invent their own procedures is that the teaching of algorithms in the primary grades is harmful for the following reasons:

1. Algorithms force children to give up their own numerical thinking.
2. They "unteach" place value and hinder children's development of number sense.
3. They make children dependent on the spatial arrangement of digits (or paper and pencil) and on other people.

This chapter elaborates on each of the preceding statements and presents the data that led us to our conclusion.

CHILDREN GIVE UP THEIR OWN NUMERICAL THINKING

When children are not taught any algorithms and are, instead, encouraged to invent their own procedures, their thinking goes in a different direction from the algorithms they are taught. For example, in addition, subtraction, and multiplication, the algorithms specify to proceed from right to left, but children's initial inventions *always* go from left to right. In division, on the other hand, the algorithm goes from left to right, but third graders' own thinking *always* goes from right to left. Figure 3.1 shows examples of what children invent for each of the four operations.

It is clear from these examples that when children are made to follow algorithms, they have to give up their own ways of thinking numerically. Because a compromise is not possible between going from left to right and going from right to left, children obey teachers by giving up their own thinking. This is in itself a sufficient reason for saying that algorithms are harmful to children.

FIGURE 3.1 Procedures invented by children for the four arithmetical operations.

---

18 +17			
	10 + 10 = 20	10 + 10 = 20	10 + 10 = 20
	8 + 7 = 15	8 + 2 = another ten	7 + 7 = 14
	20 + 10 = 30	20 + 10 = 30	14 + 1 = 15
	30 + 5 = 35	30 + 5 = 35	20 + 10 = 30
			30 + 5 = 35

44 −15			
	40 − 10 = 30	40 − 10 = 30	40 − 10 = 30
	4 − 5 = 1 below 0	30 − 5 = 25	30 + 4 = 34
	30 − 1 = 29	25 + 4 = 29	34 − 5 = 29

135 x 4		
	4 x 100 = 400	4 x 100 = 400
	4 x 30 = 120	4 x 35 = 70 + 70 = 140
	4 x 5 = 20	400 + 140 = 540
	400 + 120 + 20 = 540	

23)285   23 + 23 + 23 + 23 . . . until the total comes close to 285

46 + 46 + 46 + 46 . . . until the total comes close to 285

10 x 23 = 230, and then proceeding by addition until the total comes close to 285

CHILDREN FORGET ABOUT PLACE VALUE AND
DEVELOP POOR NUMBER SENSE

When children use the traditional algorithm to solve problems such as

$$\begin{array}{r} 987 \\ +345 \\ \hline \end{array}$$

they forget about place value and start by thinking and saying, for example, "Seven and five is twelve. Put two down and carry one (or ten). One and eight and four is thirteen. Put three down and carry one (or ten). One and nine and three is thirteen." The algorithm is convenient for adults, who already know place value. For primary-age children, who have a tendency to think about every column as ones, however, the algorithm serves to reinforce this weakness.

By contrast, if children are encouraged to invent their own procedures, they think and say, "Nine hundred and three hundred is one thousand two hundred. Eighty and forty is one hundred twenty; so that's one thousand three hundred twenty. And twelve more is one thousand three hundred thirty-two." The children who are allowed to do their own thinking thus strengthen and extend their knowledge of place value by using it.

The harmfulness of algorithms became evident from data obtained at Hall-Kent School in two kinds of situations. One was individual interviews of students, both those who had and those who had not been taught these rules. The other was observation in classrooms of constructivist teachers. Although most of the teachers at Hall-Kent School followed constructivist principles, some taught algorithms. Below is their distribution in 1989–91, when the following data were collected. It can be seen that algorithms tended to be taught more as the children grew older.

Kindergarten: None of the four teachers
First grade: None of the four teachers
Second grade: One of the three teachers
Third grade: Two of the three teachers
Fourth grade: All four teachers

All the classes were heterogeneous and comparable because the principal mixed up all the children at each grade level and divided them as randomly as possible before each school year. The transfer students from other schools were also distributed randomly among all the classes. Most of these transfer students could get right answers by using algorithms but had enormous difficulty with place value, as can be seen in Chapter 11.

Interview Data

In individual interviews in May 1990, the second graders were shown a sheet on which 19 computation problems were written. The children were asked to solve each problem without paper and pencil, give the answer, and explain how they got the answer. The interviewer took notes on what each child said.

Addition. Most of the problems presented in the interview did not yield large and consistent differences, especially when they were presented in vertical form. One of the problems, 7 + 52 + 186, was presented twice in the interview, once in vertical form and later in horizontal form. The three groups of second graders did not differ very much on the vertically written questions, but striking differences emerged when the same problem was presented horizontally.

The answers given by the three classes are summarized in Table 3.1. The teacher of the first class (labeled "Algorithms" in Table 3.1) taught algorithms, but the teachers of the other two classes did not. The two classes differed, however, in that only the teacher who had the class labeled "No algorithms" immediately called parents when children were coached at home.

Most of the children in the "No algorithms" class typically began by saying, "One hundred eighty and fifty is two hundred and thirty." This is why nearly four times as many children in the "No algorithms" class got the correct answer as those in the class labeled "Algorithms" (45% compared to 12%). (The "—'s" in all the tables in this chapter indicate children who did not even try to compute an answer and merely said "I can't do it," "I don't know," "I need a pencil to do it," "We haven't had this kind in class," "I forgot what the teacher said," and so on.)

The important difference, however, lay in the *incorrect* answers the children gave. The dotted lines in Tables 3.1, 3.2, and 3.3 were drawn to highlight the unreasonably large and small incorrect answers the children gave. These answers revealed inadequate knowledge of place value and poor number sense. For example, two children in the "Algorithms" class got 29 for 7 + 52 + 186! These children added all the digits as 1s (7 + 5 + 2 + 1 + 8 + 6 = 29). Those who gave answers in the 900s did this by adding 7 to the 1 of 186 and carrying 1 from the 10s column. All the incorrect answers of the "Algorithms" class fell in the range above and below the dotted lines.

The class labeled "Some algorithms" came out between the other two. The percentage getting the correct answer was 26, which was between 12% and 45% of the other classes. The range of incorrect answers was not as outlandish as in the "Algorithms" class but not as reasonable as in the "No algorithms" class, where only two outlandish answers were given, i.e., 617 and 138.

In May 1991, a year later, an almost identical problem, 6 + 53 + 185, was given to all the third- and fourth-grade classes. The results of these interviews

TABLE **3.1** Answers to 7 + 52 + 186 given by three classes of 2nd graders in May, 1990 (dashes indicate that the child declined to try to work the problem)

Algorithms n=17	Some algorithms n=19	No algorithms n=20
	Percentage with correct answer	
12	26	45
	Incorrect answers	
9308		
1000		
989		
986		
938	989	
906	938	
838	810	
295	356	617
. . . .		
		255
		246
		243
		236
		235
. . . .		
200	213	138
198	213	—
30	199	—
29	133	—
29	125	—
—	114	
—	—	
	—	
	—	
	—	

are summarized in Table 3.2 for third grade and in Table 3.3 for fourth grade.

All the columns except one in Tables 3.2 and 3.3 are labeled "Algorithms," indicating that the teachers of almost all third- and fourth-grade classes taught algorithms. The third column of Table 3.2, labeled "No algorithms," refers to the class taught by Sally Livingston. Although there were 22 children in her class, only 10 of them were included in Table 3.2 because only these 10 had never been taught any algorithms. The other 12 were taught these rules either at Hall-Kent School or at other schools from which they transferred.

TABLE 3.2 Answers to 6 + 53 + 185 given by three classes of 3rd graders in May, 1991 (dashes indicate that the child declined to try to work the problem)

Algorithms n=19	Algorithms n=20	No algorithms n=10
	Percentage with correct answer	
32	20	50
	Incorrect answers	
	800 + 38	
838	800	
768	444	
533	344	284
. . . .		
246	243	245
235	239	243
234	238	238
	234	
. . . .		
213	204	221
194	202	
194	190	
74	187	
29	144	
—	139	
—	—	

It can be seen in Table 3.2 that the "No algorithms" class did much better than the "Algorithms" classes. The percentage getting the correct answer was higher, and the range of incorrect answers was much more reasonable in the "No algorithms" class than in the two "Algorithms" classes. The wrong answers given by the "Algorithms" classes again revealed inadequate knowledge of place value and poor number sense.

All the fourth graders in Table 3.3 had been taught algorithms for one to four years. It can be seen in this table that the performance of the fourth graders was worse than that of the third-grade "Algorithms" classes. The percentages getting the correct answer were about the same, but the magnitude of the fourth graders' errors was greater and characterized by a new phenomenon: answers such as "Eight, three, seven," indicating that each column remained separate in these children's minds, from right to left. These students not only had inadequate knowledge of place value but also thought only about isolated

TABLE 3.3 Answers to 6 + 53 + 185 given by four classes of 4th graders in May, 1991 (dashes indicate that the child declined to try to work the problem)

Algorithms n=20	Algorithms n=21	Algorithms n=21	Algorithms n=18
Percentage with correct answer			
30	24	19	17
Incorrect answers			
	1215		
	848		
	844		
	783		
1300	783		10,099
814	783		838
744	718	791	835
715	713	738	745
713 + 8	445	721	274
. . . .			
243	245		234
	234		234
	224		234
. . . .			
194	194	144	225
177	127	138	"8, 3, 8"
144	—	134	"4, 3, 2"
143	—	"8, 3, 7"	"4, 3, 2"
134		"8, 1, 7"	—
"4, 4, 4"		—	—
"1, 3, 2"		—	
—		—	
		—	
		—	
		—	
		—	
		—	
		—	

columns. Algorithms thus appear to foster the mechanical, mindless processing of isolated columns.

By fourth grade, we expect children at least to be bothered if they add 6, 53, and 185 and get answers greater than 400 or smaller than 200. However, 39% of all the fourth graders were undisturbed by such outlandish totals, ranging from 445 to 1,215 and from 134 to 194. Nineteen percent did not even try to add the three numbers. The fourth graders who were taught algorithms for one to four years can thus be said to have done considerably worse than the second graders who were not taught these rules.

Subtraction. The addition problem discussed so far was written horizontally and was, therefore, difficult for the children who were used to algorithms. One of the other problems given in the interview in May 1991 was the following subtraction problem written vertically:

$$\begin{array}{r} 504 \\ -306 \\ \hline \end{array}$$

Most of the second and third graders who invented their own procedures said, "Five hundred take away 300 is 200. Four take away 6 is 2 less than zero; so the answer is 198." The percentages of children in the "No algorithms" classes who thus gave the correct answer were 74% in second grade ($n = 19$) and 80% in third grade ($n = 10$). The wrong answers they gave were not far from 200. They were 320, 202, 202, 200, and 194 in second grade and 202 and 190 in third grade.

The percentages in the "Algorithms" classes who gave the correct answer were only 42% and 35% in third grade and 55%, 39%, 38%, and 29% in fourth grade. These percentages were all lower than those of the "No algorithms" classes in second and third grade. The incorrect answers given by the third- and fourth-grade "Algorithms" classes are summarized in Table 3.4. It can be observed in this table that the ranges of wrong answers were again enormous and much greater than in the "No algorithms" classes.

As stated earlier, vertically written problems are usually much easier for children who are used to following algorithms. In this subtraction problem, however, the vertical arrangement did not help the "Algorithms" children. Because their knowledge of place value was poor, many of them got the answer of 108 by borrowing 10 from the 5 of 504 and subtracting 3 from 4. Others got 208 by adding 10 to 4 without borrowing it from anywhere! In Table 3.4, the large variety of answers ending with an 8 is striking, indicating that the children had learned to subtract 8 from 14 without knowing where the 10 came from.

The poor number sense of children who are taught algorithms is caused not only by inadequate knowledge of place value but also by the habit of thinking only about isolated columns. This habit is especially evidenced by the children

504

TABLE 3.4 Incorrect answers to −306 given in May, 1991 by 3rd and 4th graders who were taught algorithms. (Dash indicates that the child declined to try to work the problem)

Third grade classes		Fourth grade classes			
n=19	n=20	n=20	n=21	n=21	n=18
			898		
			808		
			498	308	
			298	298	
	1106		298	298	
	708		298	208	
	298	410	208	208	408
406	207	208	208	205	208
· · ·	· · ·	· · ·	· · ·	· · ·	· · ·
202			199	202	202
196			194	196	196
194				192	192
192					
· · ·	· · ·	· · ·	· · ·	· · ·	· · ·
108	164	189	189	148	108
106	113	108	189	108	108
"8, 0, 2"	109	108	108	108	"8, 0, 1"
"8, 0, 2"	108	108	108	"8, 0, 2"	"8, 0, 1"
"8, 10, 1"	108	19	108		"2, 0, 2"
"2, 0, 2"	108	"8, 0, 2"			—
	108	"2, 0, 2"			
	108				
	108				
	22				

in Table 3.4 who gave answers such as "Eight, zero, one" for the columns, from right to left. If these children only *thought* about whole numbers, and subtracted *about* 300 from *about* 500, they would know that the answer *has to be* about 200.

When second and third graders can perform so much better than fourth graders, we must conclude that there is something seriously wrong with using algorithms in the early grades.

Multiplication. The multiplication of a two-digit number by a two-digit number, such as 13 × 11, is not introduced in the textbook before fourth grade. This problem was, therefore, in a sense unfair for third graders because only the "No algorithms" class had been exposed to this kind of problem. This problem was nevertheless given to find out about children's number sense and their ability to invent solutions when faced with an unfamiliar problem. Some of the second graders in constructivist teachers' classrooms solve multiplication problems by addition—by adding 13 and 13 (for two 13s), doubling the result (for four 13s), adding 52 and 52 (for eight 13s), and adding 39 (for three more 13s) to 104.

Sixty percent of the third graders who had never been taught algorithms gave the correct answer to 13×11. By contrast, only 11% and 5% of the third-grade "Algorithms" classes gave the answer of 143. The important difference, however, lay in the incorrect answers the three groups produced. In the "No algorithms" class, the incorrect answers were: 79, 113, 146, and "I want to skip it." In the two "Algorithms" classes combined, the incorrect answers were: 13, 13, 13, 13, 23, 33, 33, 42, 93, 113, 113, 130, 131, 131, 133, 133, 133, 133, 133, 133, 133, 133, 155, 330, 1013, and 1133, and 10 children refused to try. It can be said again that the range of wrong answers in the "Algorithms" classes revealed poor number sense.

All the fourth graders could easily get the correct answer to this problem by using a pencil and following the algorithm. When they were allowed to use only their minds, however, the percentages getting the correct answer were only 5%, 6%, 14%, and 15% for each of the four classes. The incorrect answers produced by all four of the fourth-grade classes combined were: 11, 13, 13, 13, 13, 13, 13, 13, 13, 23, 23, 23, 26, 26, 26, 26, 33, 34, 42, 42, 44, 44, 44, 44, 45, 45, 64, 66, 113, 123, 131, 133, 133, 133, 133, 133, 133, 133, 133, 133, 135, 140, 141, 141, 141, 144, 153, 443, 1300, 1313, 1313, and 1326. (Twenty children refused to try.)

Examples of some of the ways in which these answers were obtained are the following: "Thirteen times 1 is 13, and 13 times another 1 is 13. So the answer is thirteen thirteen. One, three, one, three." "Thirteen times 10 is 130, plus 1 is 131." "Thirteen times 1 is 13. Put down the 3 and carry the 1. Thirteen times 1 is 13, so the answer is 133." "One times 3 is 3. One times 3 is another 3, and 1 times 1 is 1. So the answer is 133."

Classroom Observation Data

As stated earlier, the performance of students who had been taught algorithms before coming to classrooms of constructivist teachers also convinced us of the harmful effects of this instruction. These children could usually get right answers by using algorithms but had enormous difficulty with place value, as can be seen in Chapter 11. We let them use whatever procedure they chose as long as they could explain their steps.

Under the pressure of having to explain their procedures, above-average transfer students quickly conclude that the left-to-right method used by their classmates is easier. By contrast, average students continue to use algorithms and eventually come to understand place value. The below-average students, however, cling tenaciously to algorithms without much progress in knowledge of place value. Algorithms provide the security of producing correct answers, and below-average students continue to function like machines that cannot be unprogrammed. Their thinking remains blocked and paralyzed by the program.

The harmful effects of algorithms became even more evident when one of the fourth-grade teachers, Cheryl Ingram, decided to try the constructivist approach in 1991–92. After 10 years of teaching fourth grade, Cheryl decided to change her teaching because the children who had been in constructivist classes for one, two, or three years seemed to be better math students. I (CK) sat in her class almost every day during the math hour throughout the year to help her become a constructivist teacher and was amazed by the difficulty of unprogramming fourth graders. The following account indicates the extent to which the children did not understand place value and treated isolated columns from right to left.

One of the ways in which Cheryl tried to wean children away from algorithms was to write problems such as 876 + 359 horizontally on the chalkboard and ask the class to invent a variety of ways to solve them without using a pencil. As the children volunteered to explain how they got the answer of 1,235 by using the algorithm in their heads, she followed their statements and wrote numbers such as the following for each column:

$$\begin{array}{r} 15 \\ 13 \\ +12 \\ \hline 40 \end{array}$$

After the child finished explaining how he or she got the answer of 1,235, Cheryl said, "But I followed your way and got 40 as my answer. How did you get 1,235?" Most of the children were stumped and became silent. However, one child soon pointed out that the teacher's 13 was really 130, and that her 12 stood for 1,200.

This kind of place-value problem was relatively easy to cure. The difficulty that persisted was the column-by-column approach that prevented children from thinking about whole numbers. Presented with problems such as the preceding addition problem, the children continued to give fragmented answers from right to left, such as "5 [for 6 + 9], 130 [for 10 + 70 + 50], and 1,200 [for 100 + 800 + 300]."

In an effort to get children to think about whole numbers, we conducted an experiment on October 28, 1991. Cheryl put on the chalkboard one problem after another, such as the following, that had 99 in one of the addends: 366 + 199, 493 + 99, and 601 + 199. During the entire hour, Cheryl gave only this kind of problem for the class to solve in many different ways.

Almost all the children in the class continued to use the algorithm during the entire hour and added the 1s first, carried 10, added the 10s, and then carried 100. One of the children, however, whom we will call Joe, had been in constructivist classes since first grade and volunteered solutions like the following for every single problem: "I changed 366 + 199 to 200 + 365, and my answer is 565." After an entire hour of this kind of "interaction," only three children in the class were imitating Joe! The rest of the class continued to deal with each column separately.

In the meantime, by mid-October, Cheryl had remarked that in her 10 years of teaching fourth grade, she had never seen such excitement and enthusiasm for math. In early November, she felt the need to announce that the class *had to* invent ways of adding and subtracting without carrying and borrowing. This requirement sparked some creativity in the class, and one of the formerly passive students began to wave her hand with confidence. On November 19, she invented the following solution for 606 − 149 that indicated her thinking about whole numbers:

$$600 - 100 = 500$$
$$6 - 49 = \text{negative } 43$$
$$500 - 43 = 457$$

There were many ups and downs throughout the year, and December 20 brought a disappointment. Cheryl told the class that she had $50 to spend on Christmas presents and wanted to know if she had enough money to buy the items listed below:

3 *Battleships* (a game)	@ 7.99
2 sweaters	@11.99
1 wallet	15.00
2 dolls	@ 8.95

The first volunteer started her answer by saying, "Nine plus 9 plus 5 equals 23."

January 21 brought the first left-to-right procedure from users of algorithms. Cheryl put the following prices on the board and asked the class for the total amount:

Shirt	$5.00
T-shirt	1.95
Sweater	37.90

As usual, one student asked, "Can I start on the right?" Andrew immediately reacted by saying, "It's easier to start on the left." Rob quickly agreed. Andrew explained that 37 + 1 + 5 made 43 dollars, that 90 cents and 10 cents made another dollar, and that the answer was 44 dollars and 85 cents.

January 29, however, brought a disappointment. Cheryl wrote the following

misaligned numbers on the board, and Andrew volunteered the answer of 160
as shown below it:

$$25$$
$$3$$
$$4$$
$$+65$$

$$20 + 30 = 50$$
$$40 + 60 = 100$$
$$150 + 10 = 160$$

When Cheryl asked who agreed with Andrew, five hands went up.

The children nevertheless made considerable progress by the end of the year,
and the interviews conducted in May 1992 produced much better results than
in 1991. The percentage giving the correct answer to $6 + 53 + 185$ increased
from 17 in 1991 (see the last column of Table 3.3) to 75 in 1992. The range of
errors also decreased to 28, 202, 234, 238, and 243. Figure 3.2 shows the relationship between the use of the algorithm and the frequency of getting the
correct answer. It can be seen in this figure that 13 (76%) of the 17 children in
Cheryl's class used the algorithm in 1991 and got incorrect answers. In 1992,
by contrast, 15 (75%) of the 20 children used invented methods and got the
correct answer. This analysis indicates that children are more likely to get the
correct answer if they do their own thinking.

As for the subtraction problem, $504 - 306$ written vertically, the percentage
giving the correct answer increased from 39% (in 1991) to 80% (in 1992). The
incorrect answers in 1992 were 90, 108, 200, and 202. These were much more
reasonable than the errors of the previous year, which can be seen in the last
column of Table 3.4. As can be seen in Figure 3.3, all the children used the
conventional algorithm in 1991, and only 7 of the 18 children (39%) got the
correct answer. In 1992, by contrast, 16 of the 20 children used invented procedures, and 15 of them got the correct answer. This analysis again demonstrates
that children who do their own thinking are more likely to get the correct
answer.

The percentage giving the correct answer to 13×11 increased from 6% (in
1991) to 55% (in 1992). The wrong answers produced each year were the following:

1991: 11, 13, 42, 64, 113, 133, 133, 141, 144 (with eight children refusing
to try)
1992: 113, 133, 144, 233, 300

While the data looked much better in 1992, these fourth graders cannot be
said to have overcome the damage caused by algorithms. In class, many of them

FIGURE 3.2 The relationship between using the conventional algorithm and getting the correct answer to 6 + 53 + 185.

1991*

	Algorithm	Invented procedures
Correct answer	3	0
Incorrect answer	13	1

*One child was excluded from this analysis because she said she was thinking of multiplying 185 by 53 and of adding 6.

1992

	Algorithm	Invented procedures
Correct answer	0	15
Incorrect answer	2	3

continued to approach every addition and subtraction problem mechanically and to think about each column separately. The cognitively most advanced children came close to being unprogrammed by the end of the school year. The below-average students, however, continued to cling to algorithms and to have trouble with place value. Human beings are much harder to unprogram than computers, and children at the bottom of the class suffer the most from the damage caused by algorithms.

FIGURE 3.3 The relationship between using the conventional algorithm and getting the correct answer to $\frac{504}{-306}$.

1991

	Algorithm	Invented procedures
Correct answer	7	0
Incorrect answer	11	0

1992

	Algorithm	Invented procedures
Correct answer	1	15
Incorrect answer	3	1

CHILDREN BECOME DEPENDENT
ON THE SPATIAL ARRANGEMENT OF DIGITS AND ON OTHER PEOPLE

In interviews, children in "Algorithms" and "No algorithms" classes gave different reasons for not *trying* to compute an answer. Most of the reasons given in "Algorithms" classes were: "I need a pencil," "We haven't had this kind yet," or "I can't remember what the teacher said." While these students revealed their dependence on pencil and paper, the spatial arrangement of digits, and other people, children who have never been taught algorithms said, "I can't do it," "I don't know how," or something else that expressed their own inability to compute the answer.

Some children in constructivist classes indeed cannot solve certain problems. However, these children have at least not learned to be dependent on paper and pencil, the spatial arrangement of digits, and other people to solve problems. Algorithms enable children to produce correct answers, but the side effect is the erosion of self-reliance.

CONCLUSION

Algorithms and "alternative" or "informal" methods have been discussed in a variety of ways for many years. Some people have advocated teaching algorithms *and* encouraging "alternative" methods (Lankford, 1974; National Council of Teachers of Mathematics, 1989). Others in Brazil (Carraher, Carraher, & Schliemann, 1987; Carraher & Schliemann, 1985) and England (Jones, 1975) have questioned the desirability of teaching algorithms. A third group has urged, from a variety of perspectives, that we stop teaching algorithms. This position can be found not only in the United States (Burns, 1992a, 1992/93; Madell, 1985) but also in Denmark (Bennedbek, 1981), England (Plunkett, 1979), Holland (Treffers, 1987), and South Africa (Murray & Olivier, 1989; Murray, Olivier, & Human, 1992; Olivier, Murray, & Human, 1990, 1991). We agree with the third group but go a step further by saying that the teaching of algorithms is harmful to children in the primary grades.

CHAPTER 4

The Importance of Social Interaction

Piaget's theory is usually presented as if the child developed in a social vacuum. Some people even think that Piaget was a maturationist and that he overlooked the influence of the social environment. This misunderstanding stems partly from the fact that there is only one book by Piaget written from a sociological perspective, and this book, *Etudes Sociologiques* (1965a), has not been translated into English. In "Ecrits Sociologiques" (1976), a compilation edited by G. Busino, Piaget emphasized the parallel between the child's cognitive development and the development of objective, scientific thought in history. He also emphasized the parallel between cooperation between individuals and within an individual. This 1976 publication, too, exists only in French. Piaget (1948) also added a chapter on egocentric language and intelligence in the third edition of *Language and Thought of the Child*. This chapter, too, is not available in English.

The importance of social interaction for the child's cognitive development can nevertheless be seen in books that have been translated into English, such as *The Moral Judgment of the Child* (1932/1965b), *The Psychology of Intelligence* (1947/1963), *To Understand Is to Invent* (1948/1973), and *The Psychology of the Child* (Piaget & Inhelder, 1966/1969). The present chapter begins with highlights from these volumes and complements them with elaborations and examples from the publications in French. The chapter concludes by pointing out that although advocates of "cooperative learning" also recommend social interaction in the classroom, Piaget's rationale is different and leads to different practices in the classroom.

EGOCENTRICITY AND YOUNG CHILDREN'S REASONING

Piaget (1936/1952, 1937/1954) showed that all babies and young children begin by being egocentric and stated that "the individual, left to himself, remains egocentric" (1932/1965b, p. 400). The term *egocentric* does not mean "selfish" or "egotistical" but has two meanings in Piaget's theory. One of them refers to thinking only from one's own point of view based on one's immediate experience in a particular situation. For example, when young children are asked how many children are in their group, they often count only the others and overlook themselves. The reason for this behavior is that when they function as someone who "counts," they cannot function at the same time as someone who "is counted." The second meaning of *egocentricity* refers to a lack of differentiation between one's point of view and that of others. For example, young children often think that the moon follows them when they go on a walk and that the moon shines to show them the road (1926/1929). They also say that they have a brother named Peter, for example, but when asked if Peter has a brother (or a sister), they answer "No" (1924/1928).

The following is another example of young children's egocentricity (Szeminska & Piaget, 1968/1977). The interviewer and a 3- or 4-year-old both had three chips in front of themselves, and a box containing the same kind of chips was at the child's disposal. After the child agreed that the two people had the same number of chips, the experimenter took one chip away from the child and added it to her own set as she put her other hand over it to hide her set from the child's view. The child was then asked to take chips from the box to equalize the two sets again ("so it will be fair again"). Three- and 4-year-olds always added one chip to their own collection, and were surprised when the interviewer's set was uncovered and they saw one more chip in her set. These children did not understand what happened because they took into account only the fact that they had lost one chip. They could not reason that -1 from their own set combined with $+1$ to the adult's set made a difference of 2.

How does the child grow out of this egocentricity? Piaget's answer to this question was that through the exchange of points of view with other people, children decenter, that is, they think about another person's perspective and gradually coordinate it with their own point of view. The originality of this view lies in the two kinds of social influence he distinguished, coercion and cooperation, and their relationships to the child's construction of logic.

COERCION AND COOPERATION

In Piaget's theory, *cooperation* means something different from its meaning in common parlance. In common usage, cooperation means to comply, as in the statement "Your cooperation will be appreciated." In Piaget's theory, by contrast, to cooperate means to co-operate, or to operate or work together, which includes working things out in case of disagreement. Children's debating whether 13×11 is the same thing as $130 + (1 \times 3)$ or $130 + (1 \times 13)$ is an example of cooperation in the Piagetian sense. As we will see shortly, this kind of cooperation, or debate, or free exchanges of viewpoints without coercion, is essential for the child's overcoming his or her egocentricity.

An example of *coercion* is adults' imposition of rules and use of threats and punishment to control children's behavior. Most teachers and parents today give readymade rules in both the intellectual and moral realms and use threats, bribes, rewards, and/or punishment to enforce these rules. A mild example of intellectual coercion is the teaching of algorithms with worksheets that the teacher corrects. In the moral realm, examples of coercion are too numerous to cite. Piaget (1932/1965b, 1976) stated emphatically that coercion reinforces and consolidates children's egocentric thinking.

Cooperation, on the other hand, fosters decentering. Piaget (1932/1965b) said in the following way that children who are encouraged to agree or disagree with each other and to criticize each other's argumentation and explanation develop their logic:

> Thanks to the mutual control which it [cooperation] introduces, it suppresses both the spontaneous conviction that characterizes egocentrism and the blind faith in adult authority. Thus, discussion gives rise to reflection and objective verification. But through this very fact cooperation becomes the source of constructive values. It leads to the recognition of the principles of formal logic in so far as these normative laws are necessary to common search for truth. (p. 403)

In *The Psychology of Intelligence*, Piaget (1947/1963) further elaborated on the importance of cooperation in the following way:

> Co-operation is thus an objectively conducted discussion (out of which arises internalized [mental] discussion, i.e. deliberation or reflection), collaboration in work, exchange of ideas, mutual control (the origin of the need for verification and demonstration), etc. It is therefore clear that co-operation is the first of a series of forms of behaviour which are important for the constitution and development of logic. . . .
>
> Logic itself does not consist solely of a system of free operations; it expresses itself as a complex of states of awareness, intellectual feelings and responses, all of which are characterized by certain obligations whose social character is difficult to deny. . . . Thus, the obligation not to contradict oneself is . . . also a moral "categorical" imperative, inasmuch as it is indispensable for intellectual interaction and co-operation. And, indeed, the child first seeks to avoid contradicting himself when he is in the presence of others. In the same way, . . . the need for verification, the need for words and ideas to keep their meaning constant, etc. are as much social obligations as conditions of operational thought. (pp. 162–163)

It will be recalled from Chapter 1 on the nature of logico-mathematical knowledge that children develop logic by progressively coordinating relationships. For example, the 4-year-old who said in the class-inclusion task that there were more tulips than flowers said this because he or she could not adequately make relationships among "all the tulips," "all the roses," and "all the flowers." As this child coordinates these relationships, his or her thinking becomes more logical. Likewise, as the child thinks about the relationships other people make with the moon, that child stops thinking that the moon follows him or her. Similarly, when the boy who has a brother named Peter decenters and thinks about the relationships Peter makes, he also stops saying that Peter does not have a brother. Cooperation fosters children's development of logic because it motivates them to put different perspectives (relationships) into relationships. This is why Piaget (1947/1963) said, "Internal operational activity and external cooperation are merely . . . two complementary aspects of one and the same whole" (p. 166).

Cooperation develops earlier in interactions among peers than between a child and an adult, but it is possible for an adult to function as an equal. Children's discussion of the computational procedures they invent is an example of the exchange of points of view without any imposition of readymade rules or judgment by an adult. In children's discussions, they do not depend on adult authority to know whether they are right or wrong. They determine for themselves, by exchanging ideas among equals, whether or not something makes sense.

The Construction of Science

In *The Psychology of Intelligence* (1947/1963) Piaget pointed out the parallel between the child's construction of knowledge and humanity's construction of science in the following way:

> An exact science . . . constitutes a body of ideas whose detailed relationships are preserved and even strengthened with every new addition of fact or principle; for new principles, however revolutionary they may be, justify old ones as first approximations . . . ; the continuous and unpredictable work of creation to which science testifies is thus ceaselessly integrated with its own past. We find the same phenomenon again, but on a small scale, in every sane ["well-adjusted"] man. (pp. 39–40)

Piaget (1965a, 1976) pointed out that young children and prescientific humans are alike in that both begin or began by having subjective ideas based on immediate experiences. He went on to say that both make or made progress by exchanging viewpoints and decentering, thereby constructing increasingly objective knowledge. Scientists are critical and do not accept new discoveries without verification and debate. The importance of social interaction in humanity's construction of science can be seen in such statements by Piaget (1976) as "the triumph of collective thought is to be sought in science" (p. 115).

As Piaget and Garcia (1983/1989) emphasized, the parallel between children's construction of knowledge and scientists' construction of science is in the *process* by which theories change from one level to the next. The *content* of the ideas is not the same, as we know from the history of science and the study of how children's ideas develop. The lesson for educators to learn is that the progress from subjective experience and primitive belief to objective, scientific knowledge consists not in the elimination of the former but in the *modification* of the former through coordination with other perspectives. For example, immediate experience gives the impression that the sun revolves around the earth. When Copernicus corrected this subjective belief, he modified it by putting the planets into a broader framework of spatial relationships.

In the logico-mathematical realm, Euclidean geometry was not extinguished by non-Euclidean geometry but became part of a larger whole. When we want to build a house, for example, we still use Euclidean geometry. Newton's concept of time was likewise not eliminated by the theory of relativity. In the same way, when children invent increasingly efficient computational procedures, the previous ways of reasoning are not annihilated. They become modified and contained in the more efficient procedures.

When a scientist announces a new discovery, other scientists demand verification. This is because scientists do not accept new truths that have not been checked by others. Only when the great majority reach consensus is the new claim accepted as objective truth. Science is thus a social enterprise with strict rules of logic and empirical proof. This social enterprise does not advance through conformity, obedience, and dependence on authority. When a leader *creates* new knowledge, the others cannot depend on tradition or authority to decide whether or not the new claim is true. It follows that in math education, we must teach children so that they can create new knowledge and evaluate other people's creations without depending on the teacher's authority.

In the 1976 publication, Piaget conceptualized coercion and cooperation as two extremes of a continuum of all social processes, including those in politics and religion. Even in science, he remarked, prestige and authority have at least some influence. In reality, therefore, there are many degrees between outright coercion and true cooperation among equals. Many teachers will probably place themselves on this continuum at a point that can be called "gentle coercion."

Coercion and cooperation are both social processes that involve obligations. However, the nature of the obligation is not the same in the two situations. In coercion, the obligation is to conform and to be obedient to authority, tradition, and power. In cooperation, by contrast, the obligation is to consider all viewpoints, to be coherent and rational, and to justify one's conclusions. The teaching of algorithms may not look like coercion and may not be harshly coercive. However, children who are made to follow these rules do not have any choice and do not have the possibility of considering other viewpoints.

Experimental Evidence About the Importance of Cooperation

Piaget thus emphasized the importance of social interaction, but he never proved his theory with empirical facts except those he found in the history of science. Also, he did not specify the conditions under which children do or do not demonstrate progress as a result of social interaction.

A group of social psychologists in Geneva, such as Doise and Mugny (1981/ 1984) and Perret-Clermont (1979/1980), conducted experiments to fill in these lacunae in Piaget's theory. By encouraging children to agree or disagree among themselves in small groups of two or three, they tried to find out what kinds of children show or do not show progress in the posttest and postposttest. As the reader can see in the works discussed above and in Kamii (1985, 1989a), many children did demonstrate higher-level reasoning after experimental sessions in which sociocognitive conflict took place for only 10 minutes on average. The details of these experiments are beyond the scope of this chapter, but two conclusions seem worth highlighting:

1. A nonconserver sometimes makes progress toward conservation when he or she is encouraged to come to an agreement with another nonconserver who argues from another equally wrong point of view (see Kamii, 1989a, Chapter 3, for a summary of an experiment). In other words, in the logico-mathematical realm, it is not necessary to present or to reinforce correct reasoning. Even when the contenders both have wrong ideas, exchanges of points of view can sometimes result in the construction of a higher-level perspective that contains both of the lower-level viewpoints. (This is what Piaget called *équilibration majorante*, which has no satisfactory English equivalent and has been translated as "optimizing equilibration," "increasing equilibration," and "augmentative equilibration.")
2. Not every child makes observable progress immediately as a result of a brief session involving sociocognitive conflict. The children who make progress are generally those who are already at a relatively high level. This finding is in agreement with the conclusion reached by Inhelder, Sinclair, and Bovet (1974). In other words, children do not jump directly from a low level to a high level of reasoning. They go through a number of intermediate levels and construct each higher-level relationship out of the relationships they made before.

Differences from "Cooperative Learning"

Social interaction among peers is also advocated by supporters of "cooperative learning," such as Slavin (1990). We are delighted with the small-group activities that are increasingly taking place in classrooms but would like to point out two theoretical differences that lead to classroom practices that are different from ours.

First, advocates of cooperative learning are not aware of the nature of logico-mathematical knowledge. For example, Slavin (1990) states that one of the forms of cooperative learning is particularly suited for "teaching well-defined objectives with single right answers, such as mathematical computations and applications" (p. 4). Another method, which he calls Team Assisted Individualization, works in the following way, inspired by behaviorism:

> Students enter an individualized sequence according to a placement test and then proceed at their own rates. In general, team members work on different units. Teammates check each other's work against answer sheets [outside authority] and help one another with any monitors. Each week, teachers total the number of units completed by all team members and give certificates or other *team rewards* to teams that exceed a criterion score based on the number of final tests passed, with extra points for perfect papers and completed homework. (p. 5)

Although we agree that children learn *from* each other, we do not believe that they acquire logico-mathematical knowledge *from* other people, "single right answers," and/or well-sequenced programs. Logico-mathematical knowledge has to be constructed by each individual from the inside. When children confront an answer or argument with which they disagree, they have to think about their own thinking (the relationships they make) and about someone else's reasoning (the relationships someone else makes) and decide who is correct. If they decide that they are incorrect, they modify their own thinking. Social interaction thus stimulates critical thinking, but it is not the source of logico-mathematical knowledge.

Second, although not all cooperative learning involves rewards, its advocates do not reject the use of rewards to motivate students. For example, Slavin (1990) justifies the use of rewards cited earlier in the following way:

> Motivational perspectives on cooperative learning focus primarily on the reward or goal structures under which students operate. . . . From a motivational perspective . . . , cooperative goal structures create a situation in which the only way group members can attain their own personal goals is if the group is successful. Therefore, to meet their personal goals, group members must help their group mates to do whatever helps the group to succeed, and, perhaps more important, encourage their group mates to exert maximum effort. (pp. 13–14)

Instead of giving only one reward to a single winning team, Slavin recommends rewarding all the teams that meet specific criteria. While this practice attenuates the power of rewards, trying to motivate, or to manipulate, children with rewards is harmful to their development of autonomy (which will be discussed in Chapter 5). We find that primary-age children who are proud and excited about their inventions do not need any artificial rewards. Copernicus and Galileo were even punished for expressing their ideas, but punishment did not change the truth as they saw it. Trying to manipulate children's reasoning with rewards likewise does not change whether or not something makes sense to them.

CONCLUSION

We tried to show in this chapter that social interaction has a major part of Piaget's theory. In the various quotations we cited, he often mentioned children's moral development as he spoke of their development of logic. "Reason in its double aspect, both logical and moral, is a collective [social] product," he stated (1932/1965b, p. 400), because both logic and moral rules must be constructed from within through the exchange of points of view with other people. In the next chapter, on autonomy as the aim of education, we will see further that social interaction was of utmost importance to Piaget not only in his explanation of the nature and evolution of knowledge but also in his vision of education.

Part II

GOALS AND OBJECTIVES

CHAPTER 5

Autonomy: The Aim of Education for Piaget

Piaget's greatest direct contribution to education may well be a short chapter he wrote in a small, simple book entitled *To Understand Is to Invent* (1948/ 1973). In the fourth chapter of this book, he argued that education must aim at autonomy rather than at obedience and conformity. Since traditional education unwittingly aims at fostering obedience and conformity, changing the goal to autonomy entails changes in the way teachers make every decision from one moment to the next. This is why we believe that Piaget's conceptualization of autonomy as the aim of education may be his greatest direct contribution to education.

As can be anticipated from the previous chapter, autonomy has two aspects for Piaget, the moral and the intellectual. Since autonomy in Piaget's theory means something different from its usual meaning, we first clarify "moral autonomy" and "intellectual autonomy." We then discuss autonomy as the aim of education and show in what ways this goal changes what teachers do during every minute of the school day. We also argue that autonomy as the aim of education would drastically change the efforts being made in the name of education reform.

WHAT PIAGET MEANT BY AUTONOMY

In common parlance, *autonomy* means the *right* of an individual or group to be self-governing. For example, when we speak of Palestinian autonomy, we are referring to this kind of political right. In Piaget's theory, however, autonomy refers not to the right but to the *ability* to be self-governing. Autonomy is the ability to think for oneself and to decide between right and wrong in the moral realm, and between truth and untruth in the intellectual realm, by taking all relevant factors into account, independently of reward and punishment. A characteristic of autonomy is the ability to *cooperate,* which has a unique meaning in Piaget's theory, as we saw in Chapter 4. For Piaget, there is no autonomy without cooperation. Autonomy is the opposite of heteronomy. Heteronomous people are governed by someone else, as they are unable to think for themselves. Below is a discussion of the moral and the intellectual aspects of this difficult concept.

Moral Autonomy

A clear example of moral autonomy is Martin Luther King's struggle for civil rights. King was autonomous enough to take relevant factors into account and to conclude that the laws discriminating against African Americans were unjust and immoral. Convinced of the need to make justice a reality, he fought to end the discriminatory laws, in spite of the police, jails, dogs, water hoses, and threats of assassination used to stop him. Morally autonomous people are not governed by reward and punishment.

An example of extreme moral heteronomy is found in the Watergate cover-up. The men under President Nixon were governed by him and went along with what they knew to be morally wrong, reaping the rewards the president dispensed to those who helped him in the cover-up attempt.

In *The Moral Judgment of the Child,* Piaget (1932/1965b) gave more commonplace examples of autonomy and heteronomy. For example, he asked children 6 to 14 years of age whether it was worse to lie to an adult or to another child. Young children tended to reply that it was worse to lie to an adult. When Piaget inquired why, young children revealed their heteronomy by explaining, "Because adults can tell if something is not true and punish you." Piaget went on to ask, "Would it be OK to tell lies if you were not punished for them?" and young children answered "Yes."

Piaget (1932/1965b) also made up many pairs of stories and asked children which one of the two children in the stories was the worse. Following is an example of such a pair:

> A little boy (or a little girl) goes for a walk in the street and meets a big dog who frightens him very much. So then he goes home and tells his mother he has seen a dog that was as big as a cow.

> A child comes home from school and tells his mother that the teacher had given him good marks, but it was not true; the teacher had given him no marks at all, either good or bad. Then his mother was very pleased and rewarded him. (p. 148)

Young children systematically manifested the morality of heteronomy by saying that it was worse to say "I saw a dog as big as a cow." Why was it worse? Because dogs are never as big as cows and adults do not believe such stories. Older, more autonomous children, however, tended to say that it was worse to say "The teacher gave me good marks" *because* this lie was more believable. For more autonomous children, a believable lie is worse than one that is so outlandish as to not deceive people.

The important question for parents and teachers is: What causes certain children to become more autonomous than others? Piaget's answer to this question, found in *The Moral Judgment of the Child*, was that adults reinforce children's heteronomy when they use rewards and punishment, thereby hindering the development of autonomy. By refraining from using rewards and punishment, and by exchanging points of view with children instead, we can foster the development of autonomy, he said.

For example, if a child tells a lie, an adult could punish him or her by saying, "No dessert tonight." Alternatively, the adult can look the child straight in the eye with affection and skepticism and say, "I *really* can't believe what you are saying because (and give the reason). And when you tell me something next time, I am not sure I'll be able to believe you. I want you to go to your room (or seat) and think about what you might do to be believed." Children want to be believed, and when they are confronted with this kind of statement, they are likely, over time, to come to the conclusion that it is best for people to deal honestly with one another.

In general, punishment leads to three possible outcomes. The first outcome is calculation of risks. Children who are punished will learn to calculate their chances of getting caught the next time and the price they might have to pay if they are caught. The second possible outcome is, interestingly, the opposite of the first one—blind obedience. Sensitive children will do anything to avoid being punished, thereby giving the impression that punishment works. The third outcome of punishment is a derivative of the second, namely, revolt. Many "good," model children surprise us eventually by beginning to cut classes, take drugs, and engage in other acts characteristic of delinquency. Their reason for switching to these behaviors is that they are tired of living for their parents and teachers and think that the time has come for them to start living for themselves.

Piaget was realistic enough to say that it is sometimes necessary to impose restrictions on children. However, he made an important distinction between *punishment* and *sanctions by reciprocity*. Depriving the child of dessert for telling a lie is an example of a punishment, as the relationship between a lie and dessert is completely arbitrary. Telling children that we cannot believe what they said is an example of a sanction by reciprocity. Sanctions by reciprocity are directly related to the act we want to sanction and to the adult's point of view. They have the effect of motivating the child to construct rules of conduct from within, through the coordination of viewpoints. Other examples of sanctions by reciprocity, such as exclusion from the group, depriving the child of the thing he or she has misused, and restitution, can be found in *The Moral Judgment of the Child* and in Kamii (1982, 1985).

When adults exchange viewpoints with children, this fosters the development of autonomy by enabling children to decenter and consider relevant factors, such as other perspectives. When children can take relevant factors into account, especially other people's rights and feelings, they construct from within the rule of treating others as they wish to be treated by them. A person who has constructed this conviction from within cannot lie in situations such as the Watergate affair, no matter what reward is offered.

Many behaviorists and others believe that punishment is bad because it is negative, but that rewards are positive and good. However, rewards do not make children any more autonomous than does punishment. Children who help their parents only to get money, and those who fill out worksheets only to get a sticker, are governed by someone else just as much as those who are "good" only to avoid being punished.

Intellectual Autonomy

In the intellectual realm, too, autonomy means the ability to govern oneself by being able to take relevant factors into account, and heteronomy means being governed by somebody else. An example of outstanding intellectual autonomy is Copernicus—or the inventor of any other revolutionary theory in the history of science. Copernicus invented the heliocentric theory when everybody else believed that the sun revolved around the earth. But although ridiculed, he was autonomous enough to remain convinced of his own idea. An intellectually heteronomous person, by contrast, unquestioningly believes what he or she is told, including illogical conclusions, slogans, and propaganda.

A more common example of intellectual autonomy is a child who used to believe in Santa Claus. When she was about 6, she surprised her mother one day by asking, "How come Santa Claus uses the same wrapping paper as we do?" Her mother's "explanation" satisfied her for a few minutes, but she soon came up with the next question: "How come Santa Claus has the same handwriting as Daddy?" This child had her own way of thinking about Santa Claus, which was different from what she had been told.

Unfortunately, in school, children are not encouraged to think autonomously. Teachers use reward and punishment in the intellectual realm, too, to get children to give "correct" responses. An example of this practice is the use of worksheets. In first-grade arithmetic, for example, if a child writes "4 + 4 = ___7___," most teachers mark this answer as being wrong. The result of this kind of teaching can be seen when we walk around a first-grade classroom while children are working on worksheets and stop to ask individual children how they got particular answers. They typically react by grabbing their erasers, even when their answer is perfectly correct! Already in first grade, many children have learned to distrust their own thinking. Children who are thus discouraged from thinking critically and autonomously will construct less knowledge than those who are confident and do their own thinking.

In the next section, on autonomy as the aim of education, we argue further that we must replace an education that unwittingly aims at obedience and con-

FIGURE 5.1 Autonomy as the aim of education in relation to the goals of most educators and the public.

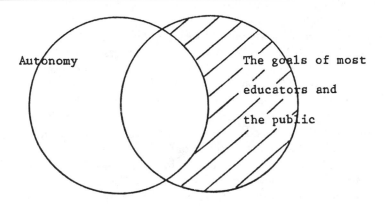

formity with one that emphasizes the honest, critical exchange of viewpoints among peers.

AUTONOMY AS THE AIM OF EDUCATION

Figure 5.1 is our interpretation of autonomy as the aim of education in relation to the goals of most educators and the public. In the shaded part of the circle labeled "the goals of most educators and the public," we include those that resulted in our memorizing words, just to pass one test after another. All of us who succeeded in school achieved this success by memorizing an enormous number of words without understanding them or caring about them. The shaded part also includes the moral heteronomy that schools generally reinforce by using reward and punishment to enforce readymade rules.

In the intersection with the circle labeled "autonomy," we list things we did not forget after each test. The ability to read and write, to do arithmetic, to read maps and charts, and to situate events in history are examples of what we learned in school that we did not forget after cramming for tests. When moral and intellectual autonomy becomes our aim, educators work hard to increase the area of overlap between the two circles.

Piaget chose mathematics as an example to argue that the atmosphere of a classroom either enhances or squelches the development of autonomy in ways that are inseparably moral and intellectual. If the classroom is governed by the authority of the teacher, children will be encouraged to conform to the teacher's wishes, without separating sociomoral issues from purely intellectual ones. If, on the other hand, the class is governed by the group, and the teacher reduces his or her power as much as possible, children will exchange points of view freely to make decisions in both the sociomoral and intellectual realms. If a teacher is coercive in one area, it is impossible for children to feel free to make decisions in the other.

Just as exchanges of viewpoints are indispensable for children to overcome their egocentricity in the intellectual realm, exchanges of points of view are essential for children to decenter in the sociomoral realm. For example, if one child complains that Johnny always goes first in a math game and Johnny disagrees, the teacher could impose a solution such as "The person who rolls the biggest number goes first." However, the teacher who keeps autonomy constantly in mind as the aim of education would suggest cooperation and say, "Can you two think of a solution that would be fair to both of you?" The children may end up making the same rule that the teacher could have imposed. From the standpoint of children's development of sociomoral autonomy, however, *who* makes rules makes an enormous difference. Children must coordinate points of view and make rules that make sense to them. They are much more likely to respect a rule *they made* than the same rule imposed by the teacher.

The essential principle for the development of autonomy is to ask children "What do you think is the right thing to do?" rather than trying to manipulate them with reward and punishment. Reward and punishment at best leads only to conformity. Children who are encouraged to debate possible solutions to sociomoral problems think about them from many perspectives and coordinate points of view. This is how, over time, these children become able to make decisions on the basis of what is best for all concerned. Autonomous people are governed by what is morally right and what is intellectually true, rather than by reward and punishment.

CONCLUSION

The reader can probably see that the teaching of algorithms reinforces children's heteronomy. By teaching readymade rules and using reward and punishment, albeit in mild forms, schools are unwittingly teaching conformity, blind obedience, and dependence on adults. By fourth grade, if we ask children to explain the steps they follow in long division, they all say, "I don't know why [I brought down this number], but my teacher said to do it this way."

The nation's schools are having enormous problems with drugs, violence, AIDS, teenage pregnancies, suicides, and so on. Most educators and the public, including the National Governors' Association (U.S. Department of Education, 1991), view these problems as being separate phenomena that are unrelated to math education. However, autonomy as the aim of education enables us to see that if children learn mathematics through blind obedience, we cannot expect them to have the judgment and autonomy to say "no" to drugs, peer pressure, and sex. Children who can take relevant factors into account do not take drugs or conform automatically to peer pressure. Those who can exchange points of view and negotiate solutions to problems do not resort to violence either. The problems of drugs, violence, and teenage pregnancies are all symptoms of heteronomy.

Autonomy as the aim of education is also important for children's self-directedness and motivation from within during the math hour. We have been amazed by the serene atmosphere in some classrooms and children's respectfulness toward one another. When some children take a long time to write all over the blackboard, for example, their classmates have surprised us by remaining keenly attentive. Such interest and respect for other students' ideas can come only from within. Teachers who genuinely respect children and make decisions with them seem to create such an atmosphere of respect.

If every school in the nation adopted autonomy as the aim of education, the work force would become more competent, racial and ethnic conflicts would be reduced, and the nation's prisons would become less crowded. It behooves us to conceptualize goals for mathematics in the context of overall long-term goals for education if we want school reform to produce more than higher test scores.

CHAPTER 6

Goals in Third-Grade Arithmetic

Having adopted Piaget's idea of autonomy as the aim of education, we hierarchically conceptualize more specific goals in the context of autonomy. In third-grade arithmetic, we begin with four broad goals and then define more specific objectives, such as multiplication.

BROAD GOALS FOR ARITHMETIC

The broad goals are listed first and elaborated on later with examples. They are that children

1. Do their own thinking and develop confidence in their own ability to figure things out
2. Become able to solve problems in many different ways
3. Develop number sense
4. Exchange points of view thoughtfully with others

Developing Independent Thinking and Confidence

This goal is rooted in the nature of logico-mathematical knowledge, discussed in Chapter 1, and is in contrast to the learning of conventional algorithms. The teaching of algorithms is based on the assumption that arithmetic consists of rules that have to be transmitted to children, as if it were social (conventional) knowledge. As stated in Chapter 1, however, arithmetic has a different source from social knowledge, and logico-mathematical knowledge must be constructed from within, through children's own thinking. The goal of children's doing their own thinking can also be justified in light of the facts presented in Chapter 3 about the harmful effects of algorithms.

An example illustrating the importance of children's doing their own thinking can be seen in their reactions to problems such as the following: "I have 275 M&M's in this bag. Do I have enough to give 15 to each person in the class [of 23]?" Traditionally instructed third graders often write

$$15\overline{)275}$$

but say that they have no idea what to do next because they have not had this kind of problem in class. Third graders who have not been taught any algorithms do not express such helplessness. Some use repeated addition and add 15 many times until they get close to 275. The most advanced students say, "Ten 23s is 230, plus half of that is 230 plus 115 equals 345. Since 345 is more than 275, you don't have enough." Others invent procedures such as the following:

$$275 \div 15$$
$$\underline{\times\ 2}$$
$$30 \times 4 = 120$$
$$\underline{\times\ \ 2}$$
$$240$$
$$\underline{+\ 30}$$
$$270 \qquad 18 \text{ r. } 5$$

They answer, "No, you don't have enough because 23 is more than 18." Children who have not been taught algorithms thus show that they have good reasons to feel confident about their own ability to solve problems. They also learn that arithmetic is logical and makes sense because, needless to say, they understand their own reasoning.

To encourage children to do their own thinking and develop confidence, the teacher must refrain from saying that an answer is right or wrong and, instead, encourage them to agree or disagree with one another. By judging the correctness of children's answers and procedures, we unwittingly stop their thinking and teach them to depend on adults to know truth. We must, therefore, avoid saying "That's right" or "That's not right" and, instead, ask the group, "Does everybody agree?" or "Does that make sense?" Children *will* eventually get to the truth if they think and debate long enough because, in logico-mathematical knowledge, absolutely nothing is arbitrary. Two and two make four in all cultures and under all circumstances (even in the dark, when nobody can see it— a bit of knowledge that is difficult to comprehend for children below the age of 5).

Solving Problems in Many Different Ways

Textbooks usually teach only one operation at a time and then present word problems as applications of the specific operation. By contrast, we let computational procedures come out of word problems and do not say what operation must be used. The reason for our approach is that, in the elementary grades, logico-mathematical knowledge is still growing out of children's mental actions on concrete objects. Below is how Piaget made this point:

> The child may on occasion be interested in seriating for the sake of seriating, in classifying for the sake of classifying, but, in general, it is when events or phenomena must be explained and goals attained through an organization of causes that operations will be used most. (Piaget & Garcia, 1971/1974, p. 17)

FIGURE 6.1 Six ways invented by four children to solve 51 × 34.

```
(a)  51                              (b)  102
     51                                   102
     51    510    51                      102
     51    510    51                      102
     51    510    51                      102
     51   1539    51                      102
     51    204   204                      102
     51   1743                            102
     51                                   102
     51                                   102
    510                                   102
                                          102
                                          102
                                          102
                                          102
                                          102
                                          102
                                         1734
```

```
(c) 51 x 10 = 510    (d) 50 x 30 = 1500      (e)  10       (f)   51
                                                 x51             34
    51 x 10 = 510        50 x 4 =    200           10            204
                                                 500             30
    51 x 10 = 510        1 x 34 =    34           510           1500
                                    1734         x  3           1734
    51 x 4 =  204                               1530
             1734                              + 204
                                               1734
```

It is best not to specify which operation to use for at least four reasons: (1) Some third graders are not yet able to engage in multiplicative thinking, as will be explained shortly; (2) children think in ways that adults cannot anticipate; (3) children who invent their own procedures use what they already know to invent higher-level procedures that contain their own lower-level procedures; and (4) children become inventive by being encouraged to be inventive.

To illustrate how differently third graders solve problems, we give in Figure 6.1 six different ways invented by four children to solve one problem. The problem made up by a student after a field trip was the following: "Fifty-one of the third graders each bought a bag of peanuts. There were 34 peanuts in each bag. How many peanuts did the third graders eat all together?" Almost all the children wrote "51 × 34." However, some used addition while others used a combination of multiplication and addition, as can be seen in Figure 6.1.

Procedures (c) and (d) were invented by the same child, and another student invented both (e) and (f). Procedure (f) illustrates especially well the point about adults' inability to anticipate children's thinking. This child partitioned (30×51) into (30×1) and (30×50) on two lines, but not (4×51). This inconsistency in notation reveals the child's awareness of potential trouble spots. The child knew that multiplying by 30 was trickier than multiplying by a single-digit number and took the precaution *she* felt was necessary (taking relevant factors into account, or autonomy, and keeping track of her own reasoning). Her procedure came very close to the conventional algorithm, but her thinking was different in that she paid particular attention to multiplying by 30 (as opposed to multiplying by 3). Procedure (d) likewise reflects a similar precaution: This child separated (50×34) into (50×30) and (50×4) but kept the 34 whole in (1×34).

Advanced students work fast, and we sometimes ask them to use the extra time to solve the same problem in another way. Procedure (d) was thus invented after (c), and (f) was invented after (e). These children both illustrate how higher-level reasoning is constructed with, and contains, previously constructed relationships.

Procedure (b) used only addition but had the potential of being instructive even to the more advanced children who were using multiplication. This child changed 51×34 to something that had the potential of becoming 102×17. If the teacher had asked him if he could do something similar by adding 204s, then 408s, and then 816s, the child might have thought of the following:

204	408	816	1,632
204	408	816	+ 102
204	408	+102	1,734
204	408		
204	+102		
204			
204			
204			
+102			

Advanced students might then have noticed that the number of addends decreased regularly and might have reinvented the method of doubling and halving described in Chapter 2.

Developing Number Sense

The third goal is related to Piaget's emphasis on the fact that precise and solid operations develop out of children's intuitive thinking about numerical quantities, which is initially hazy and only qualitative. For example, before trying to solve a problem such as 12 × ¼, it helps enormously to know whether the answer will be larger or smaller than 12. "Larger than" and "smaller than" are qualitative relationships. "Four more," "four times as many," and "one-fourth of" are examples of more precise, quantitative, numerical relationships. In other words, precise, quantitative thinking should evolve out of less precise, qualitative (but logical) thinking.

A large part of children's number sense depends on their knowledge of place value. As stated in Chapter 3, algorithms "unteach" place value and hinder children's development of number sense. If they get 154 for 51 × 34 (by doing 4× 1 = 4 and 3 × 5 = 15), for example, children who have been taught algorithms often do not sense that something is wrong. Those who do their own thinking are much more likely to sense an error and say, "That can't be right."

Intuition, or number sense, is an especially important part of arithmetic in an age of calculators. If children use a calculator and get 17,340 for 51 × 34, for example, they should sense that something is wrong somewhere. If they want to know the total of $8.99, $2.34, and $39.51, to cite another example, they should know, even when they have a calculator, that the answer should be *about* $40 + $10.

Exchanging Viewpoints Thoughtfully

To encourage children to do their own thinking, as stated earlier, the teacher refrains from reinforcing right answers and correcting wrong ones and, instead, encourages children to agree or disagree with one another. Whether they are right or wrong, we want children to speak with conviction and change their minds only when *they* are convinced that someone else is correct. In disagreeing forcefully with someone else, some students sometimes hurt other people's feelings and silence them. This is another problem that must be solved through the exchange of viewpoints. When the teacher points this problem out and asks the class what they can do to solve it, children become surprisingly respectful of other people's feelings. Learning to decenter is good for children's sociomoral development as well as their intellectual development, as stated in Chapters 4 and 5.

Becoming able to exchange viewpoints logically and diplomatically may be the most general of the four broad goals in arithmetic. Most educators and most of the public think that math education is unrelated to drug education and sex education. However, these are all related to autonomy and heteronomy. Children who cannot deal with conflicts, disagreements, and peer pressure during the math hour are not likely to deal successfully with them after the math hour either.

Having conceptualized broad goals for third-grade arithmetic, we now turn to the more specific goals involving the four arithmetical operations. It is important to define goals hierarchically because children's knowing how to compute is worthless in the long run if they cannot do their own thinking and have no confidence, no number sense, and no ability to exchange ideas with other people. If, on the other hand, children do their own thinking and interact well with others, they will all eventually become able to solve the kinds of problems found in primary arithmetic.

GOALS INVOLVING THE ARITHMETICAL OPERATIONS

Some third graders are not yet able to engage in multiplicative thinking (Clark, 1993). Because it is important not to impose multiplication prematurely on these children, we begin by summarizing what Piaget said about the difference between addition and multiplication.

Multiplication is usually presented in textbooks merely as a more efficient way of doing repeated addition. For example, third-grade textbooks typically present a picture of three plates, each containing four apples, and explain "sentences" such as the following that yield the same answer:

$$4 + 4 + 4 = \underline{12}$$

$$3 \times 4 = \underline{12}$$

Piaget, however, made a clear distinction between addition and multiplication. Some examples of the behavioral differences were given in Chapter 1 in connection with a two-to-one correspondence task. In his last writing about multiplication, he (1983/1987) described the differences between addition and multiplication as lying in the number of levels of abstraction involved and the number of inclusion relationships the child has to make *simultaneously*.

As can be seen in Figure 6.2a, repeated addition is easy because it involves only one level of abstraction besides the total (the whole). Each group of four is at the same level, and the child performs 4 + 4 first and then 8 + 4, *successively*.

By contrast, multiplication involves the making of higher-order units (units of four) and two kinds of relationships that are not required in addition (see Figure 6.2b): (1) a four-to-one correspondence between four units of one and one unit of four and (2) the inclusion of one unit of four in two units of four, and of two units of four in three units of four. Multiplication thus requires the construction of higher-order units, which have to function *simultaneously* with the lower-order units with one-to-four correspondence. The reader is reminded that hierarchical inclusion is necessary for the lower-order units, too, as we saw in Chapter 1. Children thus have to include one unit of one in two units of one,

FIGURE 6.2 The difference between 4 + 4 + 4 and 3 × 4.

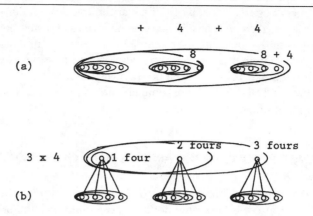

two units of one in three units of one, and so on, *as well as* one unit of four in two units of four, and two units of four in three units of four. Children who have not constructed the higher-order units often get 7 for 3 × 4 because they add 3 to 4 by thinking of all the numbers as units of one, at the same level of abstraction. The two numbers stand for the same kind of units in 3 + 4, but not in 3 × 4.

To explain the difference between addition and multiplication as clearly as possible in the preceding paragraph, we spoke of multiplication as if it involved only two levels of abstraction. In reality, however, multiplication involves a third level of abstraction—the whole that is made out of the three units of four. According to Piaget (1983/1987), addition involves two levels of abstraction (units of one and the whole) whereas multiplication involves three levels (units of one, units of four, and the whole). The reader interested in further detail and a way of assessing children's ability to think multiplicatively is referred to Clark (1993).

Solving Multiplication Problems

Because multiplication is so complicated, it is impossible for some third graders who are developing more slowly than others. We are, therefore, fully satisfied if these children can use repeated addition to solve so-called multiplication problems. On the other hand, our goal for advanced students goes considerably beyond the level usually expected in third grade. Third-grade textbooks go only as far as the multiplication of three-digit numbers by one-digit numbers. However, we find that some of our third graders are perfectly capable of multiplying two- or three-digit numbers by two-digit numbers.

As for multiplication tables, memorization of these tables is not an appropriate goal for third graders. Such memorization would crush children's excitement about what Duckworth (1987) called "wonderful ideas." Third graders come to remember easy combinations such a $4 \times 6 = 24$ and $10 \times 6 = 60$ through frequent use and will use them to deduce harder ones. Heege (1985) showed, for example, that many children deduce the answer to 8×6 from $8 \times 10 = 80$ and say that half of 80 is 40 and 8 more is 48.

Although Thornton and Noxon's (1977) workbook approach is empiricist, their sequence of easy and hard combinations is useful for reference. They began with the desirability of children's knowing the products of all the combinations of factors from 0×0 to 9×9 and made the matrices shown in Figure 6.3. Recommending that we first teach the easiest tables, those of 2s and of 5s, they darkened the cells corresponding to factors of 2 and 5 in Figure 6.3a. This figure indicates that by knowing the tables of 2s and of 5s, children will know the products for 0×2, 1×2, 2×2, and so on; of 2×0, 2×1, 2×2, and so on; of 0×5, 1×5, 2×5, and so on; and of 5×0, 5×1, 5×2, and so on.

Thornton and Noxon then recommended teaching the next easiest tables, which are those of 0s, 1s, and 9s (Figure 6.3b), and the squares (Figure 6.3c, which includes 0×0, 1×1, 2×2, and so on). Figure 6.3d includes all the cells darkened in Figures 6.3a, 6.3b, and 6.3c and indicates that there are only 20 combinations left for children to learn, but that this number becomes 10 because of commutativity (because $3 \times 4 = 4 \times 3$, $3 \times 6 = 6 \times 3$, and so on).

We agree that the tables of 0s, 1s, 2s, and 5s are the easiest, and that squares are relatively easy for children to remember through frequent use. However, we are not sure that the table of 9s is easier than those of 3s and 4s. Our preference in sequencing the difficulty for multiplication games is to increase the factors, as shown in Figure 6.4. It can be seen in this figure that we prefer to go from 0×0 to 4×4 at the beginning, besides involving the tables of 0s, 1s, 2s, 5s, and 10s. The sequence may then proceed to 6×6.

Once children can do single-digit multiplication, it is rather easy for them to invent ways of multiplying two- and three-digit numbers by one-digit numbers *if they know place value*. To solve 345×4, for example, most of our third graders who can do single-digit multiplication figure out that they must add the results of 4×300, 4×40, and of 4×5.

What is much harder is the multiplication of two-digit numbers by two-digit numbers. The problem of multidigit multipliers is discussed in Chapters 7 and 10.

Solving Division Problems

Before beginning our research, we expected children to solve division problems through repeated subtraction. We were wrong (again!). Third graders

FIGURE 6.3 Sequence of learning multiplication "facts" recommended by Thornton and Noxon (1977).

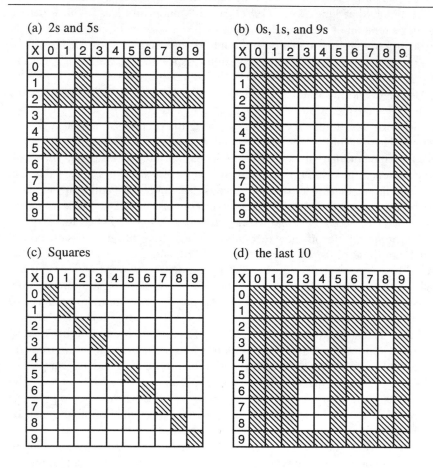

(a) 2s and 5s

(b) 0s, 1s, and 9s

(c) Squares

(d) the last 10

avoid subtraction whenever possible. Olivier and colleagues (1991) came to the same conclusion in South Africa with respect to both partitive and quotitive division problems. They stated, "We find that very few children naturally use subtraction—they rather use *building-up* or addition strategies, and if they use subtraction they quickly change to other strategies" (p. 20).

So-called division problems are thus not very different from multiplication problems. The slow-developing third graders use repeated addition, and the more advanced students invent shortcuts leading to multiplication, as can be seen in Chapter 12.

FIGURE 6.4 Sequence of factors we recommend.

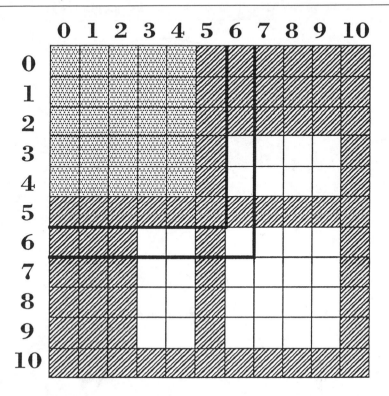

Solving Subtraction Problems

The kinds of problems that require borrowing are still hard in third and fourth grade. This difficulty lies in the fact that subtraction requires the making of two kinds of part–whole relationships, which are elaborated on below.

All part–whole relationships are hard for young children to make, as can be seen in evidence presented in Inhelder and Piaget (1959/1964) and in Piaget, Inhelder, and Szeminska (1948/1960). One of the part–whole relationships in subtraction, even with single-digit numbers, is much more complicated than in addition. In addition such as 5 + 4 (see Figure 6.5a), the child begins with two wholes, 5 and 4, at the same hierarchical level and combines them into a higher-order whole in which the previous wholes become parts. On the other hand, in subtraction, such as 9 − 5 (see Figure 6.5b), the child has to deal *simultaneously* with the whole, 9, and a part, 5, which are at two hierarchical levels.

The arrows in Figure 6.5a indicate that addition involves only "ascending"

FIGURE 6.5 Thinking in one direction (addition) compared to thinking in two opposite directions simultaneously (subtraction).

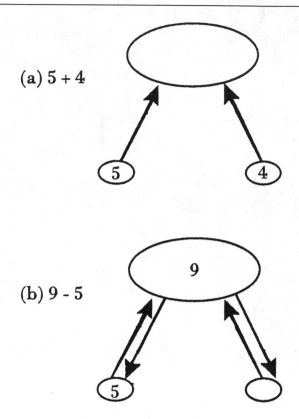

(a) 5 + 4

(b) 9 - 5

from the parts to the whole in one direction. Subtraction, on the other hand, entails both "ascending" (from the parts to the whole) and "descending" (from the whole to the parts) (see Figure 6.5b). This thinking in two opposite directions *simultaneously* is so difficult that we often hear statements such as "I took away the 5 and the 9," "I subtracted the 5 and the 9," "I subtracted the 5 with the 9," and "Five take away 9 equals 4."

Multidigit subtraction requires two more part–whole relationships—between the entire minuend and the value in a column, and between the entire subtrahend and the value in the same column (see Figure 6.6). Many children "subtract up" and get 122 for 123 − 45, as shown in this figure. This "subtracting up" would not happen if children kept in mind the whole minuend, 123, and the whole subtrahend, 45. In other words, they would not do (5 − 3)

Figure 6.6 The part-whole relationships between the entire minuend and the value in a column, and between the entire subtrahend and the value in the same column.

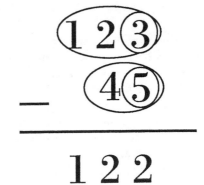

if they remembered that 5 is part of the 45, which must be subtracted from 123. When the part–whole relationships are too numerous and complicated to remember *simultaneously,* children think only about one column at a time.

Since subtraction is difficult even in fourth grade, we work on it in third grade only lightly from time to time. However, subtraction is used in a variety of other problems. For example, advanced students use it when they change 3 × $4.99 to (3 × $5 − .03). Subtraction is also used when a remainder is involved in a division problem. As can be seen in a videotape on division (Kamii, 1990b), however, third graders often use addition to figure out the remainder.

For Students Taught to Use Algorithms

If transfer students and others use algorithms, we usually do not say that they must not use them. However, we insist that all children be able to explain how they got every answer. Becoming able to explain algorithms thus becomes a goal for those who do not understand why these rules produce correct answers. We also encourage users of algorithms to invent "another way" or "a different way" of getting the answer.

Generally speaking, the advanced transfer students quickly find out that it is better to use invented procedures than to continue to use algorithms, since they can explain their own reasoning more easily and find other ways of solving problems. The slow developers, however, cling tenaciously to algorithms and continue to have enormous difficulty with place value, as can be seen in Chapter 11. We do not wish to take away the crutches that make children feel secure, but the crutches continue to block their own thinking. Slow developers especially need to do their own thinking, but these children have little reason to give up the crutches that provide the security of correct answers.

CONCLUSION

Like all other teachers, constructivist teachers push children. However, constructivist teachers do not push children in the same way as those who follow the typical textbook approach. The difference can be illustrated with such an example as the problem of knowing how many cookies there are in four boxes all together, each containing 23. If a third grader has no idea what to do, and the problem came out of a chapter in the textbook entitled "Multiplying by One-Digit Numbers," a traditional teacher would teach the child how to use multiplication. By contrast, a constructivist teacher would pose questions that might facilitate the child's invention of a solution. A constructivist teacher might say, "What are you trying to find out?" (*How many cookies all together.*) "In how many boxes?" (*Four.*) "Would it help to draw a picture to know what to do?" These questions are usually enough to enable the child to visualize the problem and to think about 23 + 23 + 23 + 23.

Hierarchically conceptualized goals are very important in order for the teacher to know how to make decisions from moment to moment. Most adults with good intentions teach children how to get a specific answer to a specific question. But the teacher who keeps in mind the long-range goal of autonomy and the general goal of encouraging children to do their own thinking is not tempted to teach such techniques.

Reform in math education is often believed to consist of better teaching methods, such as the use of computers to teach algorithms. However, the short-term objective of teaching algorithms is in contradiction with the long-range goal of developing children's autonomy and logico-mathematical knowledge. Short-term objectives must always be evaluated in light of the overall goal of turning out autonomous individuals who can think independently and creatively.

Part III

CLASSROOM ACTIVITIES

CHAPTER 7

Problem Solving

Problem solving is the main staple of third-grade arithmetic, and we devote three or four of the five math periods every week to it. The sequence of activities we generally follow with each problem is to begin by setting the stage as described shortly, giving a problem orally to the entire class, and asking each person to solve it alone first. When children have answers, they get up and compare them with those who have also finished. They also compare their methods of getting the answer, until I (SL) ask them to take their seats for the whole-class discussion.

We ask children to work alone first because we want each person to have ideas of his or her own to bring to the subsequent discussion. We also want children first to muster all the knowledge they have to invent their own solutions.

The rationales for encouraging students to talk with others who have also finished are that (1) children who have an answer get restless if they have to sit and wait for the others to finish; (2) children's time should be used exchanging ideas for reasons stated in Chapter 4; and (3) children feel more secure during the whole-class discussion if they know what others have done.

The reader may be wondering about the desirability of this whole-class approach. We use it because a feeling of community develops when the entire class works on the same problem. As for the range of abilities, below-average children can use addition to solve so-called subtraction, multiplication, and division problems, as stated in Chapter 6. We also want less advanced students to listen to the reasoning of more advanced children. The slow developers may or may not benefit from discussions, but if they are not even exposed to them, they have no possibility of benefiting from them. Slow developers often surprise us by making spectacular progress during the latter half of the school year.

This chapter is divided into two parts. The first part gives examples of interactions that took place on December 4, January 21, and January 22. In the second part, we discuss the kinds of problems we give. Since the questions we pose heavily influence what children invent, it is important that we give intriguing and challenging problems at the right level of difficulty.

INTERACTIONS IN THE CLASSROOM

I (SL) begin by asking the students to get their math folders out and to write their names and the date on a clean sheet of paper. These instructions communicate to the class that the activity for the day is problem solving rather than games or another activity. Some children beg to play games but accept my response when I tell them that what we do during the math period is a decision for me to make.

I give the problem orally to the class after setting the stage in relation to children's experiences. For example, if the problem is about money earned by babysitting, I may ask, "How many of you have earned money by babysitting?" and "How many of you babysit regularly for someone you know?" As I give the problem, I write on the board the essential information, such as the following, for the children to copy:

$3.50 an hour
4 hours every weekday
How much money in a week? 3 weeks? 6 weeks?

If children copy this information on their papers, parents can later know the problem the child worked on that day.

Working Alone

While the children are working alone, I circulate among them to interact with them individually. This is a very important part of my teaching, and more details about how I "teach" by posing questions can be found in Chapter 11. The teacher can get an enormous amount of insight about individual children during this phase. Below is an example of what I learned about Danny on December 4. He was a low-average transfer student, and I noticed that he had carried 1 as usual as follows:

$$
\begin{array}{r}
1 \\
3.50 \\
3.50 \\
3.50 \\
+3.50 \\
\hline
13.00
\end{array}
$$

He explained the 1 at the top by saying that if you get a total greater than 9, you have to carry a 1. When I asked him if he always had to carry a 1, he replied in the affirmative, and the only explanation he could give for this rule was: "Otherwise you get the wrong answer." I asked him if he would get the same answer if he added all the dollars and all the cents separately first. He tried my idea, and after getting $12.00 + 2.00 = 14.00$, he still did not see anything wrong with carrying the 1. So I asked him what answer he might get if he added the first two 3.50s first and then the last two 3.50s. Upon getting $7.00 + 7.00 = 14.00$, he still did not think there was anything funny about his "algorithm." I knew that Danny had this erroneous rule for carrying, but I did not know that his belief in it was that strong. I decided not to push him any more that day because he had had enough for one day. I made a mental note to focus next time on what to do after adding four 50¢s and getting $2.

Comparing Answers and Procedures

When children have their own answers, they get up and compare answers and procedures with others who have also finished. I continue to circulate among individuals who are still working but keep an eye on the interactions. Some children start to talk about extraneous topics, especially at the beginning of the school year, and I tell them that if they cannot remember to discuss math during the math hour, I will have to ask them to go back to their seats. The children usually form and reform groups of two or three, but some groups mushroom into "huddles" with five, six, or more, especially when a controversy develops. Some return to their seats to rework the problem.

Whole-Class Discussion

When all or almost all the children have an answer, I ask the class to "return to your seats so we can share our work." The first thing I ask for is the various answers the children got. I list all the answers that are volunteered at the upper left-hand corner of the board without saying whether they are correct or incorrect. The children sometimes react with a small chorus of "Agree" or "Disagree."

I then ask one volunteer after another to go to the board to explain how he or she got his or her answer and encourage the class to let the speaker know immediately if they disagree or do not understand something. This is a time for critical thinking about math, but it is also a time for sensitivity, respectfulness, and supportiveness. The children interact with one another critically but always in the spirit of helping the speaker make sense and trying to produce agreement among classmates.

Most children are eager to go to the board, and I try to be fair in choosing three or four among those who claim to have "a different way." However, I also keep another principle in mind: I want the class to be exposed to the high-level inventions. While children are working alone and I circulate among them, I look for those to call on later.

Following is an account of the whole-class discussion that took place on December 4. There was little discussion on that day because the problem—the one about money earned by babysitting given above—was too easy. We therefore give two other examples: January 21, when the problem was too hard, and

January 22, when the problem was more appropriate. Many other examples of whole-class discussions can be found in Chapter 10.

December 4. Whēn I asked for the answers the children got, everybody agreed that the pay would be $70 for a week, $210 for three weeks, and $420 for six weeks. I asked Lila to go to the board first to explain how she got $70 for one week. She wrote as follows as she explained that she added 3.50 and 3.50 for two hours and doubled the result for four hours per day:

$$3.50 + 3.50 \qquad \begin{array}{l} 7.00 \\ \underline{7.00} \\ 14.00 \quad \text{day} \end{array}$$

Since there are five days in a week, she went on to say, she added the amount for a day (14.00) five times. No one had any question or disagreement.

$$\begin{array}{l} 14.00 \\ 14.00 \\ 14.00 \\ 14.00 \qquad 50.00 \\ 14.00 \qquad \underline{20.00} \\ \quad 70.00 \quad \text{week} \end{array}$$

I then asked Amy to go to the board to tell us how she got $210 for three weeks. As she wrote the following numbers, I noticed that she was doing something new—adding the columns from right to left in doing 140.00 + 70.00:

$$\begin{array}{ll} & 70.00 \\ 140.00 & 70.00 \\ \underline{70.00} & \underline{70.00} \\ 210.00 & \end{array}$$

The third student I called on was Kim, who wrote as follows to get the total for six weeks and shrugged as if to say, "This was ridiculously easy."

$$\begin{array}{r} 210.00 \\ +210.00 \\ \hline 420.00 \end{array}$$

The reader has probably noticed that when small numbers (multipliers) are given, most children use addition without feeling any need to use multiplication.

"It wouldn't be bad to make $420 in six weeks," I commented and asked if anybody had gotten the amount for the first week in a different way. Peter volunteered and explained as he wrote the numbers on the board, "First I multiplied 3.50 by 4 to get the amount for four hours."

$$4 \times 3.50 = 12.00$$

$$\frac{2.00}{14.00}$$

"Since there's five days in a week," he continued, "I multiplied 5 times 14."

$$5 \times 14.00 = 50.00$$

$$\frac{20.00}{70.00}$$

Someone said, "I don't understand how you got $70," and Peter explained: "First, I split 14 into 10 and 4. Five 10s is 50 because 10, 20, 30, 40, 50 [keeping count with his fingers]. And five 4s is 20 because 5, 10, 15, 20 [again keeping count with his fingers]. So I added 50 and 20 and got 70."

I went on to inquire if anyone else had a different way of figuring out the amount for the first week. Brad raised his hand and wrote all over the board as shown in Figure 7.1 while the class watched attentively. After writing "3.50" 20 times, he explained that he first took care of all the dollar amounts and then got the total for all the cents. The dollars for each day came to 12.00, and he added five 12.00s by adding pairs of 12.00s first and getting two 24.00s. By adding the fifth 12.00 to the second 24.00, he got 36.00, and added 36.00 to the first 24.00 and got 60.00. Brad then took care of the cents for each day by writing "2.00"

FIGURE 7.1 Brad's need to write "3.50" twenty times.

Day	Day	Day	Day	Day
3.50	3.50	3.50	3.50	3.50
3.50	3.50	3.50	3.50	3.50
12.00	3.50	3.50	3.50	3.50	3.50
12.00	3.50	3.50	3.50	3.50	3.50
12.00	2.00	2.00	2.00	2.00	2.00
12.00					
12.00					

24.00
24.00
36.00

60.00

$$\underline{10.00}$$

70.00

at the bottom of each column, mentally adding the five 2.00s, and adding 10.00 to the 60.00 he had gotten for the dollar amounts.

I am careful not to say that one procedure is better than another. When third graders add 3.50 many times, it is necessary for most of them to write every single 3.50 for a long time so as not to get confused. If they are encouraged to think in their own ways, they construct progressively more efficient ways that contain the previous levels. Lila's method contained Brad's, and Peter's procedure contained Lila's. Peter was sure about when to multiply (4 × 3.50 and 5 × 14.00) and when to add (12.00 + 2.00 and 50.00 + 20.00) because he had gone through the process of reasoning that Brad and Lila had gone through, step by step.

This whole-class discussion was unusual in that it involved very little interaction. The exchanges were more typical on January 21 and 22.

January 21. The question was the following, which one of the students made up: "There are 59 cakes with 69 candles on each cake. How many candles are there in all?" These numbers were inappropriate and serve to point out that easier numbers such as 24 × 16, which I used on January 22, facilitate the invention of logical strategies.

When all the children were back in their seats for the whole-class discussion, I wrote in the upper left-hand corner of the board all the answers produced: 3,081; 4,079; 2,955; and 4,161. Since Joe volunteered the first answer, I asked him to go to the board first to explain how he got it. He wrote "59 × 69," underlining the 5 and the 6, and said, "Fifty 10 times is 500, and 500 six times is 3,000."

"How did you get that?" someone asked, and Joe wrote the following numbers on the board as he explained his partial answer:

500	10 times
500	20
500	30
500	40
500	50
500	60
3,000	

Joe then finished his explanation by writing "9" nine times in a column, adding them up, and writing "81." Returning to the "59 × 69" he had written, he drew lines from the 5 to the 6, and from one 9 to the other, as shown in Figure 7.2, and wrote "3,000" and "81" to indicate each product. He then wrote "3,000 + 81 = 3,081" as the final answer, as can be seen in the same figure.

Brad piped up and said, "I think you need to do nine 50 times," and Peter

FIGURE 7.2 Joe's way of doing 59 × 69.

```
        81
       ⌒
    59 x 69          3,000 + 81 = 3,081
       ⌣
     3,000
```

agreed. However, Kim emphatically announced that 50 × 60 and 9 × 9 were all that Joe needed to do.

I decided that this was a time for me to intervene with a question and wrote "2 × 12" on the board, asking Joe what he would do with that. "I'd do 2 times 10 and 2 times 2," Joe replied. I drew the lines that can be seen in Figure 7.3a and then wrote a "1" in front of the whole thing. My writing then looked as shown in Figure 7.3b. When I asked Joe what he would do with 12 × 12, he became silent, but Kim insisted that 10 × 10 = 100 and 2 × 2 = 4 was all he had to do, and that the answer was 104.

Brad protested, "But that's not finished. It has to be *12* twelve times."

Amy then spoke with her customary charm and confidence: "I did 12 times 12 in my head and got more than 104. You have to do 50 times 9 and 9 times 60. Can I come to the board and show you?" Joe indicated his consent (if Amy had asked *me* for permission to go to the board, I would have replied that it was up to Joe to decide whether or not *he* wanted help). Amy wrote on the board as shown and gave the following explanation: "It's easier to change 50 times 9 to 9 times 50 because you can then change 9 times 50 to 3 times 50."

$$9 \times 50 \quad \begin{array}{c} 50 \\ 50 \\ \underline{50} \\ 150 \end{array} + \begin{array}{c} 50 \\ 50 \\ \underline{50} \\ 150 \end{array} + \begin{array}{c} 50 \\ 50 \\ \underline{50} \\ 150 \end{array} = 450$$

"I then tried to find an easy way to do 9 times 60. Since I knew that 15 plus 15 is 30, and 30 plus 30 is 60, I decided to do 9 times 15 and then multiply the answer by 4."

FIGURE 7.3 The teacher's questions about how 12 × 12 might be done if 2 × 12 = (2 × 10) + (2 × 2).

(a)

(b)

$$9 \times 60 \qquad 9 \times 15 = 90 + 45 = 135$$

$$135 \times 4 = 400 + 120 + 20 = 540$$

"So you have to add 450 and 540 to the 3,081 that Joe got."

$$
\begin{array}{r}
3{,}081 \\
450 \\
\underline{540} \\
4{,}071
\end{array}
$$

I turned to Joe and the class and asked if anyone had any comment, and Kim announced, "I don't get it." It was by then unfortunately time for the class to go to gym, and I concluded the discussion by saying that we would continue with this kind of problem the next day.

January 22. The discussion that took place on this day illustrates the desirability of choosing small digits, especially for the tens, and/or numbers that are easy to partition. The problem I made up was: "Every Christmas my father gets big boxes of fruit of various kinds, like Indian River oranges, from his company. We get so many pieces of fruit that we have to give some away. This year we ended up making 24 grocery bags of fruit with 16 pieces in each bag. How many pieces did we bag all together?" I reminded the class of the previous day's confusion and said, "The numbers are smaller today, but the problem is similar." Kim was unfortunately absent on that day.

Everybody agreed on the answer of 384, and I wrote it as usual at the upper left-hand corner of the board. Lila was the first volunteer that I called on, and she wrote as follows on the board:

$$
\begin{array}{r}
20 \times 10 = 200 \\
20 \times 6 = \underline{120} \\
320 \\
4 \times 10 = 40 \\
4 \times 6 = \underline{24} \\
64 \\
\underline{320} \\
384
\end{array}
$$

To put Lila's computation into relationship with the previous day's confusion, I wrote as shown in Figure 7.4 and pointed out that Lila first did 20×10 and 20×6 (as shown in Figure 7.4a) and then 4×10 and 4×6 (as shown in Figure 7.4b). "But yesterday, some people did only this part [pointing to 20×10] and this part [pointing to 4×6]. How is Lila's way different?" I asked. Joe lost

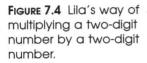

FIGURE 7.4 Lila's way of multiplying a two-digit number by a two-digit number.

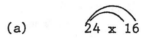

(a)

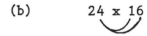

(b)

no time to say, "It's complete!" and many others agreed. It is significant that Joe's logic was correct today and also back in November (see Chapter 11), when the numbers were small. Small numbers thus facilitate the logic of multidigit multiplication.

I went on to inquire if anybody else got the answer in a different way, and Heather demonstrated the method, shown in Figure 7.5a, of adding 64 six times. Someone asked, "Where did you get the 64s from?" and Heather explained that she had first written "16" twenty-four times in a column, as shown in Figure 7.5b. (Heather was one of the many third graders who figured out the commutativity of multiplication on her own, with the greatest of ease.) She then made 32s with pairs of 16s and knew that she needed only half as many 32s as 16s, which was 12. She then added two 32s, got 64, and knew that she needed half as many 64s as 32s, so that was 6, she explained.

"That's interesting," I remarked, and pointed out as I wrote on the board that Heather had changed 24 × 16 to 32 × 12 and then to 64 × 6. (The parallel is noteworthy between these changes Heather invented and the method of doubling and halving described in Chapter 2.)

"Why didn't she multiply 32 by 24?" I asked, pointing to the 12. Randy was quick to reply that each time you double one number, you have to halve the other number because the first number becomes twice as big as it was before.

I asked who else had a different way of working the problem and called on Amy to show a third procedure. Her way, shown in Figure 7.6, came close to 4 × 24 × 2 × 2. She explained that she got the total for four 24s, doubled the 96 she got to get the total for eight 24s, and doubled the 192 she got to get the total for sixteen 24s. (The procedure invented by Amy was like the Egyptians' method of doubling described in Chapter 2.)

The fourth method was then demonstrated by Jenny. She began by writing "32" twelve times in a column and drew a line below it. She then added all the ones by counting by 2s and wrote "4" below the line. After carrying 20, she added 30 repeatedly and said, "Fifty, 80, 110, 140" and so on, all the way to 380. I commented that Jenny's way was like Heather's in that she changed 16 twenty-four times to 32 twelve times.

FIGURE 7.5 Heather's writing on the board to explain why 24 × 16 = 32 twelve times = 64 six times.

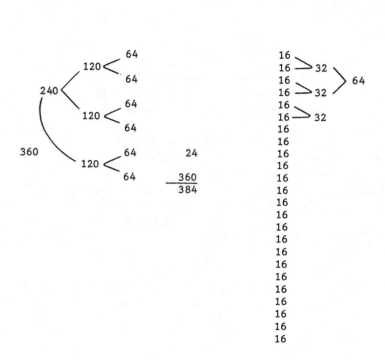

(a)   (b)

The fifth method was then offered by Randy, who explained that since half of 24 is 12, he multiplied 16 by 12 and doubled the result as follows:

$$16 \times 12 = 10 \times 12 = 120$$

$$6 \times 12 = \underline{72}$$
$$192$$
$$\underline{192}$$
$$384$$

Strictly speaking, the preceding equations are not correct, and "16 × 12" does not "say" what Randy said he had done—multiplying 16 by 12. However, I do not tell children where to write the multiplier and multiplicand in relation to spoken language, such as "12 times 16" and "multiply 16 by 12." These are bits of social (conventional) knowledge that should not get in the way of children's

Figure 7.6 Amy's writing to explain that 24 × 16 = (24 four times) × 2 × 2.

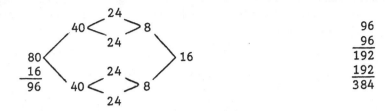

numerical thinking, that is, logico-mathematical knowledge. Randy's reasoning was conceptually deep, and I want children to be free to concentrate on reasoning.

Brad then demonstrated a sixth way, which can be seen in Figure 7.7. I pointed out that both Brad and Randy had broken one of the numbers down into groups, but that Brad changed the 16 to two groups of 8, while Randy changed the 24 to two groups of 12.

We hope the reader can see how we let computational techniques grow out of word problems. Well-chosen numbers lead to new inventions that are evidence of profound mathematical thinking. They also lead to the integration of addition, subtraction, halving (division), and multiplication. Moreover, well-chosen numbers lead to rich discussions and explanations, while numbers that are too easy or too hard lead to dead ends. Numbers such as the following are possibilities for the subsequent days, but it is necessary always to plan one day at a time in light of the previous day's discussion:

$$26 \times 34$$
$$17 \times 23$$
$$19 \times 23 \ (= 20 \times 23 - 23)$$

Figure 7.7 Brad's explanation of 24 × 16 = (four 24s) × 2 × 2.

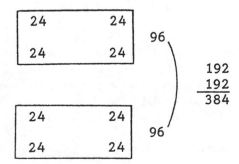

Certain contents also inspire children more than others. Since the key to constructivist teaching is to pose the right question at the right time, we describe below the kinds of contents that we have found to intrigue and motivate our group of third graders.

THE KINDS OF PROBLEMS CHILDREN LIKE

The kinds of problems that interest children can be grouped into the following categories: situations in daily living in and out of school, the teacher's personal life, problems made up by children, and situations arising in other areas of the curriculum. Holidays such as Halloween inspire attractive problems, and the teacher's personal life seems to be an endless source of interest between holidays. While textbook problems are mere excuses for practicing one operation at a time, teacher-made problems make math seem much more varied, more practical, and more interesting to children. We begin with problems that come out of life in school.

Situations in Daily Living at School

Our ancestors developed mathematics as they felt the need to count livestock and to measure land and grains. In the same way, children at Hall-Kent School construct mathematics out of daily living activities in school. Below are five examples of situations that come up naturally: breaking into small groups, making a schedule, getting enough materials for an activity, collecting money, and raising money.

Breaking into Small Groups. The class often works in small groups, especially in science and social studies. I sometimes decide how many people I want in each group and ask how many groups we will have and whether or not the groups will all have the same number of people. If the division comes out with a remainder, we negotiate a solution to this problem. At other times, I specify how many groups I want, especially when we have only three, four, five, or six sets of materials.

We follow this procedure throughout the year for all groupings. This process is good not only for arithmetic but also for children's development of autonomy. When children participate in this kind of decision making, they take relevant factors into account, such as which children are likely to work well together and what responsibility they have to assume if they decide to work with someone who is likely to tempt them into behaving in inappropriate ways.

Making Schedules. Making a schedule also involves learning to take relevant factors into account. Children need to learn to estimate the amount of time required to accomplish things. We make short-term and long-term plans together so that everybody knows what to do and what to expect.

The example described below concerns making a schedule for book reports. The children had a book report due every three weeks in two parts—a part to be handed in and a part to be presented orally to the class. Since *days* could be spent on oral reports, I asked the class to figure out the best number of minutes each person should get to make a presentation.

After some random suggestions, the children decided on ten minutes per person. There were 23 students in the class, and everybody agreed that four hours would be *much too long*. They then tried calculations for five minutes per student and concluded that that was still too long. Finally, after spending quite some time calculating, the class agreed that three minutes per person would be perfect. Three minutes would be long enough to make well-prepared points, they thought, after getting a "feel" for this duration. They also agreed that it would be good to finish all the reports in a little more than one hour ($23 \times 3 = 69$).

Discussions about schedules serve as occasions to anticipate problems and prevent them. A group that makes decisions together becomes self-directed and able to live by the rules *they* make through negotiation. Self-government is good not only for living responsibly but also for helping children to develop a profound sense of self.

Preparing Enough Materials for an Activity. Teachers often have to prepare enough materials for specific activities. When objects such as origami paper come in packages of 20, 24, and so on, questions about how many packages to buy and how much money is necessary make excellent problems.

The following example came out of a need for spoons that were to be used as rhythm instruments in a part of the spring music program. The music teacher requested that each student bring two spoons for this purpose. She put all the spoons collected by each of three classes (23, 24, and 25 students, respectively) in three boxes, and the kids asked, just for fun, how many spoons there were altogether. We, of course, sat down immediately to calculate the total in a variety of ways.

Later, the music teacher asked us to find out how many spoons she needed to provide for those who did not or could not bring any. Rather than going from class to class asking for a show of hands, we used the information we had to deduce the answer. We counted the spoons in each box and compared this number with the relevant information and gave the answer to the music teacher. (I purposely did not say what information was relevant because I wanted the children to decide what information they needed to answer the question.)

Collecting Money. Sometimes, special activities, such as field trips, cost money. These are occasions to figure out how many people have paid, how much money we have collected, how much more we need to collect, and so on.

Once a month throughout the year, as part of a schoolwide program, I send home order forms from two book clubs. The handling of these orders is the example we describe below of this kind of real-life mathematics. The books vary in price, and parents are free to order as many as they wish or none at all. The children bring the forms back with a check for each order. Since I have to list all the books on a master order form for the entire class, with the exact numbers of books and the correct amount of money, I decided to let this become the math lesson once a month.

We first check each order and make sure that each check is made out correctly for the exact amount. I do this by writing on the board the name of each child ordering books, with the amount appearing on his or her check next to it. After writing the amount on a check, I read the identification number and the title of each book the check is intended for. Since each student has a copy of a blank order form, he or she can get the price of each book being ordered. Each person must also make tally marks next to each book being ordered because the order for the entire class requires that I specify how many of each book the class is ordering.

Children have a variety of ways of ascertaining that each check is made out for the correct amount. Some mentally add the price of each book. Others at a more advanced level find out the number of books that cost $1.50 each, for example, and use multiplication.

When we agree that each subtotal is correct, each student makes an order form for the entire class. The first time I tried this activity, I made the mistake of photocopying the form supplied by each book club, so that each child would have his or her own to fill out. When we started to work on this form, I immediately realized that it took away all opportunities for inventive work and autonomy. It organized all the information in a chart, specified how to tally the books, and even indicated that $1.50 was to be *multiplied* by the number in a certain cell.

From the second time on, I let each student devise his or her own way of figuring out and reporting how many of each book we were ordering and the total amount of money the class was sending. This has been a popular activity with our children and a very good way to continue to discuss and evaluate one another's method of working.

Raising Money. Raising money is not something we do frequently, but the class feels the desirability of certain extra things from time to time. One day, for example, a class discussion led to the conclusion that it would be good to have additional books for our class library. After numerous ideas were put on the table for discussion, many were rejected and a few were investigated. Following two days of class meetings, the class voted unanimously to organize a bake sale.

The children got their parents' consent to help them make cookies, brownies, and other sweets for this purpose. Several children had the foresight to organize the class into groups so that there would be an appropriate distribution of a variety of goods.

The only choice I did not give the class was the times the sale would be held. It would be before school, from 7:45 to 8:00 in the morning, and after school, from 3:00 to 3:30 in the afternoon, I announced. The class decided to have the sale on two consecutive days. The second day was to sell what was left over.

The next question brought up by a student was "How will we tell everybody so they will know to come?" A discussion about advertising followed, and one student pointed out how stores put SALE signs in their windows. Another student reminded us of all the GARAGE SALE signs she had seen around the neighborhood. The class took the responsibility of forming publicity groups and made posters to put up around the school and wrote memos to send to every classroom in the school.

The next question was how much money to charge for each item. Several children said it depended on the size of the goods. For example, as one girl said, "It wouldn't be fair to charge the same for two big brownies as for two little cookies." The class decided to produce 25-cent bags and 50-cent bags and to ask students to bring the goods already bagged. The prices were to be marked on the morning of the sale.

The children planned the shifts of cashiers, sales assistants, and "floats," who would remind schoolmates and teachers of the sale. Others agreed to take care of the daily chores in our classroom, such as the lunch count, attendance report, and feeding the gerbil.

On the day of the sale, I helped get it started during the first 15 minutes but was not needed after that. The children had the autonomy to run the sale without me and took responsibility for *everything*. They counted money, made change, carefully recorded the names of all to whom they owed change, and took the money to them as soon as possible. This teamwork without adult intervention was something I frankly did not know was possible. The class made $48.50 and bought four beautiful books with it.

Other Examples. When a mother made 24 cupcakes for a child's birthday and sprinkled a generous amount of speckles on them, I asked the class how many speckles were used for the 24 cupcakes. (We estimated and counted approximately 40 speckles on each cupcake.) To cite another example, the day after a field trip I asked the children to make problems with the following facts: A Coke cost 55 cents a can, and peanuts cost 45 cents a bag. The third graders bought 40 Cokes and 51 bags of peanuts all together. Another source of count-less problems is the cafeteria.

Situations in Daily Living Outside School

The grocery store obviously inspires many math problems. One day in late September, I drew six small circles on one side of the board with a sign saying "McIntosh, 6 for 66 cents," and five circles on the other side with a sign saying "Granny Smith, 5 for 95 cents." The question I posed first was: "Which kind is the better buy?"—a question entailing more than one correct answer. After we came to an agreement, I asked the next question: "How much more do the Granny Smiths cost?"

We often brought newspaper ads to the class and had one that said, "Pepsi, 2 for 99 cents." When I asked how much money we would need to buy eight bottles at this price, many children wrote "99" eight times at the beginning of the year.

As stated earlier, purchases related to holidays appeal to children, and I like to make up problems that evolve from one consideration to another. For ex-ample, at Easter time, I said, "I have a friend who will have an Easter party, and she already has 15 baskets. She wants to put six chocolate eggs in each basket, and the eggs cost 35 cents a piece. What does she need to think about?" One student said "How much money will it cost altogether?" and another said "How many eggs does she need to buy?"

After the class answered both questions, I went on to say, "When my friend got to the store, she found out that the eggs sold as singles, but that they also came in boxes of 12 that cost $3.60 per box. Should she buy 90 loose eggs at 35 cents apiece, or is it more advantageous to buy some of these boxes at $3.60 a box?"

The Teacher's Personal Life

An example I gave in September was: "Yesterday, I needed some soap, and the brand I like costs $1.65 for three bars. I bought nine bars. How much did I spend on soap?" Children love to hear about the teacher's personal life and asked what brand I bought and so on.

Since I was getting married in March, I asked the class to help me plan vari-ous parts of the wedding. For example, I told the class that I had found that, with 1 yard of material, I could make 24 rice bags. My problem was how many yards I needed to buy to have 150 bags. The children loved making wedding plans with me and helped me figure out how many yards of ribbon to get for the rice bags, how many pieces of food to order, and so on.

Problems Made Up by Children

One way of asking children to make up a problem is to write "5 × 7" on the board, for example, and ask them to write a word problem that goes with this expression. (The slow developers make up revealing problems, such as "I had 5 cents, and my father gave me 7 cents. . . .") Another kind of assignment is to make up "a multiplication word problem that's not too easy but not too hard." A more open request is for "any word problem" with one condition: "You *have to* be able to answer your own question and prove it." Still another way is to give some data and ask students to make up two or three problems using these numbers.

Children learn to logico-arithmetize contents not only by solving word problems but also by inventing them. When a problem is too hard, the children can negotiate a modification—in itself a worthwhile activity.

Other Subjects in the Curriculum

Examples of the integration of math and social studies can be seen in Chapters 11 and 12, where we discuss questions related to a trip to California found in the social studies book. Another example is: "Leonardo da Vinci painted this picture [the *Mona Lisa*] about 480 years ago. About what year was that? Do you know anything else that happened about that time? What century was that in? What century is it now? Why is it called the twentieth century?"

A third example concerns packaging at factories. I asked the class what came in boxes and packages of various sizes, and the children mentioned 12 eggs in a carton, 12 doughnuts in a box, 6-packs of beverages, and so forth. I asked if somebody at some time decided how many to put in a package, and what might happen if people did not always get the same number in a package. After thus setting the stage for the world of commerce, I asked: "If you had 146 pieces of candy, and the most you could put in a package were 24, how many would you put in a package, and how many packages would you have?"

The next day, I said to the class, "Today, there are only 120 pieces of candy, and I want you to put your pens down and tell me how many boxes there would be if I told the person I hired that there had to be 10 pieces of candy in each box." As I asked similar questions about 12 pieces and then 15 pieces in a box, I made the following table on the board and asked, "If I wanted six boxes, how many pieces would there be in each box?"

10 pieces	(12 boxes)
12 pieces	(10 boxes)
15 pieces	(8 boxes)

One of the children replied that the answer was 19 pieces because the numbers decreased by 2 in the right-hand column and increased in the other column by 2 (from 10 to 12) and then by 3 (from 12 to 15). The next number had to increase by 4, she concluded, and some children agreed. A better question after the first two (10 and 12 pieces in a box) might have been 20 pieces in a box (the double of 10), followed by 5 pieces (half of 10), and then perhaps 6 or 15 pieces.

This example illustrates a principle that is worth stating: It is sometimes good to stay with the same content and situation for two or three days and vary the numbers systematically.

CONCLUSION

Unlike textbooks, we give problems that involve a variety of operations but emphasize multiplication and division. The slow developers, as we said before, use addition to solve most problems. When children are thus encouraged to do their own thinking to solve a variety of problems, they do not ask, "Am I supposed to add or subtract, . . . or multiply or divide?" Examples were given above of children who integrated division, addition, and subtraction with multiplication.

To teachers who are hesitant about throwing out the textbook, we say that children's enthusiasm about home-made problems makes the risk worth taking. It is at first difficult to think up problems every day, but math is indeed all around us. Children let us know what appeals to them and what does not and help us become better teachers.

CHAPTER 8

Group Games

Games are an essential part of constructivist teaching for many reasons. From the standpoint of children's development of autonomy, games involve rules and are therefore uniquely suited for the development of children's ability to govern themselves. When conflicts arise, the teacher can guide children in making their own decisions about sanctions and the possibility of modifying rules or making new ones.

From the point of view of arithmetic, games have long been known to motivate children to practice the four operations. Few children ever ask for worksheets, but they often beg to play math games and protest when the teacher's response is "no." For children's development of autonomy, it is important that they work and learn for their own satisfaction, without being manipulated with extrinsic motivators.

Games are better than worksheets also because feedback is immediate and from peers. Immediate feedback is obviously more effective than a reaction that comes the next day, when children do not care what happened any more. Moreover, with games, unlike with worksheets, each child has the possibility of supervising everyone else's work and learns to be critical and self-reliant. Furthermore, games provide opportunities for creating strategies, an intellectually much more demanding endeavor than completing worksheets.

Many general principles of teaching concerning rules and conflicts have been given in Kamii (1985) and in Kamii and DeVries (1980). We focus below on three specific principles that came out of our experiences with third graders: (1) The teacher needs to play with children; (2) it is desirable for the teacher to ask all the small groups at the end of the hour to tell the class how many points each player made; and (3) it is desirable that each child keep cumulative scores for all the students playing the same game.

It is easy for games to deteriorate into a time to "goof off." One of the ways of preventing this is for the teacher to take games seriously enough to play them with children. If the teacher uses this time to correct papers, children quickly get the message that games are not important enough for the teacher to bother with. Besides, it is by playing with children that the teacher can best assess how well each child reasons numerically. By playing with children, the teacher can also tell when a game needs to be modified or put away. Games must be put away when they are too difficult and when children have outgrown them.

A second way of motivating children to play games seriously is to set time aside at the end of the hour for a reporting session. By asking every group in turn to tell the class who won, by how many points, and how many points everybody else got, we make children accountable to the class. This is also a time to discuss social problems that came up, and children can offer suggestions to one another about how to resolve conflicts.

We encountered other problems: Children recorded only their own points throughout the hour, tried to total them in a rush at the end, and did not have any opportunity to check one another's arithmetic. The solution to these problems the children agreed on was to keep every player's cumulative total throughout the game in a notebook for math games. By being able to see everybody's up-to-the-minute cumulative total, children came to enjoy the excitement of the neck-and-neck competition.

The games in this chapter are described in five categories, and three more are recommended at the end as whole-class games: (1) addition games, (2) easier games involving two, three, or four operations, (3) games involving repeated addition (leading to multiplication), (4) easier multiplication and division games, and (5) harder games involving two, three, or four operations. These categories are not mutually exclusive and are intended only to facilitate the reader's comprehension.

Three points must be mentioned about the descriptions of the individual games:

1. Complete source information about the games identified as commercially made is given in the Appendix at the back of the book, as are some of the mail-order firms from which games may be purchased.
2. When the number of players is not specified, this means that the number can vary from two to four.
3. We never specify how the first player is to be chosen, and not all the details of each game are spelled out. The reason for this omission is that, for the development of children's autonomy, it is better that they make their own rules and decisions.

ADDITION GAMES

Many of the games described in Kamii (1989a) are appropriate in third grade as well as in second grade. Among the popular games in this category are the following commercially made games: *The Allowance Game* (p. 135),° *Ring Toss* (pp. 130, 131), *Safe Dart Game* (pp. 130–131), and *Shoot the Moon* (pp. 133–134). Another popular game is the Spinner Game.

°Page numbers refer to Kamii (1989a).

PHOTOGRAPH 8.1 The Spinner Game

THE SPINNER GAME

Materials: A spinner, six wooden balls, and a platter (see Photograph 8.1) similar to *Roulette* in the Hearth Song catalog and *'Round and 'Round It Goes* in the Norm Thompson catalog.

Play: The players take turns placing all the balls in the middle of the platter and spinning the spinner. The game is usually played by adding all the points indicated next to the holes in which the six balls rest. However, our Spinner Game makes the following modification: Points can be earned only in multiples of 10. For example, if the balls land in the holes marked 3, 9, 12, 4, 13, and 8, one player may think of only 20 points (12 + 8), while another may find 30 (13 + 8 + 9) or 40 (13 + 12 + 8 + 4 + 3) points. Masking tape can be used to change the numbers on the platter. It is in itself educational to have children discuss and decide which numbers to assign to the holes.

101 and O'NO99

These are two commercially made versions of essentially the same game. Teachers can make both versions with blank cards.

FIGURE 8.1 The cards used in *101* and in *O'NO99*.

Number or instruction on card	Number of cards	
	101	O'NO99
1 through 9 (3 of each)	27 cards	
2 through 9 (3 of each)		24 cards
10	6 cards	10 cards
99		4 cards
101	5 cards	
-10	4 cards	4 cards
50	2 cards	
REVERSE	4 cards	6 cards
HOLD/PASS	4 cards	4 cards
PLAY TWICE	2 cards	2 cards

Materials: 12 or more chips (or, alternatively, buttons or beans); a deck of 54 cards listed in Figure 8.1.

Play: The object of the game is to avoid totaling 101 points or more (or 99 points or more in *O'NO99*)—the number that causes a player to lose the round.

Three cards are dealt to each player in *101*, but each player receives four cards in *O'NO99*. The rest of the cards constitute the draw pile, which remains in the middle of the table.

The first player puts any card down, announcing its value (9, for example). She then takes one card from the draw pile to replace the one used. Every subsequent player plays a card (a 5, for example), announcing the cumulative total (14 in this case), and replaces it with a card taken from the draw pile. A player thus always has three cards in *101* and four cards in *O'NO99*.

Play continues, and the person who gets to 101 or above (or 99 or above in *O'NO99*) loses the round. If the players decide to give three chips to each player at the beginning of the game, the loser of a round has to lose one of them. The loser of the game is the first person to lose all three chips.

Certain cards serve specific purposes. The 101 (or 99) card can be played only when the cumulative total is negative and, therefore, generally reduces the number of cards a person can play. The −10 card is very useful when the cumulative total is close to 101 (or 99), as it reduces the cumulative total by 10. The Reverse card can be played to reverse the direction of play, and the Hold/Pass card is similar but does not reverse the direction of play. The Play Twice card is like the Hold/Pass card but makes the next player take two turns. (A player who has to play twice cannot begin by using a Play Twice card or a Reverse card because these instructions would contradict the instruction to play twice.)

Modifications: A good modification is to change this game into a subtraction game. Play begins with 101 (or 99) points, and the object of the game is not to be the one to reach 0 or below 0. The -10 cards become $+10$ cards when all the positive numbers become negative.

If 101 or 99 seems too hard, the game can be changed to 31, 50, or any other cumulative total. Children also like to go up to 50 and then down to 0. Any of the instruction cards (Reverse, Hold/Pass, and Play Twice) can be eliminated if they cause confusion.

CASINO

Golick (1973) describes the following game that many children reportedly like. We describe her version first and summarize the process we underwent to modify it considerably.

Material: A deck of playing cards with Ace = 1, and Jack, Queen, and King having no numerical value.

Play: The object of the game is to earn the highest number of points according to the following point system:

The greatest number of cards	3 points
The greatest number of spades	1 point
The 10 of diamonds	2 points
The 2 of spades	1 point
Each Ace	1 point
Taking in all the cards on the table in one play (a Sweep)	1 point

Four cards are dealt to each player, and four cards are placed face up on the table. After these are played out, four new cards are dealt again to the players, but no more to the table.

The first player may do one of the following:

1. *Match.* Playing a card of the same value as one on the table, and taking both in. For example, if there is a Queen on the table, and the player has a Queen in his hand, he puts the two together face down in front of himself to count toward his score.

2. *Combine.* The player may combine two cards *on the table* that equal the numerical value of one he has in his hand and take them in with the card in his hand. If, for example, there are a 5 and a 2 on the table, the player may take them in with a 7 from his hand. He may also take in several combinations with the same total (such as a 5 and a 2, and a 4 and a 3).

> *Note:* On each turn, a player can take more than one card from the table but cannot play more than one card from his hand.

3. *Hold.* The player may play a card of the same value as one on the table directly onto its match (or to a combination that equals it in numerical value) and say, for example, "Holding 10s." This means that he has another card of that value in his hand and plans to take in those cards on a subsequent turn.
4. *Build.* The player may combine a card or cards on the table with one in his hand to total another card in his hand. For example, if there are a 7 and a 2 on the table, the player may put them together, add an Ace from his hand, and say, "Building 10." This means that he has a 10 in his hand and plans to take in the cards on a subsequent turn.
5. *Discard.* If the player cannot match, combine, hold, or build, he discards a card face up on the table.

The second player may do any of the five things listed above as well as two other things: (1) take in any combination an opponent is holding or building and (2) build on an opponent's "build." (For example, if an opponent is building 6 with two 3s, the player may add a 4 and say, "Building 10", provided he has a 10 in his hand.)

When a player's turn comes around again, he may raise his own build if he has the appropriate cards. He does not have to take in his "hold" or "build" at once, provided he can match, take in another combination, capture another player's build or hold, or make another build or hold himself.

Modifications: While trying to play this game, some children began to say that the rules were often confusing and some did not make sense. The class then had many discussions to modify the rules, try them out, and modify them again.

The rule that seemed most devoid of sense concerned the value of the face cards. Rather than having so many cards with no point value, I (SL) suggested that all face cards should be worth 10 points. The children all agreed that this was a sensible modification.

The possibility of (1) matching, (2) combining, (3) holding, or (4) building also underwent several changes. Matching presented no difficulty, but I (SL) suggested eliminating this possibility after noticing that some players were only matching and never trying to combine or to build.

When the possibility of matching was eliminated, it did not make much sense to keep the rule of holding. Besides, the children seldom took advantage of this possibility and immediately took the cards they could take.

The rule of combining specified that a player could combine cards that are on the table but not those that are in one's hand. This rule caused much confusion, and the children decided that one should be allowed to combine cards in one's hand, too. This modification necessitated a change in the rule about what happens when a player uses up all 4 cards. The class decided that whenever the 4 cards are used up, a player should take 4 more from the top of the draw pile.

The point system, too, seemed too complicated and arbitrary to the children. After trying to modify the numbers of points by attributing 50 points for getting the most cards and 5 points to certain cards (such as the "Suicide King (of hearts)"), the class decided drastically to simplify the entire point system to: One gets only the number of points one makes, plus 5 points for a sweep because sweeps are hard to make. For example, if a player takes a 5 and a 2 from the table with a 7 from his hand, he gets 7 points (not 14). Everyone was thus to keep track of his up-to-the-minute cumulative total with only three possible moves: combining, building, and discarding.

MILLE BORNES

Material: A deck of 112 commercially made cards that can be found in large discount stores. The pictures on the cards concern an imaginary cross-country auto race filled with hazards. The following cards can be removed to simplify this game:

Hazards	Remedies	Safeties
3 "Out of gas"	7 "Gasoline"	1 "Extra tank"
3 "Flat tire"	6 "Spare tire"	1 "Puncture-proof"
		1 "Driving Ace"
		1 "Right of way"

Play: The object of the game is to be the first to have traveled 1,000 miles by playing Distance cards. There are three major categories of cards: Distance cards (of 25, 50, 75, 100, and 200 miles), Hazard cards, and Remedy cards. Hazard cards (such as Accident) are used to prevent other players from playing Distance cards. The player who has had an accident cannot play any Distance cards until she puts down a Remedy card (a Repair card in this case).

Each person is dealt 6 cards, and the remaining cards constitute the draw pile. Players take turns drawing a card from the draw pile and either playing a card or discarding one to the discard pile. A player thus always has six cards at the end of each turn.

The rules may seem complicated at first, but children master them and enjoy them.

Modification: When the numbers become too easy, it is good to change some of them to numbers such as 35 and 65.

FIGURE 8.2 The dominoes used in Twenties.

0–1	0–2	0–3	0–4	0–5	0–6̲	0–7	0–8	0–9̲	(9 dominoes)
1–1	1–2	1–3	1–4	1–5	1–6̲	1–7	1–8	1–9̲	(9 dominoes)
	2–2	2–3	2–4	2–5	2–6̲	2–7	2–8	2–9̲	(8 dominoes)
		3–3	3–4	3–5	3–6̲	3–7	3–8	3–9̲	(7 dominoes)
			4–4	4–5	4–6̲	4–7	4–8	4–9̲	(6 dominoes)
				5–5	5–6̲	5–7	5–8	5–9̲	(5 dominoes)
					6̲–6̲	6̲–7	6̲–8	6̲–9̲	(4 dominoes)
						7–7	7–8	7–9̲	(3 dominoes)
							8–8	8–9̲	(2 dominoes)
								9̲–9̲	(1 domino)
									54 dominoes

Note: It is desirable always to underline the 6 and 9 as

shown above.

FORWARD AND BACKWARD

Materials: Any board with a path, such as the *Sorry* board or a home-made board; three or four markers of the same color for each player; three dice, two of one color and one of a different color.

Play: The players take turns rolling the three dice. The two numbers on the dice of the same color are added, and the number on the third die is subtracted. If the number thus obtained is greater than 0, the player advances by that number. If the number is smaller than 0, the player moves backwards by that number. The first person to reach the goal is the winner.

Players can choose the marker they want to move, but they cannot move more than one marker during a turn.

Other rules for being sent back to Start or for being allowed to move ahead can be added to increase interest. Certain contents, such as the frogs in the next game, also increase the attractiveness of a board game. Stickers are helpful in suggesting frogs or any other content that appeals to children.

LEAP FROG (OR ODD AND EVEN)

Materials: Any commercially made or home-made board; one or more markers for each player; two 10- or 12-sided dice.

Play: The players take turns rolling the dice. If the total is an even number, the player advances by half of this total. (For example, if a 6 and an 8 are rolled, the player advanced 7 spaces.) If the total rolled is an odd number, the player does not move at all. The first person to reach the goal is the winner.

The total of 13 is lucky, and the player can advance 13 spaces.

TWENTIES

Materials: 45 counters (or tiles or buttons); the 54 dominoes shown in Figure 8.2 (the dots on plastic dominoes can be covered up with numerals written on adhesive labels).

Play: The object of the game is to make a total of 20 as often as possible, thereby being the first to get rid of one's counters.

All the dominoes are placed on the table, face down, and each player takes 5 of them. One domino is placed face up in the middle of the table to start the game. The players also divide the 45 counters equally among themselves.

The players take turns trying to make a total of 20 by putting down a domino next to one already on the table, either horizontally or vertically, as shown in Figure 8.3 and Photograph 8.2. After putting a domino down, each player takes

FIGURE 8.3 Making 20 horizontally or vertically and closing the line.

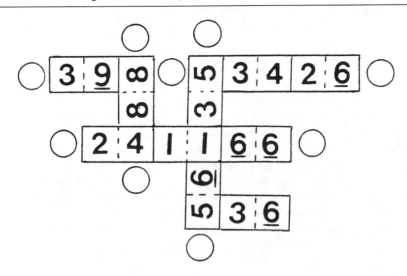

PHOTOGRAPH 8.2 Twenties

one from the face-down pile to have 5 again. When a player makes a total of 20, she closes the line with counters, as can be seen in Figure 8.3.

QUAD-OMINOS

This commercially made game is like *Tri-Ominos,* which was described in Kamii (1989a, pp. 121–122). It uses 125 plastic pieces with numerals in four corners, as shown in Figure 8.4. If the Quad-Omino with four 4s is already on the table, a player can match two 4s as shown in Figure 8.4a and get 13 points (4 + 4 + 5 + 0) for this move. Extra points can be won under various conditions, but these rules might be simplified.

Modification: An excellent modification was invented by children, who wanted to play a piece by matching only one number diagonally, as shown in Figure 8.4b. In this situation, the player would get 8 points (4 + 4). This modification turned out to be excellent because it opened up the possibility, shown in Figure 8.4c, of making matches on two sides yielding 30 points (8 + 8 + 8 + 6). It also opened up the possibility, shown in Figure 8.4d, of making matches on three sides yielding 40 points (2 + 8 + 8 + 8 + 8 + 6).

Figure 8.4 Matching Quad-Ominos according to the printed rules and invented rules.

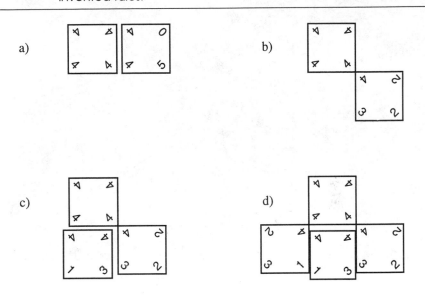

EASIER GAMES INVOLVING TWO, THREE, OR FOUR OPERATIONS

Salute! is described in Kamii (1989a, p. 138) for use with second graders but has been popular in third grade as well. It is repeated later in this chapter as a multiplication and division game, but it can also be played as an addition and subtraction game.

NUMBER RINGS (also called RING-A-ROUND)

Materials: This commercially made game is illustrated in Photograph 8.3.
Play: Each player chooses a sector consisting of 18 "bases," numbered 1–18, and takes 18 rings of one color that fit onto the bases.

The players take turns rolling three dice and can utilize one or more of the numbers rolled using addition, subtraction, multiplication, and/or division. For example, if a player rolls a 2, 5, and 6, these numbers may each be used, or the numbers may be combined to make any one of the following numbers:

3 $(5 - 2)$	9 $(5 + 6 - 2)$	13 $(5 + 6 + 2)$
4 $(6 - 2)$	10 (5×2)	15 $(5 \times 6 \div 2)$ or $[(6 \div 2) \times 5]$
7 $(5 + 2)$	11 $(5 + 6)$	16 $(5 \times 2 + 6)$
8 $(6 + 2)$	12 (2×6)	17 $(2 \times 6 + 5)$
		18 $(5 - 2) \times 6$

PHOTOGRAPH 8.3 *Number Rings*

A player who has made a number puts a ring around the base displaying that number. (There can also be a rule stating that a ring can be placed only next to a base already ringed.) The first person to ring all the bases in her sector is the winner.

THE $200 BANKER

Materials: 200 chips (or tiles or buttons); two dice; a bowl (the pot).

Play: The children in Photograph 8.4 are playing this game. One player becomes the first banker, and all the chips are divided among all the players (including the banker).

Everybody except the banker puts into the pot an amount agreed upon that is more than 1 and less than 10 (6, for example). The banker puts into the pot an amount equal to the total of all the other players (3×6, if there are 3 players beside the banker).

The banker rolls the dice. If she rolls *a double* or *a total of 3 or 11*, the banker takes everything from the pot. If she rolls *a total of 5 or 9*, all the other players divide the total in the pot ($36 \div 3 = 12$, for example). If she rolls any other total (4, 6, 7, 8, or 10), nobody gets anything, and the banker rolls the dice again. The players take turns being the banker. For example, the person sitting to the left of the first banker can be the second banker.

PHOTOGRAPH 8.4 $200 Banker

The first person to accumulate 100 chips is the winner.

The class can be asked if there is a reason for these rules. For example, is there a reason why the banker can take everything only when she rolls a double or a total of 3 or 11?

'SMATH

This commercially made game is like *Scrabble* except that equations must be made. It can be an easy game when only addition and subtraction are used.

GAMES INVOLVING REPEATED ADDITION (LEADING TO MULTIPLICATION)

The first two games described in this section use cards, and the next two use dice. *Rummikub,* the fifth game, is commercially made and involves plastic chips.

I DOUBT IT

Materials: This game was described in Kamii (1989a, pp. 136–137) for the repeated addition of 2 and 5, but a deck can also consist of four cards each of the following ten numbers:

> 3, 6, 9, 12, 15, 18, 21, 24, 27, and 30 or
> 4, 8, 12, 16, 20, 24, 28, 32, 36, and 40

Needless to say, a deck can also be made with multiples of any other number.

Play: All 40 cards are dealt to the players. If multiples of 3 are involved, the first player puts a 3 in the middle of the table, face down, saying "Three." The next person then puts a 6 on top of the 3, also face down, saying "Six." The third player continues with a 9, saying "Nine." Any player who does not have the card needed substitutes another card, hoping to get away with this bluff.

Anyone who thinks that a card other than the one announced has been played says "I doubt it." If the doubt is verified, the person caught must take all the cards on the table and add them to her hand. If the doubt is not verified, the accuser has to take all the cards. Play continues until a person wins by getting rid of all her cards.

Modification: This game can be played in descending order (30, 27, 24, and so on).

MAKING FAMILIES

Materials: A deck of playing cards with the face cards removed (alternatively, cards such as *Snap* and *Fish* can be used with "1" written on stickers placed in the corners of four identical cards, "2" placed in the corners of four cards of another kind, and so on); paper and pencil for scorekeeping.

Play: This game is like Go Fish except that all the cards are dealt. The first player begins by asking someone for a card, in an attempt to make a set of four of a kind (for example, "Suzie, do you have a 10?"). If the person addressed has the card asked for, she has to give it. As long as the first player gets the cards he asked for, he can continue asking for more. If he fails to receive a card he requested, the turn passes to the person who said, "I don't have any."

When a player has four cards of a kind (a family), he puts them down in front of himself. Play continues until someone has put down all his cards. All the players total the number of points in sets of four in front of them and subtract the number of points on cards still in their hands. The person who thus makes the most points is the winner. By making inferences from the cards people are asking for, players can collect many cards that are worth many points.

FIGURE 8.5 The combination of colors and numbers on each die in Choose.

	Green	Red	Blue	Yellow	Orange	Orange
First die	1	5	2	6	3	4
Second die	2	1	6	5	3	4
Third die	3	6	4	1	2	5
Fourth die	4	2	5	3	1	6
Fifth die	5	4	3	2	1	6
Sixth die	6	3	1	4	2	5

CHOOSE

This game was described in Kamii (1989a, pp. 137–138).

Materials: Six cubes or blank dice, each with six different numbers and five different colors on its sides, as shown in Figure 8.5; paper and pencil for scorekeeping. Self-adhesive labels in assorted colors (such as Dennison No. 43–851) can be placed on the dice, and numerals can be written on them. (Scotch tape protects the dice from wear.)

The six colors (column headings) in Figure 8.5 indicate the six sides of each die. The numerals are those that must be written on each color. For example, on the first die, 1 should be written on the green label, 5 on the red label, 2 on the blue label, 6 on the yellow label, and 3 and 4 on orange labels.

Play: The object of the game is to get the greatest number of points with dice showing the same color or the same number.

A player can roll the dice three times on each turn. After the first throw, the player decides if she will choose the same color or the same number. She sets aside those she wants to use and rolls the other dice again. She can roll all six dice again if the outcome of the first throw was not favorable.

After the second roll, the player sets aside the dice she wants to use and throws the others. She may also change her objective, depending on what she has gotten so far. If nothing encouraging has come out so far, she may roll all six dice again.

After the third throw, the points obtained are written on the scoring sheet and added to the previous total. If the player gets three 4s, one 5, and two 1s and decides to use the same *number,* her score is 12 (4 + 4 + 4). If she gets three green sides with a 6, a 5, and a 3 on them and three red sides with a 1, a

PHOTOGRAPH 8.5 *Yahtzee*

2, and a 3 on them, she may decide to use the same *color,* and get 14 points (6 + 5 + 3).

When all six dice show the same color or the same number, the number of points is doubled. For example, if the player gets six 6s, her score is 72 [(6 × 6 × 2) or (6 + 6 + 6 + 6 + 6 + 6 + 36)].

Modifications: The numbers on the dice can be changed to 2 through 7, to 3 through 8, or to 4 through 9. To change the numbers to 2 through 7, all the 1s in Figure 8.5 can be changed to 7s. To change the numbers to 3 through 8, the 1s can be changed to 7s and the 2s can be changed to 8s. To change the numbers to 4 through 9, the 1s are changed to 7s, the 2s to 8s, and the 3s to 9s.

YAHTZEE

Materials: The prevalence of this commercially made game in large discount stores attests to its popularity as a family game. A teacher may want to buy one game in order to have an instruction sheet and make a quieter, less expensive version by purchasing only a scoring pad and placing it in a shoe box with five dice (see Photograph 8.5).

Play: This is a more complicated version of Choose, and the object is to obtain the highest score by making astute decisions.

A player is allowed a maximum of three rolls of the dice on each turn but may stop after the first or second roll. For the first roll, he must roll all five dice. For the second and third rolls, he may pick up any or all the dice and roll them again.

After the third roll, the player *must* enter either the total or a 0 in one of 13 boxes. Each of the 13 boxes has a criterion for its use, and the rules are different for the Upper Section and Lower Section. The Upper Section has six possibilities: adding only the 1s, only the 2s, only the 3s, only the 4s, only the 5s, or only the 6s rolled. The Lower Section has seven possibilities: 3 of a kind, 4 of a kind, Full House (3 of a kind and 2 of another kind), Small Straight (a sequence of four such as 2, 3, 4, and 5), Large Straight (a sequence of five such as 2, 3, 4, 5, and 6), *Yahtzee* (5 of a kind), and Chance (which means any five numbers can be added).

There are strategies in deciding which box to use. For example, if the numbers 3, 3, 3, 4, and 6 are rolled, the player can get either 9 points in the "3s" box in the Upper Section or 19 points either in the "3 of a kind" box or the "chance" box in the Lower Section. How to earn bonus points is also an important consideration in this game.

The game can be further complicated with chips and other rules, but our third graders play *Yahtzee* without the chips.

RUMMIKUB

Materials: This popular, commercially made game, which can be found in large discount stores, uses 106 tiles numbered 1 through 13 in four different colors and two Jokers. We have simplified the rules, especially regarding the Joker, and do not use the stand, as can be seen in Photograph 8.6. Without the stands, children can help one another and anticipate the next player's move.

Play: The object of the game is to win the greatest number of points.

Setting up. The tiles are mixed, face down, on the table. Each player picks 14 tiles.

Beginning. A player must make an initial meld of at least 30 points in one or more sets to place tiles on the table. These points must come from tiles in a player's hand, not from those already on the table. Each tile is worth the number of points on it. A Joker may substitute for any tile, and its point value is the same as the tile it represents when melding, and worth 30 points when held in one's hand if another player wins. A meld is either a RUN or a GROUP.

A RUN consists of at least 3 consecutive numbers of the same color, such as
Red 4, 5, and 6 (15 points); or
Orange 1, Joker (substituting an orange 2), orange 3, and orange 4 (10 points)

PHOTOGRAPH 8.6 *Rummikub*

A GROUP consists of at least 3 tiles of the same number but all of different colors, such as

Red 12, blue 12, and black 12 (36 points)

Playing the table. Once a player has put down the initial 30 points, she is free to play on the table and rearrange melds. If it is impossible to make a run or a group or to add onto a run or a group already on the table, the player must pick a tile from the face-down pile. This person must then wait until her next turn to play. She continues to pick tiles until she can play. Two examples of playing the table follow:

On the table are 4 orange, 4 black, 4 red. A player can add a 4 blue (and get 16 points).

On the table are 6 red, 7 red, 8 red. A player can add a 5 red (and get 26 points), a 9 red (and get 30 points), or both (and get 35 points). If she has a Joker and a red 4, she can get 30 points with the red 4, the Joker, and the red 6, 7, and 8.

The game is rich in a host of other possibilities.

Ending. The game ends when one player uses up all of her tiles. The player who thus Rummikubs gets 100 extra points. Each of the others adds up the value of the tiles left in her hand, counting 30 points for a Joker and the face value of all the other tiles, and subtracts it from her total.

EASIER MULTIPLICATION AND DIVISION GAMES

Involving One Multiplication Table at a Time

RIO

Rio is the easiest game that can be played with the tiles shown later in Photograph 8.9. The children in the picture are playing a more advanced version, which we call Multiplication Bingo. This commercially made game was called *Loto Calcul* or *1 × 1 Bingo* in French (Ravensburger, 1984) but has been discontinued. The following materials, however, are easy to make (attractive stickers make the game much more appealing than mere numerals on the tiles).

Materials: Two 12-sided dice (with the numbers 0–10 and a J on the sides); 64–100 chips; 86 tiles (two sets bearing the following 43 numbers): 0, 1, 2, 3, 4, 5, 6, 7, 8, 9, 10, 12, 14, 15, 16, 18, 20, 21, 24, 25, 27, 28, 30, 32, 35, 36, 40, 42, 45, 48, 49, 50, 54, 56, 60, 63, 64, 70, 72, 80, 81, 90, and 100.

Play: For the table of 6s, for example, the players take 11 tiles numbered 0, 6, 12, 18, 24, 30, 36, 42, 48, 54, and 60 and scatter them in the middle of the play area. Each player takes 5 chips, and the object of the game is to be the first to get rid of them.

Rio is played with one die, and the players take turns rolling it. If the first player rolls a 4, he must multiply it by 6 and can place one of his chips on the tile numbered 24. If the next person rolls a 6, he places one of his chips on 36 (6 × 6 = 36). If the third player rolls a 4 again, this person has to take the chip that is on 24.

On the first round, each player can roll the die only once. From the second round on, a player can roll it as often as he wishes, provided he continues to put a chip on a tile. If the player gets a product that is covered with a chip, he has to take the chip, and the turn passes to the next person.

Each player must roll the die at least once when his turn comes. If a Joker comes up, the player can make the Joker stand for any number he wishes.

Involving Parts or All of More than One Multiplication Table at a Time

The difficulty of games in this category can be varied by choosing certain cards or tiles so that only easy combinations are involved, as discussed in Chap-

PHOTOGRAPH 8.7 Salute!

ter 6 (Figure 6.4). If the numbers on the cards go only up to 5 in Salute!, for example, the number of cards bearing the same number must be increased so that there will be at least 40 cards in the deck. If all the cards up to 10 are used, Salute! or any other game becomes classified in the next category, games involving all the multiplication tables.

SALUTE!

Number of players: Three.

Materials: At least 40 playing cards or home-made cards.

Play: The cards are dealt to two of the three players. The two players sit facing each other, and each holds her stack face down. Simultaneously, the two players both take the top cards of their respective piles and say, "Salute!" as they hold them next to their faces in such a way that they can see only the other person's card. In Photograph 8.7, for example, one player can see that her opponent has a 10 (and the hand-against-chest salute is not very conventional).

The third player uses the two numbers turned up and announces the product, such as "40." Each of the other two players tries to deduce the number on her own card by dividing the product by the opponent's number. The person who shouts the correct number first takes both cards. The winner is the person who collects the most cards.

MULTIPLICATION WAR

Number of players: Two.

Materials: The same as for Salute!

Play: All the cards are dealt and kept face down in stacks in front of each player. Simultaneously, each player turns over the top two cards of his stack and announces the product of the two numbers. The person whose product is larger takes all four cards. The winner is the player who collects more cards.

Variation: The person who states the product first gets all four cards.

REVERSE RIO

Materials: The tiles used in Rio and Multiplication Bingo; a six-sided, eight-sided, or ten-sided die.

Play: If a six-sided die is used, any number of tiles bearing numbers up to 60 can be scattered in the middle of the table. (For an easier game, any number of tiles bearing numbers up to 30 or 35 can be used.)

The players take turns rolling the die. If a 6 is rolled, the players try to be the first to find a tile showing a number that is a multiple of 6 and to announce, "I found one!" If she can prove that the number on the tile is a multiple of 6, she can keep the tile. The winner is the player who collects the most tiles when all have been taken.

THE AREA GAME

Materials: Two sets of Perceptual Puzzle Blocks, which can be seen in Photograph 8.8 and Figure 8.6a (Creative Publications catalog No. 34460); paper and pencil for scorekeeping. The Perceptual Puzzle Blocks in Figure 8.6a are all ¾-inch thick. Block *a* is a cube (¾-inch × ¾-inch × ¾-inch). The letters *a* through *i* on the blocks have no significance in this game.

Play: Each person takes a set of nine blocks (one block each from *a* through *i*). The players first agree on the dimensions of the square or rectangle they will try to make.

The 7 × 7 version. The object of the game is to be the one who completes the 7 × 7 square. The first player puts down any block of his choice. The two players then take turns putting one block down. A block can be put down only

PHOTOGRAPH 8.8 The Area Game

by making it touch at least one unit of length of a block that is already on the table (as shown in Figure 8.6b). The person who completes the 7 × 7 square gets 49 points (because 7 × 7 = 49). The other player gets no points for the first round. Play continues for the number of rounds agreed upon.

The 6 × 6 version. The object of the game is to score 36 points (6 × 6) by being the one to complete a 6 × 6 square.

The 6 × 7 version. The object of the game is to score 42 points (6 × 7) by being the one to complete a 6 × 7 rectangle.

TABLE SHAPES

Materials: Three sets each of 24 commercially made triangles, shown in Figure 8.7. If only the red set is used, the tables go only up to 4. If the red and blue sets are used, they go up to 7. If the red, blue, and green sets are used, the tables go up to 10.

Play: All the triangles are divided equally, face down. The players take turns trying to put down a triangle that matches one that is already on the table. A match is made when one side has a multiplication problem and another side has the answer, as can be seen in Figure 8.7. Anyone who does not have a

FIGURE 8.6 (a) Perceptual Puzzle Blocks and (b) two blocks touching each other along a unit of length.

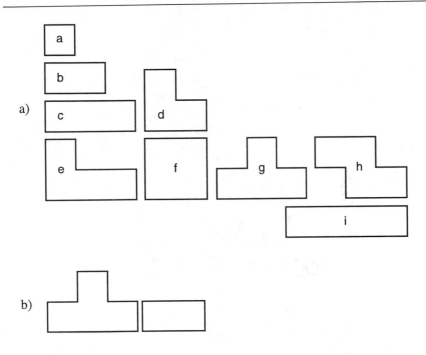

triangle that matches has to pass. The person who uses up all of her triangles first is the winner.

MULTIPLICATION DOMINOES

Materials: Commercially made Multiplication Dominoes (the yellow set is for the tables of 2s and 3s, the red set for the tables of 4s and 5s, the green set for the tables of 6s and 7s, and the blue set is for the tables of 8s and 9s).

Play: Each domino has a multiplication problem on one side and a product on the other side. The players first divide all the dominoes and then take turns putting one down that matches a domino that is already on the table. To make a match, a player must put the answer next to a multiplication problem, or vice versa.

This has not been a popular game in our classroom, but the fact that it has been in the Didax catalog for many years suggests its commercial success.

FIGURE 8.7 Triangles used in *Table Shapes.*

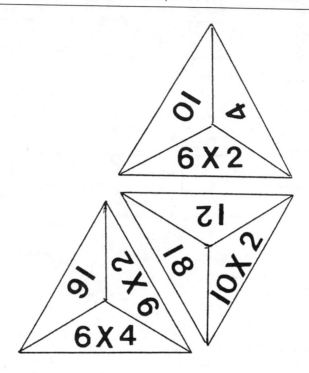

Involving All the Multiplication Tables Simultaneously

As stated earlier, any one of the games described in the previous category can be played with all the multiplication tables. Below are two other games that cannot be partitioned into parts.

TABBY CATS

Materials: This commercially made game is no longer available through the Didax catalog, but a teacher can make it. Needed are a board for all the players with 55 spaces around it with the problems shown in Figure 8.8; a scoring board for each player with two cats on it (Figure 8.9, in which one cat has the 21 products up to 28, and the other cat has the 21 products 30 through 100); a die; a marker for each player; 168 or more chips.

Play: The players take turns rolling the die and moving the marker the corresponding number of spaces. The numbers appearing in the space where the marker comes to rest are multiplied (for example 6 × 6), and a chip is placed

FIGURE 8.8 The fifty-five problems appearing in the spaces around the Tabby Cat board.

1x1	2x1	3x1	4x1	5x1	6x1	7x1	8x1	9x1	10x1
	2x2	3x2	4x2	5x2	6x2	7x2	8x2	9x2	10x2
		3x3	4x3	5x3	6x3	7x3	8x3	9x3	10x3
			4x4	5x4	6x4	7x4	8x4	9x4	10x4
				5x5	6x5	7x5	8x5	9x5	10x5
					6x6	7x6	8x6	9x6	10x6
						7x7	8x7	9x7	10x7
							8x8	9x8	10x8
								9x9	10x9
									10x10

FIGURE 8.9 Scoring board used in *Tabby Cat*.

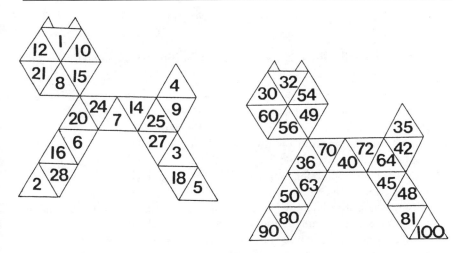

Photograph 8.9 Multiplication Bingo

in the appropriate triangle (36) on the player's scoring board. The first player to cover either cat completely is the winner.

MULTIPLICATION BINGO

Materials: All the tiles listed in the description of Rio; two 12-sided dice (each with the numbers 0–10 and a J); 64–100 chips.

Play: Each player takes 16 tiles *without looking at them* and makes a 4 × 4 arrangement with them (see Photograph 8.9). The rest of the tiles are set aside. Each player also takes 16 chips. The object of the game is to be the first one to make a line with 4 chips horizontally, vertically, or diagonally.

The players take turns rolling two dice. The numbers rolled are multiplied. If a 2 and an 8 are rolled, for example, the player and anybody else who has a 16 covers it with a chip.

The J on a die is the Joker, which can stand for any number. For example, if a player gets a 5 and a J, and he wants to cover a tile with 30 on it, he can make the J stand for a 6, and anybody else who also has a 30 can cover it. If two Js come up, the player can choose a number and square it (5 × 5, 6 × 6, or the square of any other number from 0 through 10).

Variations: Each player takes 25 tiles and makes a 5 × 5 arrangement. The person who makes a line of 5 chips horizontally, vertically, or diagonally is the winner.

The first person to make two lines can be the winner. The lines do not have to be parallel.

The first person to cover up all his tiles can also be the winner.

HARDER GAMES INVOLVING TWO, THREE, OR FOUR OPERATIONS

X FROM OUTER SPACE

This popular, commercially made game has been discontinued, and it is mentioned in the hope that it will become available again. Essentially, it uses a board suggesting a journey in outer space and three dice—a white one and two red ones (see Photograph 8.10). The white die indicates the number of spaces to advance on the board. Many of the spaces are squares with a small number (such as a 6) in big print in the middle and a larger number (such as 42) in small print in the upper right corner. Upon landing on one of these spaces, the player adds the numbers on the red dice and multiplies the total by the small number in big print (6 in this case). If the product is the same as the number in the

Photograph 8.10 *X From Outer Space*

corner (42 in this case), the player can advance five more spaces. If the product is larger than 42, she can move forward one space; but if the product is smaller than 42, she has to move backward one space.

The first person to get to the Sun is the winner.

TRIBULATIONS

Materials: This is another discontinued commercially made game, but a teacher can make the necessary materials. Needed are 50 cards bearing the numerals 1–50; 49 tiles bearing the numerals 1–8 in the following quantities:

Number	Quantity	Number	Quantity
1	5	5	6
2	6	6	10
3	6	7	5
4	6	8	5

Play: The tiles are mixed and randomly arranged in a 7 × 7 square as shown in Figure 8.10. The numbers can face in different directions.

The first player draws a card, announces the number on it, and places it where all the players can see it. Looking at all the tiles, all the players silently try to find three numbers in a row that will produce the number on the card. *The first two numbers are multiplied, and the third number is then either added or subtracted* to produce the number on the card. The three numbers must be in order vertically, horizontally, or diagonally in either direction. The 6s and 9s are interchangeable.

The first person to find a correct number combination announces it and collects the card if he can prove its correctness.

A new card is then drawn, and play continues. The person who collects the most cards is the winner.

TIGUOUS

This is the easier version of Contig (Broadbent, 1975). It can also be modified to make a board-game version of *Number Rings* (also called *Ring-a-Round*).

Materials: Three dice; 20 chips; the board shown in Figure 8.11.

Play: The players divide the chips. The first player rolls the three dice and has to use the three numbers rolled with any operation(s) to make one of the numbers on the board and covers it with a chip.

FIGURE 8.10 Examples of three numbers used to make 14 and 29 in *Tribulation.*

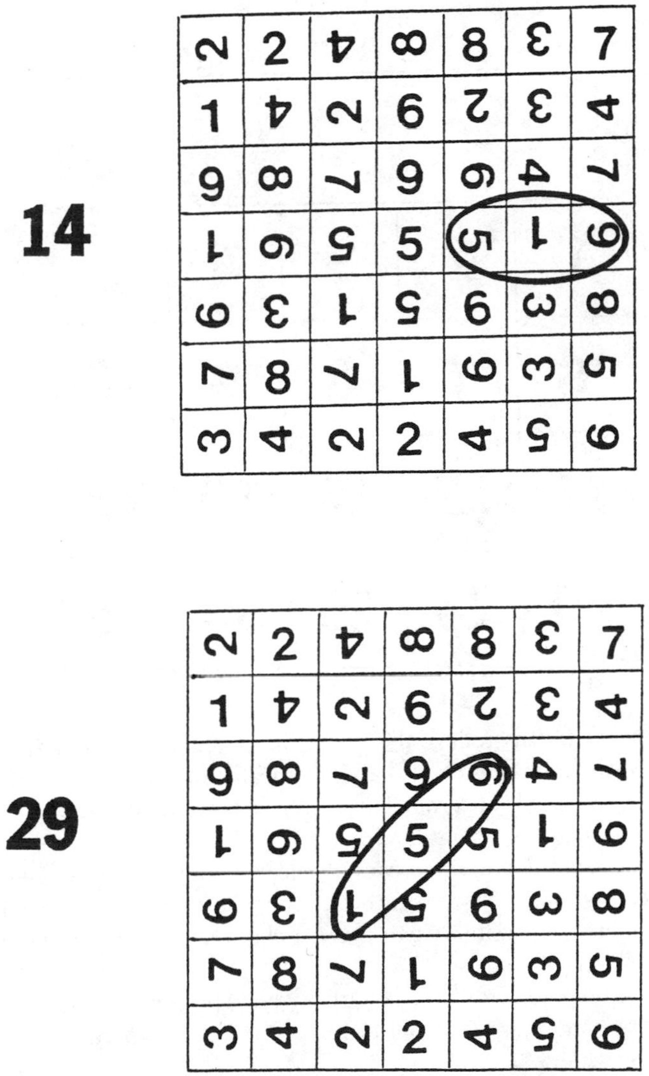

14

29

FIGURE 8.11 A Tiguous board.

TIGUOUS

1	2	3	4	5
6	7	8	9	10
11	12	15	16	18
20	24	25	30	36

The players take turns rolling the three dice. The second and subsequent players can cover only a number that is vertically, horizontally, or diagonally next to one that is already covered. This number has to be made with the three numbers rolled using any operation(s).

When a player rolls the dice and cannot make a number that can be covered, she must pass. If another player can think of a way to cover a number, the first person to announce a possibility can place a chip on the appropriate number. *This does not affect any turns.*

A player is eliminated from further play when she *fails in three successive turns* to produce a number that can be covered. The first player to use up all her chips is the winner.

NUMBERS CHALLENGE and TWENTY-FOUR

These are similar commercially made games, but the numbers to be made can vary from 1 to 24 in *Numbers Challenge,* whereas it is always 24 in *Twenty-*

PHOTOGRAPH 8.11 *Numbers Challenge*

Four. The latter has cards of three difficulty levels that are worth 1, 2, or 3 points.

Materials: Commercially made cards each bearing four numbers (see Photograph 8.11); four different dice in *Numbers Challenge.*

Play: The object of the game is to win cards by being the first to use all four numbers (such as 5, 7, 7, and 2) with addition, subtraction, multiplication, and/ or division and make 24 in *Twenty-Four* (or the number between 1 and 24 indicated by dice in *Numbers Challenge*). All four numbers must be used only once [$7 + 7 + (5 \times 2) = 24$, for example].

The top card of the stack is turned over. The first person who has made 24 (or any other number rolled) says, "I've got it," and explains his solution. If the explanation is accepted by the other players, he can keep the card. The winner may be the person who collected the most cards or the first player to win 5 cards.

This game can be played as a whole-class game as can be seen near the conclusion of the present chapter.

WHOLE-CLASS GAMES

AROUND THE WORLD

Materials: Flashcards involving selected multiplication problems.

Play: Two children compete at a time. Child A and child B stand up to compete first, and when a flashcard is shown, they both try to say the product first. If A wins, A moves next to C, and B sits down. A and C stand up to compete next. If C then wins, C moves next to D to compete with D. If, however, A keeps defeating every subsequent opponent, she is designated as the big winner who has gone "around the world."

For children's development of autonomy, and for their learning of multiplication, it is important to let children be in charge of the game and flash the cards. Another child can be the judge who determines who gave the correct answer first.

TIC-TAC-30

Materials: Chalkboard and chalk of two colors.

Play: The class is divided into two teams. A Tic-Tac-Toe grid is drawn on the board, and the children take turns writing numbers in the spaces. Each team tries to be the first to make 30 in a way similar to Tic-Tac-Toe, using only five numbers such as the following: 4, 6, 8, 10, and 12, which are available to team A, and 5, 7, 9, 11, and 13, which are available to team B. Members of each team consult one another before going to the board to write the number decided upon. As in Tic-Tac-Toe, a team has to make 30 with three of its own numbers in a row vertically, horizontally, or diagonally.

Figure 8.12 illustrates a game in progress. Figure 8.12a shows that team A first wrote "8" with white chalk and that team B then wrote "9" with red chalk. Team A has decided to use the 10 as indicated because it will then be possible to make 30 on the next turn by using the 12. When team B sees the numbers in Figure 8.12b, we hope that it will "see" the need to put *something* between the 10 and the 8. The numbers already used are crossed out and no longer available.

Variations: Tic-Tac-45 with the numbers 10, 12, 14, 16, and 18 available to team A, and the numbers 11, 13, 15, 17, and 19 available to team B.

Tic-Tac-55 with the numbers 16, 18, 20, 22, and 24 available to team A, and the numbers 17, 19, 21, 23, and 25 available to team B.

FIGURE 8.12 A Tic-Tac-30 game in progress.

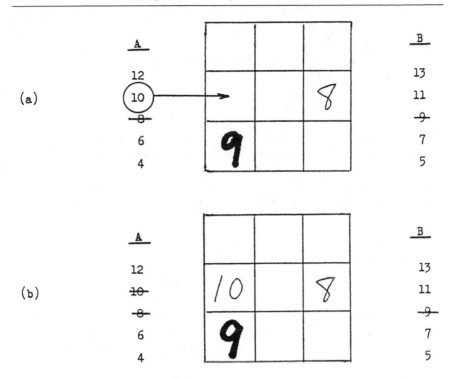

NUMBERS CHALLENGE or *TWENTY-FOUR*

Material: The commercially made game described earlier for small groups.

Play: The class is divided into three or more teams, and the teacher lists the teams on the board to record their cumulative scores.

The teacher then draws a card and copies the four numbers on it as shown in Figure 8.13, for example. As soon as a player thinks of a combination, he or she announces, "I've got it," and goes to the board to write equations such as

$$7 + 2 = 9, 9 - 6 = 3, 3 \times 8 = 24$$

If everybody agrees that this is a valid solution, the person who offered the first solution earns 10 points for his or her team. Every subsequent valid solution earns 3 points (such as the following two):

$$7 - 6 = 1, \quad 1 + 2 = 3, \quad 3 \times 8 = 24$$
$$8 + 7 = 15, \quad 15 \times 2 = 30, \quad 30 - 6 = 24$$

FIGURE 8.13 An example of *Numbers Challenge* or *Twenty-Four.*

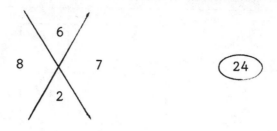

If a player claims to have a solution, but it turns out not to be valid, his or her team loses 5 points.

The class tells the teacher how many points to add or subtract from each team's cumulative score on the board.

CONCLUSION

It is important from the standpoint of children's development of autonomy that they be allowed to choose from a variety of games. But it is also important for the teacher to choose the variety offered to children. Enjoyment is a necessary but not a sufficient condition in any educational activity. Some children get stuck on games that have become too easy. Some never seem to notice card games. The teacher's use of games is thus an art that requires reflection and experimentation to maximize their potential value.

CHAPTER 9

Other Activities

A constructivist approach to arithmetic is not a "package" or "method" of teaching because constructivism only *explains* how children acquire knowledge. Each teacher must, therefore, figure out how to use the basic principles of constructivism with different groups of children. The kinds of problems and group games described in Chapters 7 and 8 are essential components of primary arithmetic based on Piaget's theory, but other activities can and must also be used within a constructivist framework.

Independently of Piaget's theory, many math educators have been developing classroom activities to improve upon instruction based on textbooks and workbooks. It behooves us to study the work of these educators and to benefit from their reflection and experimentation. Many of their activities are compatible with constructivism, although some require modification. This short chapter gives examples of the kinds of activities not included in Chapters 7 and 8 that we devised or adopted from various sources. We apologize for not always being able to give proper credit to the creators of these activities, as we often learned about them in conference presentations, casual conversations, and classroom observations.

WARM-UPS

"Throwing" Numbers on the Board

At the beginning of the math hour, I (SL) sometimes write three to six numbers on the board, such as the following that I presented on September 23, asking the class to add them without using paper and pencil:

$$50$$
$$50$$
$$15$$
$$49$$

After giving plenty of "think time," I ask for and list all the answers the children got in the upper left-hand corner of the board. I then ask for volunteers to explain the different ways in which the answers were obtained.

Our rationales for this activity are that it is good for children to have to think without recourse to paper and pencil, and it is particularly important for users of conventional algorithms to have to deal with numbers that are not aligned in columns. Many users of algorithms know the rule of working from right to left and of carrying but cannot apply it when the numbers are not arranged in columns. This difficulty is illustrated by Kimberly, who tried to deal with the next problem.

On September 23, the most advanced transfer student, Jack, was weaning himself from the algorithm and volunteered the following explanation in response to the preceding problem. (As stated earlier, we do not tell transfer students that they must *not* use algorithms. However, we often ask them to solve a problem in two different ways and always insist that everybody be able to explain *how* an answer was obtained.)

$$50 + 50 = 100$$
$$100 + 49 = 149$$
$$149 + 15 = 159 + 5 = 164$$

As each volunteer speaks, I connect the numbers added by drawing lines between them or by circling some of the numbers. I make these marks on the board so that the speaker can tell that his or her statements are being understood and everybody else can follow each step of the explanation.

When the next problem was given on the same day, Jack went back to the conventional algorithm. The next set of numbers was the following:

$$2.25 \qquad\qquad 2.99$$
$$1.95$$

Kimberly tried to use the algorithm to add 2.25 and 1.95 first. She began by getting "one dollar" for "five plus five," revealing her poor knowledge of place value. She then mentally carried 1 to the tens column, added it to the 2 and the 9, and got "a dollar and two cents." She finished by adding the "two dollars and one dollar" correctly but forgot to carry the 1.00 from the "dollar and two cents" that she had gotten.

The children who had been in constructivist classes in the first two grades proceeded in a wide variety of ways, sometimes zig-zagging from right to left, from left to right, or starting in the middle. Below is what Arthur did, adding 2.25 and 1.95 first:

$$.20 + .90 = 1.10$$
$$1.10 + (.05 + .05) = 1.20$$
$$1.20 + (2.00 + 1.00) = 4.20$$
$$4.20 + 2.00 = 6.20$$
$$6.20 + .90 = 7.10, \text{ plus } .09 \text{ is } 7.19.$$

Amy was more methodical and got 5 for all the dollars, and 2.00 for (.95 + .05 from the .25) + (.99 + .01 from the .20 that was left over), and then added .19.

It is easy to let these warm-ups become 20- or 30-minute activities, as both the children and I become fascinated by all the different ways that are invented.

What's My Rule?

In this activity adopted from the constructivist project at Purdue University (Cobb & Merkel, 1989; Cobb et al., 1991), I ask the class to say the number that comes after the arrow, not the rule that I am following. For example, I may write the following on the board:

$$3 \longrightarrow 6$$
$$5 \longrightarrow 10$$

When I write the third line as follows, and ask what number comes after the arrow, many volunteers raise their hands:

$$10 \longrightarrow$$

After the answer is given, I write it to the right of the arrow. If no one disagrees with the answer, I go on to pose the next question, and the class sees the following:

$$3 \longrightarrow 6$$
$$5 \longrightarrow 10$$
$$10 \longrightarrow 20$$
$$16 \longrightarrow$$

What's My Rule? is a particularly good activity because the teacher can keep writing problems for a long time until almost all the hands go up. Advanced children can keep participating, while the slower ones can take more time to figure out the relationship between the pairs of numbers. If the teacher writes the next problem faster and faster, the class gets excited trying to give the answer equally fast.

This activity can be used for any other operation. A more difficult example with subtraction follows:

$$25 \longrightarrow 10$$
$$32 \longrightarrow 17$$
$$51 \longrightarrow 36$$
$$43 \longrightarrow 28$$
$$36 \longrightarrow 21$$
$$84 \longrightarrow$$

QUANTIFYING GROUPS OF OBJECTS

Many educators believe in giving manipulatives to children whenever students have difficulty with "regrouping," division, or any other aspect of arithmetic. However, when children are given objects, they often focus on moving them around and stop thinking numerically. As Olivier and colleagues (1991) also stated, when children do not know what to do with a partitive division problem, for example, their thinking is facilitated much more by *drawing* 18 cookies for three children than by manipulating 18 counters.

The preceding point, however, does not imply that we always avoid the use of objects. Objects are important for children's development of number sense. There are also times when objects help children to think. For example, in A Two-Dice Game, which will be discussed shortly, objects are indispensable for enabling children to think about probability. Below are two other activities in which we use objects to foster children's development of number sense.

Estimation

Either a child or I bring a quantity of candy, nuts, shells, or any other objects in a container. The container may be sealed or unsealed, transparent or opaque, but children are always allowed to see what kinds of objects are in the container. A ballot box is prepared, with the lid taped shut. At their convenience during the day (or week), the children each write on a piece of paper the number estimated and their name and drop it in the ballot box.

Two children open the ballot box at the end of the day (or week) and count the objects in such a way that others can quickly check the accuracy of the count. Making groups becomes necessary in this situation, and children have to make other decisions as well, such as how to keep pieces of candy clean and edible. The person whose estimate was the closest is the winner. What to do with the objects after counting them is a sociomoral problem, as well as a mathematical one, that the class has to solve through discussion.

Estimation also offers a reason for making graphs. Some graphs come out with a central tendency, that is, the tendency for more people to make similar estimates in the middle of the range than at either end.

Collecting 10,000 Objects

This activity was inspired by Bickerton-Ross (1988), who began by discussing with her third graders the curriculum requirement of understanding numbers up to 10,000. She guided her students to use the guess-and-check method to determine how many objects each of the 15 members of the class had to bring from home in order to have 10,000 objects. After the students decided that they each needed to bring 666, and that the teacher would bring 10, Bickerton-Ross asked: How would other people be able to look at the display and know for sure that there were 666 objects in each collection?

I decided to modify this activity to maximize children's possibility of developing number sense. Since 1,000 seemed big enough to be at the frontier of my students' "number sense," I divided 1,000 by 21—the number of children in the class—and got 48. I thought I would build the number up from 1,000 to 2,000 or 5,000 before getting to 10,000.

I asked all the children in the class the next day to each bring 48 things from home. The objects should be small and 48 of the same thing in a zip-lock bag, I told the class. The children immediately wanted to know what my purpose was and why I wanted 48. I purposely did not answer these questions and said only that I wanted the students to be creative. "Look in kitchen cabinets, in desk drawers, in the playroom, or even outside," I told them.

The children were buzzing around the next day showing each other the variety of objects they had chosen to bring—macaroni, cotton balls, lentils, beans, rice, Cheerios, acorns, broken crayons, popcorn kernels, Q-tips, beads, paper clips, pebbles, and so on. I first asked the class what they thought we were going to do with all these objects. Among the responses were "Make a problem with them" and "Divide them up." As I expected, the children's curiosity resulted in excitement and their undivided attention.

I asked the children to write down *how* they counted the objects and how they were *sure* they had 48 things. Some of the responses were: "I counted by 1s," "I counted by 2s," and "I counted by 3s and that didn't work right. I think because 3 is an odd number and 48 must not be." The method I particularly noted for discussion later was: "I made piles with my objects. I knew that 6 × 8 is 48 so I made 6 piles with 8 and I did it again making 8 piles with 6. I proved it."

The kids guessed my next question before I asked it—"How many do we have altogether?" Before they began to work on this problem, I asked if they *thought* we *might* have enough to make 1,000 and display them on the wall outside. The children were astonished to find out that there were 1,008 objects, and we shared all the different ways in which the total of 1,008 was calculated. Some used repeated addition (writing "48" twenty-one times), but most made groups of two, three, four, five, or eight 48s. I was pleased that several children volunteered to remove 8 objects to make an even 1,000.

We displayed the 1,000 objects on the wall in the hallway with the written descriptions of how the children counted the 48 objects in each transparent bag. Just like the students in Bickerton-Ross's school, the passers-by at Hall-Kent School were intrigued by the display of 1,000 curious objects and accompanying write-ups. Many students went back to their respective classrooms talking about 48 (which seemed "like nothing") and 1,000 (which seemed colossal).

Over the two weeks that followed, we built on the 1,000 objects to work up gradually to 10,000. For example, my next question was: "How many more objects do you each need to bring to have 5,000 things to display?" Although the numbers at times became difficult to work with, the kids never gave up. They were so excited to actually *see* so many objects on their wall that they begged to go to a million! (However, some third-grade classes are not as strong as this one and can barely get to 2,000.)

A COLLECTION OF MATH LESSONS

Burns (1987) in *A Collection of Math Lessons from Grades 3 Through 6* presents ingenious activities that involve many strands and emphasize reasoning. For example, Chapter 1, dealing mostly with estimating the number of raisins in a ½-ounce box, as well as in a 1½-ounce box, includes addition, multiplication, division, statistics (central tendency), proportionality, and reasoning about volume and weight. The activities in this book are also appropriate for a wide range of developmental levels.

The book is unusual also because of the pedagogical tips given by the author, who is a superb teacher. It describes in detail the steps she went through to carry out each activity with a class organized into small groups. The children's reactions and statements are also described in detail so that the process of teaching by emphasizing children's thinking can be understood. For example, in Chapter 2 Burns describes children's reactions to her request that each group divide a large sheet of paper into 10 sections to list objects that come in groups of 3, 4, 5, 6, 7, 8, 9, 10, 11, and 12. Burns could have given a dittoed form to each group, but this would have robbed children of an opportunity to think. She noted that "several groups folded the paper in half, folded it again, and folded it again, each time opening it to count how many spaces there were. After three folds, there were eight spaces, in a four by two array. This was perplexing to them, and they dealt with it in several different ways" (p. 26). The author goes on to describe many inelegant solutions the children devised.

A Two-Dice Game, which Burns describes in Chapter 4, is ingenious and different from the games we present in Chapter 8 in that it focuses on probability. Burns gave 11 counters to each pair of students and asked them to put the counters on the numbers of a number line that went from 2 to 12. The children could arrange the 11 counters in any way they liked—all on a different number, all on one number, or a few on some of the numbers. She told the class that she would roll two dice and call out the sum (5 + 3 = 8, for example). "If you have a counter on that number (on 8 in this case), you remove it, and if you have more than one counter on that number, you take off only one of them," she told them. The first group to remove all 11 of the counters would be the winner.

Almost all the children put one counter on each number, expecting the sum of 7 to come out as often as 2 and 12. After playing the game and making a graph of the sums made with two dice, the author asked the children why the sum of 7 was made more often than 9, 11, 12, or 2. A leader soon explained that there was only one way of making 2 (1 + 1) but that 7 could be made with 6 + 1, 5 + 2, and 4 + 3. Many other ingenious activities can be found in *About Teaching Mathematics* (Burns, 1992a).

OTHER FAVORITE ACTIVITIES

Flashing Frames

Flashing Frames and the Balance Beam, which follows, are two other activities adapted from the constructivist project at Purdue University (Cobb & Merkel, 1989; Cobb et al., 1991). In Flashing Frames, I use an overhead projector and flash a transparency for less than a second, and the children figure out how many circles they think they saw. Figure 9.1a is an example of a transparency, and two children explained their answers in the following ways: "I saw 5 circles going down, and I saw 2 rows. That means that there had to be 10 squares in each box. And 10, 20, 30, take away 2, 4, 6 is 24." "I saw 5 on one side, and that's 5, 10, 15. And I saw 3 on the other side, and that's 3, 6, 9, plus 15 is 24."

As the level of difficulty increases, more time is allowed for viewing, but the exposure is still "a quickie." I modified this activity by asking children to invent similar problems to give to one another. ("Similar" includes taking into account the fact that it is difficult to know at a glance the exact number in a collection of more than five objects.) These modifications are good because children invent much harder problems than I do. Figure 9.1b is an example that yielded the following two solutions:

$4 \times 2 = 8$ Three 4s is 12.
$8 + 1 = 9$ Four 12s is 48.
$9 \times 4 = 40 - 4 = 36$ Four 3s is 12 empty spaces.
                    $48 - 12 = 36.$

The Balance Beam

I draw a balance beam on the chalkboard with various weights on it as illustrated in Figure 9.2 (invented by G. Wheatley and described in Cobb & Merkel, 1989). Children are asked to figure out and discuss the number(s) necessary to make the two sides balance.

This activity, too, can continue for a long time. For example, the last problem

FIGURE 9.1 Examples of Flashing Frames problems.

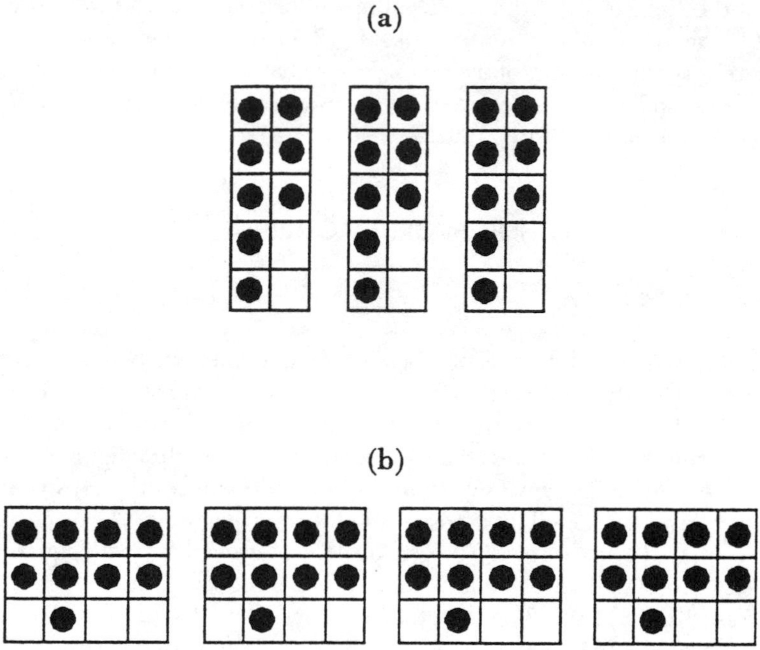

(a)

(b)

in Figure 9.2 with 186 on one side developed into another activity we call Make This Number. Make This Number in turn developed into the reading of a big book. We now describe Make This Number, which grew out of The Balance Beam.

Make This Number

All the different ways of making 186 volunteered by the class are listed below.

$$100 + 86$$
$$186 + 0$$
$$176 + 10$$
$$106 + 80$$
$$185 + 1$$
$$186 \times 1$$

FIGURE 9.2 Examples of Balance Beam problems.

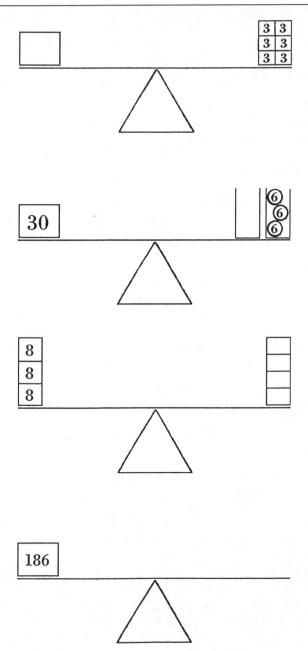

200 − 14
190 − 4
78 + 108
196 − 10
386 − 200
93 + 93
486 − 300
189 − 3
1,086 − 900
198 − 12
206 − 20
3,086 − 2,900
4,086 − 3,900
5,000 − 3,900, no, 4,900, no, 5,086 − 4,900
A million minus nine thousand ninety-nine, wait, one million eighty-six minus ten thousand.

Randy responded by saying, "There's a lot of thousands in a million, more than ten thousand." I decided to shift into a different activity and said to the class, "We are kind of confused. Maybe this is a good time to read *How Much Is a Million* by David Schwartz (1985). Maybe it will help us figure out what a million is in relation to 186." The Balance Beam thus moved into a third kind of activity—the use of children's books.

USING CHILDREN'S BOOKS

The use of children's books is becoming well known through workshops and books such as *Math and Literature (K–3)* (Burns, 1992b). We will therefore give only one example to show that we agree that children's books are excellent sources. Books are often uniquely suited to stimulate thinking in specific ways. For example, in *How Much Is a Million?* the author says, "If this book had a million tiny stars, they would fill seventy pages. Climb aboard!" (p. 8). The illustrator then shows four children traveling in a balloon through seven pages of tiny stars. At the end on the seventh page, the adult in the balloon says, "There you have one hundred thousand stars. If we take this seven page journey ten times, we'll pass a million stars" (p. 15). This book thus helps children visualize and feel what is meant by "one hundred thousand stars," "a million stars," "seven pages," and "seventy pages."

CONCLUSION

We tried to show in this chapter that a constructivist program is not a packaged set of activities, and that constructivist teachers study and adopt many of the ideas developed by other educators. Some practices become obsolete in light of constructivism, but others are validated and strengthened by this scientific theory.

Part IV

QUESTIONS
FREQUENTLY
ASKED

CHAPTER 10

How Do You Approach Multidigit Multiplication?

Textbooks introduce multidigit multiplication with easy problems like

$$\begin{array}{cc} 23 & 26 \\ \underline{\times 3} & \underline{\times 4} \end{array}$$

Problems such as the one on the left come first because they require no regrouping and are, therefore, much simpler. This is a good, behavioristic approach to teaching the conventional algorithm of multidigit multiplication. However, we do not believe in teaching conventional algorithms, and our ancestors did not invent multiplication for such small numbers. Telling children to use multiplication for such small numbers is an arbitrary imposition because addition is perfectly adequate when the multiplier is small. Our children do 3×23 in their heads. They also do 4×26 by doubling the double of 26 or by thinking that since four quarters make a dollar, four more cents make $1.04, or 104 cents.

In second grade, we give problems such as: "How much money do you need to buy five packs of gum if one pack costs 23 cents?" Second graders usually get the answer by writing "23×5," writing "23" vertically five times, and then using addition. Some, however, begin to say, "Five 20s is 20, 40, 60, 80, a dollar," and "Five 3s is 3, 6, 9, 12, 15 . . ." [Children's writing "23×3" instead of "3×23" is probably based on the fact that they write as they think and say "23 three times." We do not tell them that they have to write "3×23" because we want them to concentrate on numerical thinking (logico-mathematical knowledge), without the extra burden of conventions (social knowledge).]

Later in second grade and early in third grade, we increase the multiplier to 12 packs, for example. Our hope is to motivate children to use multiplication in computation, rather than using only the word *times* in speaking and the symbol $\times$ in writing. In 1991–92, however, most of our third graders continued to use the tedious, two-at-a-time addition illustrated in Figure 10.1. Many of them seemed to like the ease and security of writing and adding numbers.

By November 20, 1991, we had decided that almost half the class were stuck on addition and needed a push toward multiplication. Addition had become much too easy and boring for them. In this chapter, we discuss two ways in which we pushed children toward using multiplication in computing answers

FIGURE 10.1 A two-at-a-time additive procedure

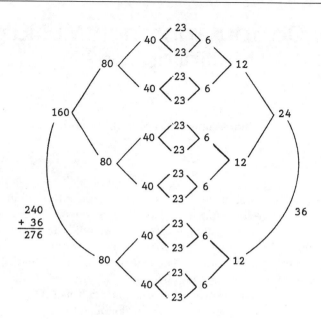

to problems: (1) by encouraging them to think of the *fastest* and *easiest* ways that require *as little writing as possible* and (2) by encouraging them to use the properties of our system of writing.

ENCOURAGING CHILDREN TO THINK OF THE FASTEST WAYS

We have two reasons for pushing children to think of the fastest ways that require little writing instead of telling them to use multiplication. First, many slow-developing third graders are not yet able to think multiplicatively (Clark, 1993), as stated in Chapter 6. Second, before using multiplication, children make smaller subgroups than tens and use only addition. To do 12 × 23, for example, many third graders break 12 down into 4, 4, and 4 (rather than into 10 and 2) and do 23 + 23 + 23 + 23 = 92, and 92 + 92 + 92 = 276. For most children, this is a necessary step on the way to multiplication, and children should not be deprived of the time they need to construct this level. The idea of making small, equal subgroups (e.g., 4 + 4 + 4) seems to come before that of making unequal subgroups such as 10 + 2. As children try to think of more efficient ways than repeated addition, they make progress toward multiplication. After making pairs of 23s, they often make groups of three, four, or five 23s.

November 20

By November 20, as stated earlier, we had decided that almost half the class needed a push. Children like Joe were especially manifesting their readiness for multiplication, as can be seen in the following interaction that took place on that day. To do 12 × 23, Joe first wrote "23" twelve times (see Figure 10.2a), added three numbers at a time, beginning with the 20s, and then combined the results two at a time. After explaining to me (SL) how he got the answer of 276, he remarked, "There *has to be* an easier way to do 23 twelve times." Picking up on this opening, I pointed to the column of 20s and said, "You added all these twenties. Can you think of an easier way?"

Joe did think of an easier way, but it was *not* multiplication. Keeping count with five fingers, he said, "Twenty, 40, 60, 80, 100." I wrote "100" in the margin of his paper (see Figure 10.2a) and asked, "Then what?" Joe continued, keeping count with his other five fingers, "A hundred twenty, 140, 160, 180, 200." I wrote "200" under the 100 I had written, crossed the 100 out, and told Joe, "You have 200 so far." "Two more is 220, 240," Joe continued, and I wrote "240" under the 200 and crossed out the latter, as shown in Figure 10.2a.

I then wrote on Joe's paper the conventional form for multiplication (see Figure 10.2b). "You've just done this part," I told him, circling three of the numbers as illustrated in Figure 10.2c—"20 (pointing to the 2 of 23) twelve times (pointing to the 12)."

"What else do you need to do?" I inquired. Joe put out all ten fingers and counted by 3s as he kept count with them, "Three, 6, 9, 12, 15, 18, 21, 24, 27, 30, 33, 36." I circled the 3 and the 12 as shown in Figure 10.2d and told Joe that he had just done "this part—3 (pointing to the 3 of 23) twelve times (pointing to the 12)."

I wrote "36" in the margin under the 240 that I had written (Figure 10.2a) and waited for Joe's next move. He said, "Two hundred seventy-six," and remarked with pleasure that this was the same answer as the one he had gotten before and that the 240 and the 36, too, were the same.

Joe thus demonstrated his readiness for a push. *He* was the one who expressed a desire for "an easier way," and I only asked one question after another and related *his* thinking to the social, conventional knowledge about writing that he already had.

November 22

I started the math hour by asking the class to get yesterday's papers out. My plan was to get all the children to rethink yesterday's problem in *different, faster,* and/or *easier* ways.

FIGURE 10.2 Joe's additive procedure (a) and the correspondence between his reasoning and the parts of a written multiplication problem (b, c, and d).

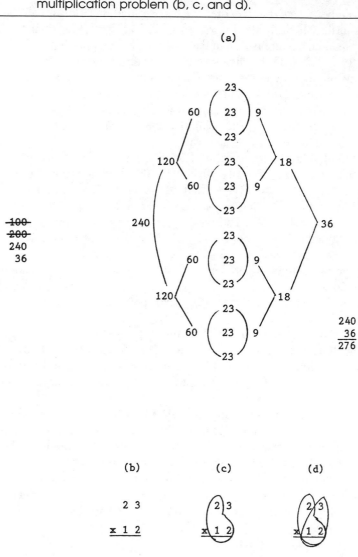

12 × 110. The problem (part of a social-studies unit) was: "How much should we budget for lodging and food for our pretend vacation in California?" I told the class that a motel costs about $60 a night, food costs about $50 a day, and we should plan for 12 days because we could probably stay at friends' houses 3 days out of the 15-day vacation.

"This is what most of you did yesterday," I said to the class and quickly wrote on the board the two-at-a-time addition shown in Figure 10.3. "What are some of the other ways you solved this problem?" I asked, hoping to bring out the more efficient procedures I had seen. Amy announced that she had written "110" six times for 6 days and doubled the result for 6 more days as follows:

$$
\begin{array}{r}
110 \\
110 \\
110 \\
110 \\
110 \\
\underline{110} \\
\end{array}
\qquad
\begin{array}{r}
600 \\
\underline{60} \\
660 \\
\underline{660} \\
1{,}320 \\
\end{array}
$$

FIGURE 10.3 The two-at-a-time additive procedure used by most students.

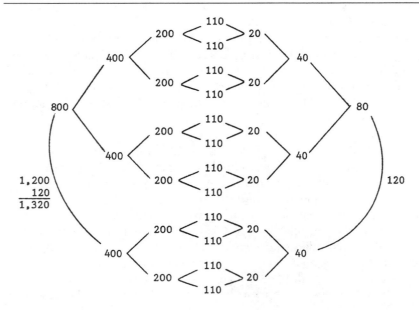

FIGURE 10.4 The correspondence between Amy's reasoning and the parts of a written multiplication problem.

"Who did it like Amy?" I asked, and several hands went up.

"Who did it a different way?" I went on to ask as usual and asked Jenny to show us her way.

Jenny had written "110" twelve times in a column. Pointing to each 1 in the tens column, she said, "Ten, 20, 30, 40, 50, 60, 70, 80, 90, 100, 200," whereupon someone pointed out, "It's 110, not 200." Jenny was puzzled but soon agreed, and went on to say, "One hundred ten, 120," and wrote "120" on the side. She went through a similar procedure for the hundreds column beginning with "One hundred, 200, 300" and ending with "ten hundred, eleven hundred, twelve hundred."

Since many in the class were unsure about the relationship between twelve hundred and the thousands, I asked Jenny, "How do you write 'twelve hundred'?" Jenny was stumped and was glad for Cathy's help. She finished by adding 1,200 and 120 and getting 1,320.

"Is it correct to say that ten hundreds is one thousand?" I asked the class and proceeded to another question: "If I pay sixteen hundred dollars for a piece of furniture, is there another way to say 'sixteen hundred dollars'?" Only half of the hands went up. After this discussion of a social-knowledge (linguistic) aspect of place value, I returned to the math problem: "All these ways are great, but is there an even *faster* way?"

Immediately, Amy announced, "A hundred 12 times, and ten 12 times." "What Amy said was this," I told the class as I wrote the numbers shown in Figure 10.4a. "Amy said, 'A hundred [underlining the first 1 of 110 as shown in Figure 10.4b] 12 times [circling the 12].' Amy then said, 'Ten [underlining the 10 of 110 as shown in Figure 10.4c] 12 times [circling the 12 again].'"

Amy blurted out, "You add a zero when you multiply by ten, and two zeros when you multiply by a hundred." Not wanting children to memorize such a rule without understanding *why* it works, I turned to the class and asked, "Who can explain what Amy said—without talking about adding zeros?"

Heather responded with "We said one hundred 10 times is one thousand. So one hundred 12 times is two more hundreds, and that's one thousand two hundred."

I wrote "1,200" on the board and said, heavily underlining the first 1 of 110, "We have done the hundreds; so now we have to take care of the tens [underlining the 10 of 110 again]." Jack offered, "10 ten times is a 100; so 10 twelve times is 120." With the help of the class, I added 120 to 1,200, and everybody agreed that the result was the same as the answer we had been getting.

After commenting that Amy's second procedure was a much faster way, I ended the discussion with one of my rare speeches to the class: "I want you to *look at the problem* and trust yourself to think about the *fastest* way. There's nothing wrong with adding, but think about what you can do in your head before you start writing. Use your head, and write down only what you have to. You might save a lot of time by taking a few minutes to think before you start writing. I won't give you any timed tests, but I want you to think about the *fastest* way. Now, how would you work the next problem by writing as little as possible?"

125
× 11. I wrote this problem on the board and noted the solemn silence and concentration that reigned. Everyone was thinking and not writing. After 10 minutes of individual work and exchanges among friends, a variety of new procedures appeared. Kim and Amy reported their methods orally, and Brad and Lila in turn went to the board to show off their inventions.

Kim, who had been stuck on the two-at-a-time method of addition (like Figure 10.3), got the answer without writing anything! She said, "A hundred 11 times is one thousand one hundred. (I wrote "1,100" on the board.) Twenty-five cents 4 times is a dollar; so 25 cents 8 times is 2 dollars. Twenty-five cents 3 times is 75 cents; so eleven 25s is 275. (I wrote "275" under the 1,100 I had written.) And one thousand one hundred plus 275 is 1,375."

Amy was next and reported that she got 1,000 for 100 × 10, and 300 for 25 × 12 (because 12 quarters make $3.00). She then added 1,000 and 300 (and got 1,300), added "one more hundred" (and got 1,400), and subtracted 25 (thereby getting the final answer of 1,375).

Brad wrote the following on the board:

$$
\begin{array}{r}
125 \\
125 \\
125 \\
+\,125 \\
\hline
500
\end{array}
$$

"How did you get 500?" I inquired, and he explained, "One hundred 4 times is 400. Twenty-five 4 times is 100. So 100 and 400 is 500."

I had another question for my benefit as well as that of the class: "Why did you add 125 four times?" Brad's explanation was: "Because it would be easy to

FIGURE 10.5 the correspondence between Lila's reasoning and the parts of a written multiplication problem.

(a)	(b)	(c)	(d)

$$
\begin{array}{cccc}
1 \ 2 \ 5 & 1\,②\,5 & 1\,②\,⑤ & ①\,②\,⑤ \\
\underline{\times \ \ 1 \ 1} & \underline{\times \ \underline{1} \ 1} & \underline{\times \ \underline{1} \ 1} & \underline{\times \ \underline{1} \ 1}
\end{array}
$$

add two 500s." He finished by writing the following on the board and explained that 4 times plus 4 times plus 3 times made 11 times 125:

$$
\begin{array}{llll}
500 & - \ 4 \ \text{times} & & \\
500 & - \ 4 \ \text{times} & 125 & \\
\underline{375} & - \ 3 \ \text{times} & 125 & 300 \\
1{,}375 & & \underline{125} & \underline{75} \\
& & & 375
\end{array}
$$

Lila split 11 into 10 and 1 and did $(10 \times 20) + (10 \times 5) + (10 \times 100) + 125$. She began her explanation by writing as follows:

$$
\begin{array}{ll}
10 \times 20 & 10 \times 10 = 100 \\
& 10 \times 10 = \underline{100} \\
& 200 \\
10 \times 5 = 50 &
\end{array}
$$

I wrote on the board the numbers shown in Figure 10.5a and told Lila and the class, "You have done 20 [circling the 2 as shown in Figure 10.5b] ten times [underlining the first 1 of 11]. You've also done 5 [circling the 5 as in Figure 10.5c] ten times [underlining the first 1 of 11 again]. What are you going to do now?"

Lila replied, "A hundred 10 times is a thousand," and wrote:

$$10 \times 100 = 1{,}000$$

I circled the 1 of 125 and underlined the first 1 of 11 again, as can be seen in Figure 10.5d.

Lila went on to write:

$$
\begin{array}{l}
200 + 50 + 1{,}000 = 1{,}250 \\
1{,}250 + 125 = 1{,}375
\end{array}
$$

I then underlined the second 1 of 11 and pointed out that that 1 stood for the one 125 that Lila had set aside to do 10×125.

I concluded the math hour by writing the problem once again on the board as follows to compare the ways in which the four children had broken the numbers down into parts. (On subsequent days, I asked the children to find similarities and differences among the procedures put on the board.)

$$\begin{array}{r} 125 \\ \times 11 \\ \hline \end{array}$$

"Kim and Amy and Brad and Lila all broke one of the numbers or both of them down into parts. Kim broke 125 down [pointing to 125] into 100 [pointing to the 1 of 125] and 25 [pointing to 25]. She did this," I said and wrote "100 + 25" to the right of 125.

"Amy did the same thing, but she also broke the 11 down [pointing to 11] into 10 [pointing to the first 1] and 1 [pointing to the second 1]. So she did this [pointing to 100 + 25] as well as this," I said and wrote "10 + 1" to the right of 11. The board now looked as follows:

$$\begin{array}{r} 125 \\ \times\ 11 \\ \hline \end{array} \quad \begin{array}{l} (100 + 25) \\ (10 + 1) \end{array}$$

"Amy did 10 times 100, 12 times 25, and 1 time 100, and then subtracted one 25 because she had multiplied it by 12 instead of by 11," I explained as I pointed to the various digits.

"Brad broke 11 down, too, but he changed it to 4 plus 4 plus 3," I remarked and wrote "4 + 4 + 3" to the right of (10 + 1).

"Lila's way was like Amy's way but different. She broke the 125 down into 100 and 20 and 5 [pointing to each digit]," I remarked and wrote "100 + 20 + 5." The board now looked as shown below:

$$\begin{array}{r} 125 \\ \times 11 \\ \hline \end{array} \quad \begin{array}{l} (100 + 25) \\ (10 + 1) \end{array} \quad \begin{array}{l} (100 + 20 + 5) \\ (4 + 4 + 3) \end{array}$$

My final statement was: "Any way you work the problem is OK, but I want you to *think about* the fastest and easiest way to break the numbers down and look for those tens and hundreds."

Logico-Mathematical and Social Knowledge in Multiplication

The reader may have noted that while we never transmit the logico-mathematical aspects (reasoning) of multiplication, we bring out children's inventions (logico-mathematical knowledge) and compare them. We also relate children's inventions to the social (conventional) aspects of our base-10 place-value system of writing so that they will use its properties as Hermina Sinclair suggested (personal communication, April 1992). The vertical form of writing multiplication problems is social knowledge that children did not invent. The preceding account included many examples of how we relate the social knowledge of written parts to the thinking that children do. We also look for moments to review terms (social knowledge) related to place value and multiplication such as "twelve hundred" and "one thousand two hundred." This social knowledge is very helpful for knowing that 12×100 = twelve hundred = one thousand two hundred.

We saw with reference to 12×110 and 125×11 on November 22 that Amy's knowledge that "You add a zero when you multiply by 10, and two zeros when you multiply by 100" helped her enormously. These rules about adding zeros use the properties of our base-10 place-value system of writing (social knowledge) and greatly simplify computation with large numbers. We want children to use these rules *if they can explain them* (logico-mathematical knowledge).

A key to constructivist teaching is the posing of the right question at the right time so that children will think. One of the outcomes of their thinking can be higher-level reasoning. We experimented with various approaches to these rules about zeros, and a way developed by Philip Westbrook seems worth experimenting with further. Westbrook is a teacher at Shades Cahaba Elementary School in Homewood, Alabama, and we describe his approach below.

FURTHER ENCOURAGING CHILDREN
TO USE THE PROPERTIES OF OUR SYSTEM OF WRITING

It is important to emphasize first that there is a heavy amount of social knowledge involved in Westbrook's approach, but there is also a large amount of reasoning (logico-mathematical knowledge) because he insists on children's justifying every answer. Because the possibility of children's learning tricks is great, Westbrook constantly asks them, "How do you know?"

Dividing 123 by 10 and Multiplying the Result by 10

Certain combinations of factors involving tens and hundreds seem much easier than others for third graders. Among the relatively easy combinations are: 1×10 (or one 10) = 10, 2×10 (or two 10s) = 20, 3×10 (or three 10s) = 30, and so on. Combinations such as 1×100 (or one 100) = 100, 2×100 (or two 100s) = 200, 3×100 (or three 100s) = 300, and so on are also relatively easy.

Knowing that children already have this knowledge, Westbrook asks questions that enable them to use this knowledge and go further. After writing "123" on the board, for example, he asks children how many ones there are in one hundred twenty-three. If they answer "Three," he reacts by saying, "Yes, there are three ones in the ones place, but how many ones are there in the whole

FIGURE 10.6 Lines indicating how many ones, tens, and hundreds are in 123 and why 12 tens ends with a zero.

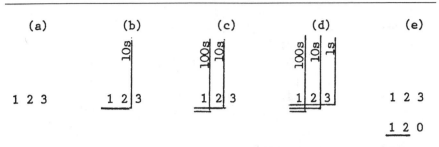

number, one hundred twenty-three?" Children quickly realize that there are 123 ones in 123.

Westbrook's next question is "How many tens are there in one hundred twenty-three?" If the answer is "Two," he responds, "Yes, there are two tens in the tens place, but how many tens are there in the whole number, one hundred twenty-three?" If necessary, he may ask if there are any tens in one hundred.

Children are thus led to figure out that, in 123, there are 123 ones, 12 tens, and 1 hundred. At the appropriate moments, Westbrook draws the lines that can be seen in Figure 10.6 showing 12 *tens* (Figure 10.6b), 1 *hundred* (Figure 10.6c), and 123 *ones* (Figure 10.6d).

After thus drawing lines to highlight the number of tens that are to the left of the vertical line (Figure 10.6b), Westbrook changes his question from division to multiplication: "What's twelve times ten?" The class is likely to say "A hundred twenty," whereupon Westbrook asks as usual, "How do you know?" (Most children explain that if 10 tens is 100, two more tens is 120.) Westbrook then writes "123" and "120" (see Figure 10.6e), underlines the first two digits, 1 and 2, of 120 (1*2*0), and points out the correspondence between the 12 in 123 and the 12 in 120. He thus explains that the zero in 120 means that there are 12 tens in 120 and no ones.

"What's fourteen times ten?" he may then ask, requesting a proof for every answer. By thus using what children know (10 tens = 100), Westbrook tries to get them to generalize about zeros by *reasoning* as follows:

$$12 \times 10 = 12 \text{ 10s} = 100 + 20 = 12\underline{0}$$
$$14 \times 10 = 14 \text{ 10s} = 100 + 40 = 14\underline{0}$$
$$15 \times 10 = 15 \text{ 10s} = 100 + \text{half of } 100 = 15\underline{0}$$
$$20 \times 10 = 20 \text{ 10s} = 100 + 100 = 20\underline{0}$$

Needless to say, Westbrook asks the same kinds of questions about 10 hundreds, 12 hundreds, 14 hundreds, 15 hundreds, 20 hundreds, and so on, and encourages children to exchange points of view.

Figure 10.7 Lines indicating how many thousands, hundreds, tens, and ones are in 2,147.

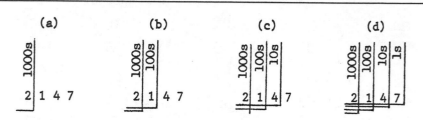

Dividing 2,147 by Powers of 10 and Multiplying the Result by Powers of 10

Westbrook then goes through similar exercises with larger numbers such as 2,147 and asks questions such as the following:

How many *ones* are there in two thousand one hundred forty-seven?
How many *thousands* are there in two thousand one hundred forty-seven?
How many *hundreds* are there in two thousand one hundred forty-seven?
How many *tens* are there in two thousand one hundred forty-seven?

As the children answer, Westbrook draws the lines that can be seen in Figure 10.7 showing 2 *thousands* (Figure 10.7a), 21 *hundreds* (Figure 10.7b), 214 *tens* (Figure 10.7c), and 2,147 *ones* (Figure 10.7d) to the left of each vertical line, respectively.

The next step is to work back from division to multiplication by asking questions such as the following, writing the answers, asking for explanations, and underlining the zeros as shown below:

What's 2147 times 1?   (2,147)
What's 214 times 10?   (2,140, with nothing in the ones place)
What's 21 times 100?   (2,100, with nothing in the tens and the
                          ones places)
What's 2 times 1000?   (2,000, with nothing in the hundreds, the
                          tens, and the ones places)

He goes on to vary the numbers in the multiplication problems over months, beginning with multiples of 10 (51 × 30, for example) and ending with more complicated problems, such as 51 × 34. Four children's solutions to 51 × 34 were discussed in detail in Chapter 6. The reader may recall that when the teacher asked for two different ways of getting the answer to this problem, two children invented a higher level immediately after producing a lower level of multiplication. The two levels produced by one of the children were the following:

Lower level	Higher level
51 × 10 = 510	50 × 30 = 1,500
51 × 10 = 510	50 × 4 = 200
51 × 10 = 510	1 × 34 = 34
51 × 4 = 204	1,734
1,734	

CONCLUSION

Multiplying a two-digit number by a single-digit number or by a multiple of 10 is not very difficult for advanced third graders. However, when neither of the two two-digit numbers ends with a zero, they become confused, as we saw in the example of 59 × 69 in Chapter 7. The reader may recall that some children argued that 50 × 60 and 9 × 9 were all they needed to do.

When children are confused about the logic of multidigit multiplication, a good way to facilitate inventions is by giving problems, such as 125 × 11, that have small, easy-to-multiply digits. These numbers are much easier than 59 × 69, as we noted in Chapter 7. Another way to facilitate the invention of cross-multiplication is to have children discuss only procedures, without worrying about exact numbers. If the teacher says, "Let's just discuss what and what we need to multiply," children will make statements such as the following, without getting lost in the details of computation: "I'd do 50 × 60, 50 × 9, 9 × 60, and 9 × 9."

The rules about zeros are seldom invented even by advanced third graders. However, there always seems to be at least one child in the class who has heard these rules about zeros and uses them without knowing why they work. Since these rules make computation much easier, we decided to experiment with focused exercises to encourage children to figure them out. Note, however, that we never give these rules in readymade form.

Once advanced third graders have figured out these rules about zeros, they propel themselves to new heights. To solve problems such as 52 × 49, for example, some change it to 52 × 50 − 52, and then to 52 × 10 × 5 − 52 = 520 × 5 − 52. Subsequently increasing the difficulty to 123 × 52 does not cause undue confusion, as children invent 123 × 10 × 5 + 246. Some children become able to solve many problems all in their heads, as we saw in the example of 125 × 11, which Kim solved without writing anything. Another example is the child who wrote only "240" on his paper for 15 × 16. His explanation was: 16 × 10 = 160, plus half of that is 160 + 80 = 240.

In November 1991, and repeatedly thereafter, we had to push children to give up addition in favor of multiplication. We daily reminded children that if they spent a few minutes thinking about faster ways instead of starting to write immediately, they could save a lot of work. Whether or not this pushing is appropriate depends on children's cognitive levels and personalities. In 1990–91, pushing did not seem advisable because the children in the class did not seem to be advanced enough to be bored with addition. In 1989–90, pushing was not necessary because the advanced children began to use multiplication on their own. Constructivism thus does not provide a recipe. Because it is not a pedagogical method, each teacher must decide what to do depending on the particular group he or she has.

CHAPTER 11

What Do You Say to Children When You Work with Them Individually?

After I (SL) give a problem to the class, I want children to work alone to get their own answers before they get up to exchange points of view with friends. While they are working independently, I walk around to see what individual children are doing and to "teach" without teaching in the traditional sense. This "teaching" is a very important part of what I do as a teacher, and I say different things to different children, depending on where they are. Knowing where each child is depends on the theory that is in the teacher's mind, and assessment is discussed as a separate topic in Chapter 12.

In the present chapter, I describe videotaped conversations that took place on November 21 with four children at various levels of development—Kim, Jenny, Joe, and Cathy. I conclude with some of the principles of teaching that I keep in mind as I talk with individual children.

CONVERSATIONS WITH FOUR CHILDREN

The first problem I gave on November 21 came from the social studies project referred to in Chapter 10 involving the making of a budget for a vacation in California. I told the class that one of the decisions each person had to make was whether or not to rent a car. By checking around, I told them, I had found out that the best price was about $35 a day. The question was: "How much would it cost to rent a car for 15 days?" If renting a car for 15 days would cost too much, people might decide not to rent one for the entire trip.

As usual, all the children started to work individually, and I first stopped to see what Cathy was doing. She said she was writing "35.00" fifteen times, and I told her that I would be back to see her progress. I then stopped to see what Kim was doing.

Talking with Kim

Kim was one of the top students in the class and had been in classes of constructivist teachers at Hall-Kent School since first grade. Like many others in the class, Kim was stuck on the two-at-a-time additive procedure illustrated in

FIGURE 11.1 Kim's finished paper.

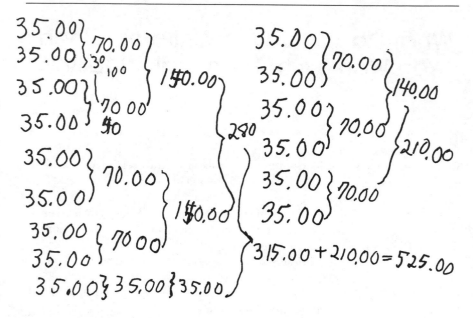

Figure 11.1 instead of advancing to multiplication. As I expected, she explained that she had written "35.00" fifteen times and that she was bracketing them in groups of two.

For the first pair of 35.00s, she said, "Thirty and 30 is 60, and 5 and 5 is 10, and 60 plus 10 is 70." She wrote "70.00" for the first bracket and repeated this writing for all the other pairs of 35.00s.

Kim then bracketed all the 70.00s in pairs. Pointing to the second 70.00, she explained, "I take 30 from 70 to make 100 with the other 70. That makes this 70 [the second 70] 50." She wrote "50" below the second 70.00, as can be seen in Figure 11.1, and went on to say, "One hundred plus 50 is 150." She thereupon wrote "150" for the first pair of 70.00s.

When she started to write "150" for all the other pairs of 70.00s, I stopped her by saying, "Tell me what you did right here [pointing to the first 70.00, the second 70.00, and her sum of 150.00]." To my surprise, Kim confidently repeated the same explanation with the same error.

Knowing that this error was an unusual one for Kim, I reacted by saying, "I disagree with that. There's something right here [pointing to the 150] that I am not sure about." Kim did not realize her error and repeated herself again by explaining that she had taken 30 out of the second 70 to make 100.

"I agree with that," I told her, "But this part down here [pointing to the 50 and the 70 above it] is what I am not sure about." Kim exclaimed, "Now, I see!"

and corrected herself. She continued by bracketing the 70.00s in pairs, and I knew that she would get the final answer without difficulty. "We'll share our answers in a few minutes," I told Kim after thanking her for her explanation.

When I looked around, I saw Jenny walking toward me seeking my help.

Talking with Jenny

Jenny was one of the less able children who had transferred to Hall-Kent School in September. She could use the algorithm of carrying perfectly and got correct answers most of the time, but her knowledge of place value was very poor. The strong point in her favor was that she was confident and explicit about what made sense to her and what did not. When she understood something, she said so clearly, and when she did not, she also said so without hesitating.

"Tell me what you have done," I said as I noticed her customary place-value errors (see Figure 11.2, top right corner). She had written "6," "12," "18," "24," "30," "36," "42," and "45" for the column of 10s and added 45 to 75, as if these were all 1s.

Jenny explained that she had put down "35" fifteen times, covered up all the 5s for the time being, and added only the 30s. "Thirty and 30 is 60. I did it again," she announced.

"What did you do again?" I asked, and she replied, "Not putting zeros on." "Is that going to matter?" I inquired, and her response was a definite "Yes."

FIGURE 11.2 Jenny's paper when she sought help.

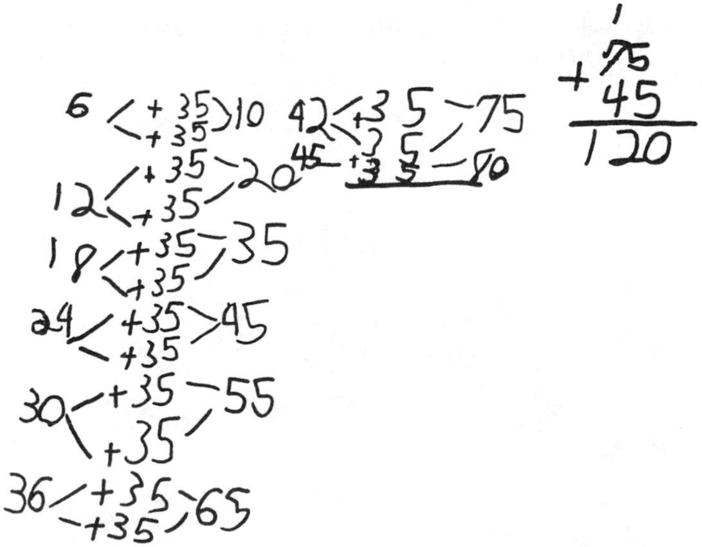

"Would it help to change those as you talk to me?" I asked, and Jenny wrote zeros after the 6, 12, 18, and so on as she went down the column of 30s explaining her corrections:

30 and 30 is 60.
60 plus 30 plus 30 is 120.
120 plus 30 plus 30 is 180.
180 plus 30 plus 30 is 240.
240 plus 30 plus 30 is 300.
300 plus 30 plus 30 is 360.
360 plus 30 plus 30 is 420.
420 plus 30 is 450.

On her own initiative at this point, Jenny crossed out all the numbers in her previous computation,

$$\begin{array}{r} 75 \\ +45 \\ \hline 120 \end{array}$$

and wrote "450" away from these numbers.

"What did you do next?" I asked, and Jenny explained, "I added all my 5s." "What did you get from all the 5s?" I inquired, and Jenny replied, "I messed up." When I asked what she meant, she said that she sometimes got 75 and sometimes 80. "Go through the 5s," I suggested, and she counted by 5s in various faltering ways. She sometimes counted rhythmically by combining two 5s in the same decade and sometimes changed this pattern ("5, 10—15, 20—25, 30, 35, 40—45 . . .").

When she finally reached 75 with satisfaction, and without stumbling any more, I asked, "Do you feel good about the 75?" Jenny responded with a confident "yes."

"What are you going to do next?" I asked, and Jenny wrote the following as she explained her rationale:

$$\begin{array}{r} 450 \\ + \ \ 75 \\ \hline 5 \end{array}$$

She then said, "Seven and 5 is 12; so I put my 2 down and carry my 10," writing "2" below the 7 and "10" above the 4 as follows:

$$\begin{array}{r} 10 \\ 450 \\ + \ \ \ 75 \\ \hline 25 \end{array}$$

"Four hundred and 10 is," Jenny continued, and I interrupted with, "You said, 'put my 2 down [pointing to the 2] and carry my 10 [pointing to the 10],' but I don't see 12 here [pointing in general at all the writing]."

"What I could do is add 400 and 10," Jenny repeated. I responded by saying,"Show me what you mean. I'm not sure I understand."

Jenny repeated herself again by saying, "I could add this 400 [pointing] with the 10 [pointing], and that would be 410."

Zeroing in on the 10, I said, "OK, but are you sure that's a 10 [pointing]? Where did it come from?" With certitude, Jenny answered, "From the 12."

Place value is one of the hardest problems for children who have been taught algorithms (see Chapter 3). When a child mistakenly focuses on a single column as if each were an isolated column of ones, I often try to focus his or her attention on the entire numbers, 450 and 75 in this situation. "You said this [circling 75] was seventy-five, and that this [circling 450] was four hundred fifty. So how can you possibly get 12 from this [the 5] and this [the 7]?"

"Oh, that's a seventy and a fifty!" Jenny exclaimed, and I tested her by asking, "Are you sure?" "Yes," Jenny replied with certitude, and I continued with "How do you do that [70 + 50]?"

"I'd add 70 and five 10s," Jenny answered, and counted on five fingers, "Eighty, 90, 100, 110, 120."

"So would you still put 2 right here [under the 7]?" I asked, and Jenny informed me, "This 2 is a twenty, and I'm going to carry a hundred."

"You are not going to add 400 and 10?" I asked to ascertain her conviction. "I'm going to add 400 and 100," she replied firmly.

"So what will your answer be?" I asked, and Jenny emphatically stated, "Five hundred and twenty-five." When she finished writing "5" in front of the 25 under the line, completing her answer of 525, I asked, "Five hundred twenty-five what?" "Five hundred twenty-five dollars," Jenny replied, and I thanked her for talking to me.

I was especially curious about what Joe had done in light of the interaction we had the day before (November 20 in Chapter 10). My next stop, therefore, was at Joe's place.

Talking with Joe

Joe had been in constructivist classes at Hall-Kent School since kindergarten and was one of the more advanced, inventive children in the class. When I asked him what he had done, he explained that the car would cost $175 for 5 days; so he added $175 three times for 15 days and got a total of $525.

"Do you remember what you did yesterday? You got the same answer by doing something else, and you said that way was faster. Can you do that just to

FIGURE 11.3 Joe's paper at the end of the conversation.

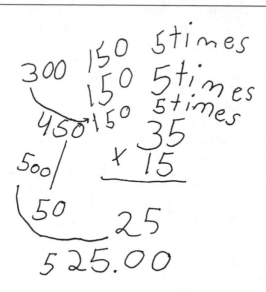

see if you get the same answer?" I asked. Joe thought a minute and wrote the following, which can be seen in the middle of Figure 11.3:

$$
\begin{array}{r}
35 \\
\times 15 \\
\end{array}
$$

He then tried to count by 30s keeping count with his fingers: "Thirty 10 times is 30, 60, 90, 120, 150, 190, no, 180, 190, 200. This is hard."

"Do you need to write it down when you get to a point where you can't hold it any more?" I suggested. Joe ignored me at first but ended up accepting this suggestion. "Thirty times 10, 30 ten times. I'm going to do it again," he said, and counted by 30s, keeping count with five fingers, "Thirty, 60, 90, 120, 150." He stopped, wrote "150," reflected, and wrote "5 times" next to it (see Figure 11.3). He then wrote "150 5 times" two more times, and subtotals of 300 and 450.

Moving to the 5 in 35, Joe said, "Five 10 times is" and used ten fingers to keep track: "Five, 10, 15, 20, 25, 30, 35, 40, 45, 50."

He wrote "50," as can be seen in Figure 11.3, added it to the 450 he already had, and wrote "500."

He went on to say, "Five 5 more times," and counted by 5s to 25. He finished by writing "25," adding it to the 500 he had gotten, and writing the final answer of 525.00 (see Figure 11.3).

"Does that check with the other answer you got?" I asked, and Joe replied in the affirmative with satisfaction. "That's interesting. Thanks, Joe," I said and walked over to Cathy as I had promised.

Talking with Cathy

Cathy was like Jenny in that she had transferred to Hall-Kent School in September, could use the algorithm of carrying perfectly, but did not understand place value and why the algorithm produced the correct answer. However, Cathy was different in two ways: She was intellectually more limited and became passive when she did not understand something.

I asked Cathy what she was doing as I noticed the second column of 35.00s that she had forgotten about (see Figure 11.4). "I added 30 and 30 and got 60, and I added the 5s and the 5s and got 10," Cathy explained as she pointed to the two-at-a-time addition she had done. "Now, I'm going to add the 10s, and there'll be a 5 left over," she said as she ran her finger down the vertical lines she had drawn to make pairs of 5s. The leftover 5 that she mentioned referred to the 5 in the last 35.00 of the column. Treating the column of 10s as 30s rather than as 3s was a major achievement for Cathy!

Figure 11.4 Cathy's paper at the end of the conversation.

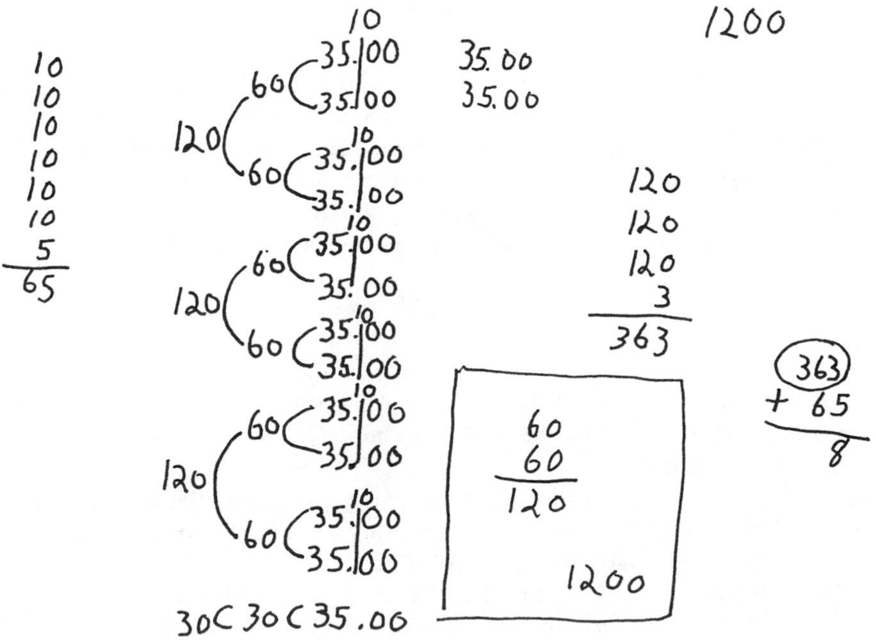

"I'm going to add my 10s up," she said and carefully counted the 10s she had written at the top of each vertical line in the column of decimal points.

She started to make a column of six 10s on the left-hand side, and I requested, "Can you think out loud for me so I'll know what you are doing?"

Cathy obliged by explaining, "I'm writing it [10] six times 'cause that's how much 10s I've got." After writing "5" and drawing a horizontal line at the bottom of the column, she used the algorithm by saying, "Zero, zero, zero, zero, zero, zero, five," and wrote "5" below the line. She continued with the algorithm by counting the 1s in the 10s column as 1s, wrote "6" below the line, and announced, "Sixty-five."

"I heard you counting these as ones," I told her, pointing to each 1 and repeating what she had said—"One, two, three, four. . . ." I then pointed to the first 1 and asked, "What is this one?" "A ten," Cathy replied. "A ten? So that's 10, 20, 30, 40, 50, 60, 65?" I asked as I pointed to each 10 and the 5 at the bottom of the column. Cathy answered, "Yes," and I told her, "That's what I get, too. Then what?"

"I'm going to add it [the total of 65] to this," Cathy continued, pointing to the following, which she had written for the column of 30s (see Figure 11.4):

$$\begin{array}{r} 120 \\ 120 \\ 120 \\ \underline{3} \\ 363 \end{array}$$

Cathy had copied the 30 from the last 35.00 of the column as a 3, but I decided not to point out this error. The 60s and 120s she had written correctly seemed like plenty of progress for Cathy for the time being, and I thought that this progress would generalize soon. Besides, pushing children when they have already done enough hard thinking is counterproductive.

Cathy went on to write the following numbers using the algorithm:

$$\begin{array}{r} 363 \\ +65 \\ \hline 8 \end{array}$$

"I added the 3 and the 5, and I got 8," she explained and went on to say, "I add the 6 and the 6, the sixty and the sixty, and get . . . [long silence] . . . twelve hundred, no, hold on."

Cathy became silent, and I asked, "How much is twelve hundred? Can you write 'twelve hundred' for me up here?" pointing to an empty space at the top of Cathy's paper. To my surprise, she wrote "120."

"That says 'one hundred and twenty,'" I remarked, even though I knew that reading "120" was easy for her. "Do you want me to show you how to write 'twelve hundred'?" I asked, and upon hearing a "yes," I wrote a zero after her "120." I asked her to read it [1200] and Cathy obliged by saying, "Twelve hundred."

"Do you know the other way to say it [1200]? Remember the discussion we had the other day in class?" I asked, and Cathy was silent.

"You can also say 'one thousand two hundred,'" I informed her as I pointed to the 1 and the 200 in 1200.

"Let's go back to the problem," I suggested. "You said this [drawing a circle around 363] was three hundred sixty-three. And you were adding 65 to it [circling the 65 with a finger]. You were adding sixty and sixty [pointing to the two 6s] and said that was twelve hundred. Do you still agree with that?" Cathy's response was a definite "yes."

"You do? OK," I said, and gently went on to say, "It seems funny to me, Cathy. Twelve hundred is one thousand two hundred [pointing to the 1200 on her paper]." Cathy interrupted at this point by saying, "I think it's thirty-six hundred and three [referring to the 363 that I had circled]."

"Why? What's this number?" I asked, circling the 363 with my finger and asking her to read it. "Three hundred and sixty-three," she said this time.

Since this was an impasse I wanted Cathy to get out of somehow with some feeling of success, I decided to do something I would normally not do: I drew a large square in an empty part of her paper and said, "Can you show me here in any way you know what 60 plus 60 is?"

Cathy wrote the following with ease:

$$
\begin{array}{r}
60 \\
\underline{60} \\
120
\end{array}
$$

After writing this answer, she read it as "a hundred twenty."

"Can you tell me how you got a hundred twenty?" I asked, and her explanation revealed confusion springing from a variety of sources: "I added the zero and the zero and got zero. Then I added the sixty and the sixty and got twelve hundred. That's really going to be one hundred and twenty, without two zeros."

"How do you know it's just one hundred twenty, and not any more than one hundred twenty?" I asked, and Cathy's answer showed her focus on numerals without numerical thinking. "Because you know that twelve hundred would have to have two zeros like this," she said as she wrote "1200" inside the square (see Figure 11.4). "Sixty and sixty equals a twelve. But you can't add two more zeros because it's not like six hundred; so it's going to be only one zero. So a hundred and twenty is what I got."

Noticing that the class was waiting for the usual discussion to begin and knowing that Cathy could not make any more progress that day, I concluded our conversation by saying, "I'm going to let you finish and come out with the final answer. I agree with you that sixty and sixty is a hundred and twenty."

I turned to the class and asked everybody to take a seat to share "what we have done."

A few words about Cathy's thinking may be in order before a discussion of principles of teaching. Cathy was just beginning to show enormous progress by thinking about the 3 in 35.00 as 30, by getting 60 for 30 + 30, and by getting 120 for 60 + 60 on her paper.

However, the algorithm she was taught at another school existed side by side with her newly acquired knowledge of tens. When she added the column of tens, she thought about the 1s as ones. The "dance of the digits" came out in full force when she gave her explanation of why 60 + 60 was one hundred and twenty and not twelve hundred: "Because you know that twelve hundred would have to have two zeros like this [1200]. . . . Sixty and sixty equals a twelve. But you can't add two more zeros because it's not like six hundred; so it's going to be only one zero. So one hundred and twenty is what I got." If Cathy had not learned to write digits in a certain sequence and in specific places like dance steps, she would not have given such an "explanation" based on how many zeros must be written to the right of 12.

Her repeated statement that 60 + 60 was twelve hundred is an example of the conflict between two ways of thinking: thinking about every column as ones (6 + 6 = 12) and thinking that 60 + 60 = maybe 1,200, or maybe 120 (she did write "120" at one point). Cathy is like all the other below-average children, who demonstrate that they are hurt much more by algorithms than above-average students such as Jack (see Chapter 9).

PRINCIPLES OF TEACHING

I would now like to highlight some of the principles of teaching I kept in mind in the preceding conversations with individual children. The basic principle is to treat children with respect as fellow human beings, not like pets to be trained with rewards. In fact, I am careful to keep each child in the driver's seat and to follow his or her thinking instead of leading them to *my* ways. Below are three of the specific principles that I followed.

Avoid Saying "That's Right" and "That's Not Right"

This is one of the hardest principles to remember. Instead of saying "That's right," I asked Jenny if she felt good about the 75 she got for fifteen 5s. Likewise, I asked Joe if the answer he got by using a different procedure checked with the first answer he had gotten. We want children to satisfy themselves and to judge whether or not things make sense *to them*. By trying to reinforce correct answers, we encourage children to please the teacher and to depend on the teacher to know whether or not an answer is correct. The closest we come to reinforcement, therefore, is to say, "I agree with you," "That's what I get, too," or "That makes sense to me." Agreeing with children on an equal footing is very different from being the omniscient authority who decrees that an answer *is correct*.

When children make errors, we try to get them to correct themselves by reacting in one of several ways. The most indirect way is to say, "Would you explain to me how you got this number?" Children often correct themselves while trying to explain their thinking to someone else. For example, Jenny corrected herself when she said, "Thirty and 30 is 60. I did it again," while trying to explain the 6 she had written.

When this approach does not result in self-correction, we may say, "I don't understand" or "I am not sure about that." This is what I said to Jenny when she repeatedly added 10 to 400 instead of adding 100 to 400.

The most direct way of reacting is to say "I don't agree," as I implied when Kim repeatedly said that $70 + 70 = 150$. I used this approach with Kim because this was a superficial error for her, and she was an outgoing child full of confidence in her own ability to think. I was nevertheless vague in my disagreement because I wanted her to find *her own* error rather than answering *my* specific question. This is why I said, "This part is what I am not sure about," pointing to the 50 and the 70 above it, instead of asking, "What's 70 minus 30?"

Whenever possible, I try to bring out conflicting elements that are already in the child's mind to encourage him or her to make higher-level relationships. For example, when Jenny kept thinking $5 + 7 = 12$ instead of $50 + 70 = 120$, I said, "You said that this [circling the 75] was seventy-five, and that this [circling 450] was four hundred fifty. So how can you possibly get 12 from this [the 5] and this [the 7]?"

The conflicting element sometimes comes from my perspective. For example, when Jenny put down a 2 and carried a 10 in the preceding situation, I said, "But I don't see 12 here [pointing in general to all the writing]." The reader may have noticed that this element from *my* perspective was much less effective than ideas from Jenny's own perspective (5 as part of 450 and 7 as part of 75).

Individualize Objectives

To insure that I help children on *their terms*, I frequently make statements such as: "Tell me what you have done," "What did you do next?" and "What are you going to do next?" As they speak, I carefully assess each child's *process* of thinking before saying anything and formulate different objectives for different children.

Kim's error of 70 + 70 = 150 was a superficial and rare mistake for her, and my objective for her was to get her beyond the two-at-a-time additive procedure that we saw. However, my plan was not to push her individually but to push the entire class the next day (see Chapter 10 about November 22) because many other students were in the same boat.

Jenny's problem was place value. However, she was clearly on her way to knowing 10s and 100s solidly, and a few questions sufficed for her to correct herself.

Joe was the most advanced of the four children, and my objective was to push him toward the multidigit multiplication that *he* had initiated the day before (November 20 in Chapter 10).

Cathy's problem was obviously place value. Her concept of 10s was very weak, and she needed time to strengthen her own thinking to overcome the foreign rules that made no sense but produced correct answers.

"Teach" by Asking Questions

I try to "teach" only by asking questions. For example, although my objective for Joe was multidigit multiplication, I never suggested multiplication. Instead, I asked him if he could do what he had done the day before that *he* said was faster. Likewise, I asked Jenny, "Would it help to change those [the 6, 12, 18, and so on, to 60, 120, 180, and so on] as you talk to me?" I wanted *her* to decide whether or not the zeros would help *her.* In the realm of logico-mathematical knowledge, telling children *what* to write and *how* to get the answer prevents them from doing their own thinking. I want children to feel free to reject my ideas because only when they have this freedom are children free to do their own thinking, honestly.

I thus avoid direct instruction but make an exception for social knowledge. For example, I showed Cathy how to write "twelve hundred" and told her another way for saying "twelve hundred." My hope was not merely to teach these bits of social knowledge but to enable her to use this information to strengthen her knowledge of place value.

CONCLUSION

All the preceding principles flow from constructivism (Chapter 1) and autonomy as the aim of education (Chapter 5). I always try to develop children's own thinking starting with what *they* are doing. I do not always succeed but get better at what I strive to do. During the past year, which was my fourth year of teaching third grade, I finally had the feeling of knowing precisely what I was doing. I knew the variety of levels to expect in third grade and the sequence of development that was likely to evolve. Just as children invent new ways of thinking, I, too, keep inventing and experimenting with the knowledge that I construct each year.

CHAPTER 12

How Do You Assess Children's Thinking in Problem Solving?

The way we assess children's progress depends on the theoretical framework that is in our minds. For the addition of two-digit numbers, for example, it is important from an algorithmic point of view that children write numerals in neatly aligned columns, with all the 1s in the ones column and all the 10s in the tens column. From the viewpoint of constructivism, however, such a concern is completely unimportant as long as children know to add the 10s together and the 1s together. To discuss how we assess children's thinking, therefore, we give examples of word problems and the theoretical reasons for our categorization of children's responses. Since multiplication and division are the main concerns in third-grade arithmetic, this chapter focuses on these operations, starting with multiplication.

At the beginning of the year, we ask children to bring a folder that has two pockets so that they can keep filler paper in one pocket and their finished work in the other. The reason for using loose sheets instead of a notebook is that we want to collect children's papers from time to time to analyze them or to return them with comments. Math folders are also useful for parent conferences, when we want to discuss the kinds of problems the class has been solving and the progress each child has made since the beginning of the year. These folders also serve to let parents know that their children are getting everything that others are getting from the textbook and more (such as confidence, inventiveness, and liking for math).

Before getting down to the first problem of the day, we always ask the children to put their names and the date on a new sheet of paper. This routine permits us to collect specific papers and to ask children to arrange them in chronological order after we return them. Collecting all the papers from the class on certain days allows us to sort them according to types of strategies used. By studying each folder chronologically, we gain insight into the constructive process over time.

A detail that is important to us is that we ask children to write with a pen rather than with a pencil during the math hour. The reason for this request is that we do not want children to erase their work, but they seem to have a strong desire to erase their errors out of existence. We are interested in their thinking, we tell them, and if they cross out their first attempt instead of erasing it, we can know how they thought before changing their minds.

MULTIPLICATION PROBLEMS

The line of demarcation between addition and multiplication cannot be drawn clearly in third graders' invented computational procedures. Early in the year when children encounter so-called multiplication problems, they use mostly addition and a mixture of multiplication and addition. We therefore first describe the types of addition and multiplication we found on November 21, when the problem was 15 × 35. In the second part of this section, we discuss the types of addition and multiplication procedures that appeared later in the year in response to 5 × 245 and 51 × 34.

Strategies Conceptualized Early in the Year

As stated in Chapter 11, the first problem given to the class on November 21 was: "If it costs $35 a day to rent a car on our social-studies vacation in California, how much will it cost to rent one for 15 days?" The analysis of the class's written responses to this question is discussed below. Chapter 11 described the teacher's interactions with four children before the collection of these papers. We hope Chapter 11 and this one will complement each other in explaining how we assess children's levels of thinking.

The aspects of assessment described below include the following four: logical conceptualization of numbers and operations, knowledge of place value, ability to remember and carry out one's own plan, and accuracy in computation and knowledge of sums and products. We begin by discussing children's logic about numbers and operations.

Logical Conceptualization of Numbers and Operations. The most obvious types of strategies we looked for on November 21 were those using addition and multiplication. Within the type using addition were writing "35" fifteen times, as shown in Figure 11.1, and the more efficient use of addition. These are outlined first and then discussed.

A. Writing "35" fifteen times but not adding anything (one child)
B. Writing "35" fifteen times and using addition (sixteen children)
   1. Making pairs of numbers, pairs of pairs, and so on (thirteen children)

2. Making identical subgroups of more than two numbers, writing a total for every subgroup, and adding all the subtotals (three children)

C. Writing "35" only five times and adding the subtotal as many times as necessary (four children)

   Note: A more general description of this type is "writing '35' fewer than fifteen times and adding the subtotal as many times as necessary." Writing "70" seven times and "35" once would belong to this type.

D. Writing "35" only once and using addition-multiplication (two children)

The child in the first type (A), who wrote "35" fifteen times in a column without adding anything, was a very slow developer who counted on her fingers even to do 5 + 3 and treated all the columns as ones. She usually got the correct answer by using the algorithm that she had learned in second grade but had no idea how "regrouping" worked. Although her work was at the lowest level of the class on November 21, it represented enormous progress over the "35 + 15" that she would have written earlier in the year.

The majority of the class (16 of 23, type B) wrote "35" fifteen times and used only addition. Within this type, most (13 of 16, type B.1) added pairs of numbers, pairs of pairs, and so on, as can be seen in Figure 11.1. Even some of the highest-level children in the class had endlessly been doing this two-at-a-time addition since the beginning of the school year, and we wanted them to move on to a more efficient procedure, as stated in Chapter 10. Some of these children added 35s, then 70s, and then 140s as Kim did (Figure 11.1), but others

FIGURE 12.1 Writing "35" fifteen times making identical subgroups of more than two numbers.

(a)

35	35	35	35	35		
35	35	35	35	35		
35	35	35	35	35		
105 +	105 +	105 +	105 +	105 =	525	

(b)

1				
35	35	35		
35	35	35	11	
35	35	35	165	
35	35	35	165	
35	35	35	165	
165	165	165	495	

added each column separately—an even more tedious procedure. Only one child, Jenny, added each column cumulatively and wrote "6, 12, 18, . . ." and "60, 120, 180 . . ." later for each pair of 30s rather than "60, 60, 60 . . ." (see Figure 11.2). She did more in her head and wrote much less than the other 12 children.

The next two types (B.2 and C) are instructive—writing "35" fifteen times in equal subgroups of more than two numbers (type B.2) and writing "35" only five times (type C). The new common element here is that the children broke 15 down into equal subgroups. The difference between the two types is that "35" was written fifteen times in type B.2 but only five times in type C. Figure 12.1 shows two examples of type B.2. The second example (Figure 12.1b) in this figure was supplied by Danny, a transfer student who had been taught algorithms, as stated in Chapter 7. The rule he learned from this instruction was that when he carried, he always had to carry 1! This rule worked well for adding three 165s but not for adding five 35s.

Below is an example of type C, writing "35" only five times and adding the subtotal as many times as necessary:

$$
\begin{array}{ll}
35 & \\
35 & \\
35 & \\
35 & \\
\underline{35} & \\
175 & 300 \\
175 & 210 \\
\underline{175} & \underline{15} \\
525 & 525 \\
\end{array}
$$

This example clearly illustrates constructive (reflecting) abstraction. This child did not feel the need to write "35" fifteen times because once she got 175 for five 35s, she could think *simultaneously* about one 175 and about five 35s. Because she solidly made a higher-order unit (175) out of five lower-order units (five 35s), she could iterate the higher-order unit (175 + 175 + 175) knowing that each 175 included five 35s.

The next type (D), writing "35" only once, *may* or *may not* represent a step further in the constructive process. The two children in this type wrote "35" only once and knew that 35 stood for thirty-five 1s and that 15 stood for a different kind of unit—the number of times thirty-five 1s were to be taken. While third graders write "15 × 35," which denotes multiplication, they often continue to use addition for a long time to compute the answer. This is why we used the term *addition-multiplication* in the preceding outline and said that type D *may* or *may not* represent a step further in the constructive process.

FIGURE 12.2 Writing "35" only once and using addition-multiplication with commutativity.

```
 35
x15
```

```
15 15     15 15     15 15     15 15     15 15     15 15     15 15
15 15     15 15     15 15     15 15     15 15     15 15     15 15
  60        60        60        60        60        60        60


                                                    60
15 15     15 15                                     60
15 15     15                                        60
  60        45                                      60   240
                                                    60
                                                    60
                                                    60
                                                    60   240
                                                         480 + 45 = 525
```

The addition-multiplication of one of the children, Joe, was described in detail in Chapter 11. Figure 12.2 shows the addition-multiplication of the other child in type D, Brad. (Although we could have categorized Brad in type B.2 because he wrote the same addend 35 times in subgroups of four, his use of commutativity, which will be discussed shortly, was clearly at a higher level than type B.2.)

Brad wrote "15" thirty-five times because he obviously thought that thirty-five 15s was the same thing as fifteen 35s. The commutativity of multiplication is easily invented by advanced third graders and discussed lightly in class as it appears. For the children who can generalize from $2 \times 3 = 3 \times 2$, $3 \times 4 = 4 \times 3$, $2 \times 6 = 6 \times 2$, $3 \times 5 = 5 \times 3$, and $4 \times 5 = 5 \times 4$, the commutativity of multiplication is obvious. For others, however, this commutativity is a mystery. We will have occasion to return to this topic later in this chapter.

As can be seen by comparing the last three types (B.2, C, and D), it is impossible to draw a clear line of demarcation between addition and multiplication. On November 21, all the children in the class would have agreed that the answer could be obtained with "35 fifteen times," "15 times 35," or "35 times 15," or by "timesing 35 by 15." However, they all used addition to compute the answer.

Two points must be made about the preceding analysis. One is that although we stated that writing "35" only five times represents progress over writing it fifteen times, the difference in what children write is often a manifestation of their personality rather than of their cognitive level. Some advanced children continue to write "35" fifteen times because they like the ease and security of the old habit, as we stated before. Others are prudent and want to prevent all possible confusion. Some anticipate having to produce a proof and feel that by showing fifteen 35s, they can prove the soundness of their reasoning.

The second point to be made is that although it is necessary to analyze the class's written work to understand children's progress, assessment requires talking frequently to children and knowing what lies behind their writing. We saw in Chapter 11, for example, that Kim, Jenny, and Cathy were at very different levels of cognitive development. In the present chapter, however, they were all categorized in type B.1 because they all wrote "35" fifteen times and added pairs of numbers, pairs of pairs, and so on. Children's written work is, therefore, necessary to analyze but not sufficient for an assessment of their numerical thinking.

Knowledge of Place Value. The second major aspect of assessment is children's knowledge of place value. By November 21, the great majority of those who had been in constructivist classes were simply not making place-value errors any more. However, most of the children who had learned algorithms came to third grade with serious place-value problems, and only the cognitively most advanced students in this group had overcome this handicap. As the reader saw in Chapter 11, Jenny, a transfer student, had made considerable progress, but another transfer student, Cathy, still showed many difficulties.

Execution of Plan. A child's not remembering his or her own plan often looks like simple forgetting. However, when children add many numbers but have no idea what their purpose was in adding them, this is likely to reflect an inability to organize their actions. The ability to coordinate a subgoal with the ultimate goal is one more example of a part–whole relationship (being able to think *simultaneously* about a part and the whole). As explained by Inhelder and Piaget (1959/1964), part–whole relationships are very difficult for young children. Another example of children's difficulty in remembering their plan is their getting a numerical answer such as 525 without any idea whether it means 525 days or 525 dollars.

Accuracy in Computation and Knowledge of Sums and Products. Finally, children's accuracy in computation and their knowledge of specific sums and products must also be assessed. For most children, sums were like second nature to them by November, but a few were still counting on fingers even to do 5 + 3, as stated previously. Children should eventually overcome this difficulty, but we have not studied this problem longitudinally and systematically enough to know what happens to them in the long run. As for products and multiplication tables, when children have solidly constructed the logic of multiplication, they will remember many products through frequent use. We hope they will also be motivated from within to learn other combinations by heart and to deduce the difficult combinations from the easier ones that they remember (Heege, 1985).

The four aspects just discussed overlap considerably because knowing place value and specific sums (such as $6 + 6 + 6 = 18$) helps multiplication enormously. Above-average students are generally highly competent in all four areas, but some children who can reason logically well have poor knowledge of place value. We therefore keep all four aspects in mind as we interact with children both individually and as a class.

Strategies Conceptualized Later in the Year

The preceding discussion of 15×35 concerned the beginning of third grade, and some children make dramatic progress later in the year. We therefore describe below the subsequent development of multiplication with one- and two-digit multipliers.

Multiplying Multidigit Numbers by One-Digit Numbers. Inventing a way to solve 5×245, for example, is fairly easy for children who know place value and can think multiplicatively. They simply break 245 down by digits and do the following, which is similar to "the expanded form":

$$
\begin{array}{rr}
5 \times 200 = & 1,000 \\
5 \times 40 = & 200 \\
5 \times 5 = & \underline{25} \\
& 1,225
\end{array}
$$

Multiplying Multidigit Numbers by Two-Digit Numbers. Two-digit multipliers are much harder, as we saw in Chapter 10. The various types of approaches to 51×34 are outlined first and then discussed.

    A. Incomplete attempts
    B. Breaking only one of the numbers down
       1. Into equal subgroups smaller than 10 and using addition-multiplication
       2. Into tens and ones and using addition-multiplication
    C. Breaking both numbers down into tens and ones and using addition-multiplication

Type B.1 in the preceding outline corresponds roughly to types B.2, C, and D that we saw on November 21. On November 21, the children were partitioning only one of the two numbers into subgroups smaller than 10. In the new types B.2 and C, which appeared later in the year, the children broke one or both numbers into subgroups of tens and ones.

An example of the first type in the new outline (type A, incomplete attempts) is trying to solve 51 × 34 with (50 × 30) + (1 × 4). A debate over this procedure was described in Chapter 7. This kind of incompleteness can appear only after children partition both numbers into subgroups of tens and ones.

The next type (type B.1, breaking only one of the numbers down into subgroups smaller than ten) was already seen on November 21. Two examples with respect to 51 × 34 are shown in Figure 12.3. Multiplication begins to appear more prominently in Figure 12.3b than in Figure 12.3a. In Figure 12.3b, 51 is partitioned into 50 and 1, but only as a subsequent step after partitioning 34 into 5 × 6 + 4.

In the next type (B.2), children make subgroups of 10 from the beginning. The example given in Figure 12.4 is self-explanatory and has already been presented in Chapter 6. Multiplication appears even more explicitly here than in Figure 12.3b.

Generally speaking, the next more sophisticate procedure (type C) is to break both numbers down into digits and essentially to cross-multiply, as shown in Figure 12.5a. The child here partitioned 51 into 50 and 1, and 34 into 30 and 4, and multiplied the appropriate numbers directly by 30 and by 50 instead of multiplying them by 10 many times and adding the results (as in Figure 12.4). It is important to point out that breaking both numbers down by digits and cross-multiplying is not necessarily the most sophisticated procedure. For example, the child who produced Figure 12.5b, sometimes partitioned both 34 and 51 but kept 34 whole in 1 × 34. The most efficient way thus depends on the specific numbers involved in the problem. To do 52 × 34, many children do (50 × 30) + (50 × 4) + 68.

The procedures shown in Figures 12.4 and 12.5 clearly indicate the advantages of knowing how to use the properties of our base-10 place-value system of writing. The child who produced Figure 12.4, for example, knew that to do 51 × 10, all she had to do was to write a zero after 51. It is important to point out again that in assessment we must talk to children to find out what lies behind their writing. The rule about writing a zero is worthless unless children can explain why it works. Those who have gone through the following constructive process, described in Chapter 10, can explain why 51 × 10 equals 510:

$$50 \times 10 = (10 \times 10) + (10 \times 10) + (10 \times 10) + (10 \times 10) + (10 \times 10)$$
$$= 100 + 100 + 100 + 100 + 100$$
$$= 500$$
$$1 \times 10 = 10$$
$$500 + 10 = 510$$

Figure 12.3 Breaking only one of the numbers down into subgroups smaller than ten.

```
(a)                    51
                       51
                       51
                       51
                      +51
                           250      51
                           + 5      51
                           255      51
                           255     +51
                           255      204
                           255
                           255
                           255
                          +204
                                  1,400
                                    300
                                  +  34
                                  1,734
```

```
(b)          5 x 51 = 250 + 5 = 255

        255
        255
        255
        255
        255
       +255      1,200
       1,530       300
                 +   30
                 1,530

        4 x 51 = 200 + 4 = 204
                         +1,530
                          1,734
```

We conclude this discussion of multiplication by reiterating that analysis of children's written work is necessary to conceptualize types of solutions, but that we can overestimate or underestimate children's knowledge by examining only what they write. Just as we can overestimate children's numerical thinking by looking at Figure 12.4, we can underestimate their reasoning by interpreting Figure 12.3a at face value. This computation may or may not be the highest level of a cautious child who prefers to prevent all possible confusion.

Unlike the textbook approach, teaching based on constructivism treats divi-

FIGURE 12.4 Breaking only one
of the numbers down into
subgroups of tens and ones.

```
51 x 10 = 510
51 x 10 = 510
51 x 10 = 510
51 x  4 = 204
          1734
```

sion and multiplication together as complementary processes. To illustrate the assessment of children's reactions to a division problem, we now present examples collected on April 15.

FIGURE 12.5 Breaking both numbers down into tens and ones.

(a)	(b)

```
   (a)                          (b)

50 x 30 =1500           50 x 30 = 1500

50 x 4 =  200           50 x 4 =   200

1 x 30 =   30           1 x 34 =    34

1 x 4 =     4                     1734

         1734
```

DIVISION PROBLEM

The problem given to the class on April 15 was: "There are 251 pieces of candy in the bag. How many will each person get if 22 people in the class want to share them equally?" It was not easy at first to sort the papers, and we could initially identify only one outstanding paper and four at the lower end. The two extremes are described below, beginning with the upper end.

The paper showed only the writing that can be seen in Figure 12.6. This child tried 10×22, saw that he could add another 22, and got up to 242. He then tried to give half a piece to everybody, found out that there were not enough to do that, and tried to give one-fourth to each person. The surprising thing about this paper was that we had always been satisfied with a remainder and had never worked on fractions in the context of division. This child figured out that with a remainder of 9, he could not give half a piece of candy to everybody, but that he could give one-fourth. Just as children, on their own initiative, often think of doubling, and of doubling the double, they think of a half, and then of half of a half.

Figures 12.6 Solving a division problem by explicitly using multiplication and fractions.

```
20 x 10 = 200
 2 x 10 =  20
          220
         + 22
          242  + 5 1/2 (1/2 of 11) = 247 1/2
         + 11 (1/2 of 22)
         too much           Answer:  11 1/4 r. 3 1/2
```

At the other extreme of the class was a child who wrote "251" vertically 22 times and tried to add each column. (This was also the child who was at the lowest level in the multiplication problem, 15 × 35.) Three others wrote "251 × 22" but attempted to figure out how many times 22 went into 200 and into 51.

The other 17 papers at first all looked different from one another and impossible to categorize except for the two or three here and there that were the same. By reading and rereading the papers, imagining how each child thought, and sorting and resorting the papers, it was possible tentatively to conceptualize the following types. They are outlined below and explained later.

A. Writing "251 ÷ 22" or something else that fitted the problem but having no idea how to compute the answer (three children)
B. Adding 22 repeatedly until the total reached 242 (five children)
   1. Without making subgroups (four children)
   2. Making subgroups (one child)
C. Estimating before using addition-multiplication (eight children)
   1. Adding 10 twenty-two times and being satisfied with a remainder of 31 (two children)
   2. Trying various estimates (six children)
      a. Without making subgroups (one child)
      b. Making subgroups (five children)
D. Explicitly using multiplication some of the time (two children)

It is interesting to note that repeated subtraction is seldom seen among children who invent their own procedures. The infrequent use of subtraction was also noted in South Africa by Olivier and colleagues (1991).

Type A is self-explanatory, and type B.1, repeated addition of 22, is familiar to the reader. Type B.2 (adding 22 repeatedly by making subgroups) is also familiar. As can be seen in the example in Figure 12.7, the child in type B.2 got 132 for six 22s, knew that doubling 132 would go over 251, and therefore tried adding five 22s (110) to 132. Having gotten 242 for eleven 22s, he added one more 22 to 110, got 264 by doubling the result (132), and concluded that the answer had to be 11 r. 9.

The next type (C.1), estimating 10 pieces, adding either 10 twenty-two times or 22 ten times, and being satisfied with a remainder of 31, is clearly a different approach. It is important to point out that neither type C.1 nor type C.2 is necessarily an advance over type B because estimating is simply a different strategy. One of the two children in type C.1 wrote as shown in Figure 12.8. He made a subgroup of five 10s for 5 people (and got 50), doubled the subtotal for 10 people (and got 100), doubled that subtotal for 20 people (and got 200), and added two more 10s to get the total (220) for 22 people.

In the procedures of the next subtype (C.2), the type-C.1 strategy was extended to deal with the remainder. For example, one child (see Figure 12.9) tried 10 × 22 and got up only to 220, tried 15 × 22 and went over 251, tried 13 × 22 and went over 251 again, tried 11 × 22 and got too little, and then tried 12 × 22 and went over 251. While this guess-and-check method is well known, this child's method of working is noteworthy because she made estimates for only 11 people and doubled the result. As can be seen in Figure 12.9, she essentially did 11 × 10 and doubled the result in order to try 22 × 10. To try 22 × 13, she likewise did 11 × 13 and doubled the result. However, she had a different strategy for 22 × 15: Having done 22 × 5 = 110 and 22 × 10 = 220, she simply added 110 and 220.

One of the two examples of the highest type (D), explicitly using multiplication some of the time, has already been given as the first example of solutions found on April 15. The other example can be seen in Figure 12.10. This child

FIGURE 12.7 Solving a division problem by using addition-multiplication and making subgroups.

22		22		
22		22		
+22		22		
66 (3)		22		
+66 (3)		+22		
132 (6)	+	110	=	242
		+22		
		132	=	264	Answer: 11 r. 9

FIGURE 12.8 Solving a division problem by estimating 10 and being satisfied with a remainder of 31.

10

10

10

10

+10

50 + 50 = 10 times   100

                       +100

                        200

                        +10

                        +10
                        220   **Answer: 10 r 31**

used multiplication, a higher-level operation, but was satisfied with a remainder of 31. There seems to be some inhibition to doing 22 × 1 or 1 × 22. Multiplying by 1 is perhaps felt not to be multiplication. Like many other third graders, this student used addition to get the remainder rather than using subtraction.

Division problems naturally suggest the commutativity of multiplication to children who are "ready." To solve the preceding division problem, the children thought either about how many 22s they could make or about giving 10, 15, or some other number to each person. In the process, some noticed that 11 × 22 was the same thing as 22 × 11.

CONCLUSION

Up to this point, we have discussed assessment from the standpoint of individual children and teaching. It is possible to use interviews and the types conceptualized in this chapter to report the progress over a year quantitatively to administrators and the public. The reader may have noticed that after each type outlined earlier, we sometimes gave in parentheses the number of children in that type. We can change these numbers to percentages, and by comparing the percentages at the beginning and the end of the school year, we can report the progress made during the interval. For example, with respect to the multiplica-

FIGURE 12.9 Solving a division problem by estimating 10, 15, 13, 11, and then 12.

22 x 5 = 110					
22 x 10 = 220	(less)	10	13	11	12
22 x 15 = 330	(too much)	10	13	11	12
22 x 13 = 286		10	13	11	12
22 x 11 = 242		10	13	11	12
22 x 12 = 264		10	13	11	12
		10	13	11	12
		10	13	11	12
		10	13	11	12
		10	13	11	12
		10	13	11	12
		_10_	_13_	_11_	_12_
		110	143	121	132
		_110_	_143_	_121_	_132_
		220	286	242	264

FIGURE 12.10 Solving a division problem by explicitly using multiplication.

Well theres 22 people get <u>10</u>

10 ten times is 100 then double it

200.   then thats Just 20 people.   200 + 10 = 210 + 10 = 220

220

+31
―――

251

tion problem 15 × 35, if the percentage in type B.1 (the two-at-a-time, additive procedure illustrated in Figure 11.1) went down from 60% to 20%, with corresponding increases in the higher-level types, this would evidence considerable progress.

This chapter focused only on the cognitive aspects of children's thinking. Before concluding, we would like to make another point about children's development of autonomy and personality that greatly influences their intellectual development. Children who are confident about their own ability to think and are autonomous and inventive are more likely to develop intellectually in the long run than those who lack confidence, are passive, and are concerned mainly about pleasing the teacher.

CHAPTER 13

Have You Done Any Evaluation of Your Program?

The program was evaluated by analyzing the responses of Sally's third graders to a variety of problems and comparing them with what children did in another school after three years of traditional instruction. A significant limitation of this evaluation is the small sample of children in Sally's class who had consistently had constructivist arithmetic in grades 1–3. The performance of this small group nevertheless indicates that a constructivist approach produces better results and that a similar study on a larger scale is urgently needed.

I (CK) have worked closely with the principal and some of the teachers at Hall-Kent School since 1984, but by 1991–92, only the following numbers of teachers at various grade levels did *not* teach algorithms:

> First grade: Five out of five teachers
> Second grade: Two out of four teachers
> Third grade: One out of three teachers
> Fourth grade: One out of three teachers
> Fifth grade: None of the four teachers

The reader may have noted that these proportions did not differ markedly from those of 1989–1991, reported in Chapter 3.

The preceding numbers may lead the reader to expect an entire class of third graders who had had three years of constructivist math. Since there were two second-grade teachers who did not teach any algorithms, it should have been possible to make one third-grade class with these second-grade classes. This did not happen, however, and there were only 13 children in Sally's class who had never been taught any algorithms.

The reason for this small number was that, at the end of each school year, as stated in Chapter 3, the principal mixed all the children at each grade level and assigned them to classes for the next year as randomly as possible. Some teachers in the school felt so strongly about the desirability of this annual redistribution that the principal felt compelled to go along with their demand. These teachers felt that this procedure insured heterogeneous classes with a fair distribution of easy- and hard-to-teach children.

Sally thus had 22 children in her class at the end of 1991–92, but 9 of them were either transfer students or Hall-Kent students who had been taught algorithms. Although the sample of 13 is too small for respectable statistical analyses, this is probably the only group in an American public school who had never been taught algorithms in grades 1–3 and had been encouraged to invent their own procedures. To the best of my knowledge, Piaget's theory about the nature of logico-mathematical knowledge has never been used consistently in primary arithmetic in any other public school.

To compare the outcome of three years of constructivist math with that of three years of traditional instruction, I asked two third-grade teachers in another school to let me test their children. Their school was like Hall-Kent School in that it was in a suburb of Birmingham, Alabama, but its scores on the Stanford Achievement Test were consistently much higher. The two teachers were highly respected and conscientious, and I promised to keep them and their school anonymous. Since the findings from their classes were very similar, their classes were combined to constitute a Comparison Group of 39 children.

All the children in the Constructivist Group ($n = 13$) and the Comparison Group ($n = 39$) were individually interviewed three times and given a group test of word problems in April and May of 1992. The data thus obtained do not adequately cover all the goals and objectives described in Chapters 5 and 6, but they provide enough information to indicate that children do better if they are encouraged to do their own thinking and that traditional instruction harms most children.

The data are presented in three parts. Findings about word problems are presented first to compare the two groups mostly in ability to reason logically. We then discuss data from an interview focusing on children's ability to explain *how* they got answers to easy computational problems, such as 4×13 and $32 - 18$. The third part consists of findings from two interviews about computational problems in which children's numerical reasoning was assessed. Previous comparisons had indicated that students in the two groups did equally well in pencil-and-paper computation, and I was interested in evaluating their *processes of thinking* rather than the correctness of their answers.

TESTING ABILITY TO REASON LOGICALLY USING WORD PROBLEMS

The two groups were given a test consisting of the following six word problems:

1. There are 4 people in the group. Each person has 3 pencils and 5 books. Which one of the following gives the total number of books?

———4 + 5
———4 × 3
———4 × 5
———4 + 3 + 5

2. After 4 children divided some marbles equally among themselves, there were 2 left over. Joan (one of the 4 children) got 12 marbles. How many marbles were there altogether?
3. I saw a sign saying, "Coca-Cola, 2 cans for 55 cents." How much money would I need to buy 8 cans?
4. My mother is planning a picnic for 26 people and wants to have 2 hotdogs for each person. The hotdogs come in packages of 12. How many packages does she need to buy?
5. Fifty people came to the meeting, and my father wanted to know how many of them would vote for Mr. Clinton. Eight said they did not know yet, and the others were divided equally into those who would vote for Mr. Clinton and those who would vote for Mr. Bush. How many would vote for Mr. Clinton?
6. There are 155 M&M's in a bag. If we divide them equally among the 25 people in the classroom, how many M&M's will each person get?

The six questions were photocopied on five sheets of paper stapled together, and a researcher read each problem to the class. There was a line for the answer after each question, and the children were asked to use the empty space on each sheet to show all their work. There was no time limit, and the entire class waited until everybody finished each problem and was ready to go on to the next one.

Children's ability to give correct answers was not the focus of this test, but the percentages giving correct answers do give indications of how well children reasoned logically. The percentages, presented in Table 13.1, show that the Constructivist Group reasoned significantly better than the Comparison Group in all the word problems.

The important question here is how the two groups produced wrong answers. Table 13.2 shows that the incorrect answers of the Comparison Group were due mostly to poor logic. This group did make many computational errors, but computation was not the focus of this test of word problems. The reasoning of children in the Comparison Group is discussed below in further detail with respect to each question.

Question 1

This multiple-choice question was a modification of an item included in the National Assessment of Educational Progress (Lindquist, 1989). The question

TABLE 13.1 Percentages in the Constructivist and Comparison groups giving correct answers to the word problems

	Constructivist group (N=13)	Comparison group (N=39)	Difference	Significance (2-tailed)
1. Books	100	69	31	.05
2. Marbles	92	46	46	.01
3. Coca-Cola	92	41	51	.001
4. Hot dogs	77	23	54	.001
5. Mr. Clinton	92	62	30	.05
6. M&M's	85	33	52	.001

given in its 1989 report to illustrate the item without divulging it was: "Pam has 4 pictures. There are 3 trees and 5 cars in each picture. Which number sentence gives the total number of cars in the pictures" (followed by the same four possible answers)?

This question was included in our evaluation as a means of having some basis for comparing the Alabama samples against national norms. In the National Assessment, only 69% of the third graders responded to this item, and only 32% of the 69% got the correct answer (Lindquist, 1989). Since 69% of the Comparison Group in Alabama got the correct answer to this item (refer to Table 13.1), it can be said that the Comparison Group was a superior sample considerably above the national norm.

As can be seen in Table 13.2, 26% of the Comparison Group and no one in the Constructivist Group chose the answer of "4 + 3 + 5." This was the most popular choice in the National Assessment and was selected by 41% of the 69% of third graders who responded to this item (Lindquist, 1989). The question that must be raised here is why so many third graders, both in the Comparison Group and in the National Assessment, chose such a nonsensical answer when the correct choice was in front of their eyes.

Question 2

This question was invented to assess children's understanding of division with a remainder. Although the Constructivist Group had never been given such a contorted question in class, only one child, 8%, got an incorrect answer (refer to Table 13.1). By contrast, as can be seen in Table 13.2, 54% of the Comparison Group got incorrect answers through poor logic. Some (21%) got as far as 4 × 12, but 33% gave a wide variety of incorrect answers with different kinds of faulty reasoning. Figure 13.1 shows the variety of wrong answers given by 33% of the Comparison Group and how each answer was obtained (sometimes by two children).

Table 13.2 Percentages in the Constructivist and Comparison groups evidencing poor logic in approaching word problems

	Constructivist group (N=13)	Comparison group (N=39)
1. Books		
Completely illogical procedure i.e., choosing "4 + 3 + 5"	0	26
2. Marbles		
Partly logical procedure i.e, getting as far as 4 x 12	8	21
Completely illogical procedures e.g., 4 x 10 + 2=42	0	33
3. Coca-Cola		
Partly logical procedure i.e., 8 x .55	0	33
Completely illogical procedures e.g., .55 + .55	0	13
4. Hot dogs		
Partly logical procedure e.g., getting as far as 52 hot dogs	23	21
Completely illogical procedures e.g., 12 + 12 = 24	0	46
5. Mr. Clinton		
Partly logical procedure i.e., getting as far as 50 - 8	0	23
Completely illogical procedures e.g., 25 + 4 = 29	8	15
6. M&M's		
Partly logical procedure e.g., guess-and-checking, trying 5 and then 7	8	5
Completely illogical procedures e.g., trying 155 - 25, then 155 x 25, etc.	8	54

Questions 3–6

The children in the Constructivist Group were often given questions in class similar to Questions 3, 4, and 6. The differences between the two groups can, therefore, perhaps be attributed to experience. We must nevertheless ask why the Comparison Group did so poorly.

It can be seen with respect to Question 3 in Table 13.2 that most of the errors

FIGURE 13.1 The variety of illogical responses given by 33% of the Comparison Group to Question 2. (*After 4 children divided some marbles equally among themselves, there were 2 left over. Joan (one of the 4 children) got 12 marbles. How many marbles were there altogether?*)

Answers	Procedures
56	14 x 4
42	4 x 10 + 2
	3 (children) x 10 + 12
38	12 x 3 + 2
28	4 +2 +12 28
24	12 x 2
18	4 + 2 + 12
16	12 2 x 4 16
14	12 + 4

(33%) made by the Comparison Group were produced by multiplying 55 cents by 8. The errors in Question 5 were likewise not completely nonsensical, and 23% of the Comparison Group got at least as far as 50 − 8. Question 6 may have been difficult because of the large numbers that the Comparison Group was not used to encountering.

Question 4 (hotdogs) was the hardest one for both groups, and only 77% and 23%, respectively, of the two groups got the correct answer. (It would have been better to specify that hotdogs came *only* in packages of 12 and that the mother did not mind having leftovers.) While the proportions using partly logical procedures were about the same in the two groups (23% and 21%), the majority of the Comparison Group (46%) got a large variety of wrong answers with completely illogical procedures. Figure 13.2 shows the variety of wrong answers and procedures found on the papers of the Comparison Group (sometimes more than once).

It can be seen in Figure 13.2 that, in addition to errors in logic, the Comparison Group made many computational errors. The latter will be discussed elsewhere when findings from computational problems are analyzed.

In conclusion, the Constructivist Group did better on word problems mostly because of the poor logic of the Comparison Group. Traditional instruction seems to interfere with children's development of logical reasoning by not allowing them to do their own thinking. If children's logic is poor in word problems, ability to manipulate numbers on paper is not of much use.

ASSESSING ABILITY TO EXPLAIN HOW ANSWERS WERE OBTAINED

An interview was conducted to assess children's ability to explain how they got answers to easy problems, written vertically, in multiplication and subtraction. The materials used in this interview were a blank sheet of paper, a pen, and 52 chips.

Interview About an Easy Multiplication Problem

Procedure. The procedure for the first question was the following:

1. On a blank sheet of paper, the interviewer wrote

$$\begin{array}{r} 13 \\ \times\ 4 \\ \hline \end{array}$$

and said, "Thirteen times 4." She asked the child to "work this problem," offering her pen to the child. If the child asked any question—such as "Do you want me to add or multiply?"—the interviewer replied, "I want you to do it in any way that's best for you."
2. When the child finished writing the answer, the interviewer brought the chips out and asked, "If we make four piles of 13 and 13 and 13 and 13 chips (indicating four different locations on the table in front of the child), will we have what this problem says?" All the children replied in the affirmative, and the interviewer asked the child to make two piles of 13 while she also made two piles.
3. When four piles of 13 chips each were made, the interviewer asked, "If we pushed all these together, how many chips would we have?" All the children replied, correctly, "Fifty-two."
4. The interviewer then asked the child to explain with the chips (which were still in four piles of 13 each) "how all this works" (pointing to what the child had written).
Note: The interviewer purposely did not ask the child to show her "what you

FIGURE 13.2 The variety of illogical responses given by 46% of the
Comparison Group to Question 4. (*My mother is planning a
picnic for 26 people and wants to have 2 hotdogs for each
person. The hotdogs come in packages of 12. How many
packages does she need to buy?*)

Answers	Procedures
48	12 + 12 + 12 + 12
34	1 26 12 x 2 ――― 34
24	12 x 2
14	26 -12 ――― 14
13	I counted by twos.
8	I don't know how to show you. I just got it.
4	I multiplied it.
3	12 + 12 + 12 = 36

3	Tried 12 then 26 then 12 then 12
	       x 2 +12 +26 x26
	       ――― ――― ――― ―――
	        24 38 38 32

3	12 +12
3	26 ÷12 ――― 3
2+	12 + 12 = 24 + 2 = 26

I don't know	Tried 12 then 13 then 26
	       ÷ 2 ÷12 ÷ 2
	       ――― ―――
	        26 13
	       ÷ 6
	       ―――
	        20

meant when you wrote this" because she knew that many children were following rules they did not understand.

If the child did not seem to know what to do or explained his or her writing only with words, the interviewer said, "I noticed the first thing you did was to do 4 times 3 [pointing to the respective numerals]. Could you show me *with the chips* what the 4 times 3 means?" (If, however, the child began by writing "40," the interviewer asked him or her to explain where the 40 came from.)

Some children took 3 chips from each of the four piles of 13. Most, however, made four groups of 3, or three groups of 4, with chips from only one pile of 13 and announced, "Twelve." All of these responses were accepted as good enough to be considered correct.

When a child showed a set of 4 chips and one of 3 chips (oooo   ooo) (see Figure 13.3a) to explain the meaning of 4 × 3, however, the interviewer said, "I see only 7, but you said 4 times 3 made 12. Can you show me how 4 times 3 makes 12?"

5. The interviewer then asked the child to explain with the chips every subsequent step of the written procedure. For example, if the child got 12 for 4 × 3 and wrote "2" below the line and "1" above the 1 of 13, the interviewer asked him or her to show with the chips what "this part [pointing to the 2]" meant and what "this part [pointing to the 1 carried]" meant.

Note: The interviewer was careful to use the term "this part," rather than "one" or "ten."

6. If the child showed only 4 chips (oooo) to explain 4 × 1 (see Figure 13.3b), the interviewer remarked, "You used all these [pointing to the chips the child had used to explain 4 × 3 and 4 × 1] to explain how 'all this' works [pointing to the child's writing]. But you didn't use any of these [pointing to the unused chips]. Were you supposed to use all of them, or were you not supposed to?"

The interviewer thus asked questions that might prompt a better explanation if the child did not adequately explain the written procedure on his or her own.

Findings. Before presenting the results, it is important to point out that these tasks and materials were completely unfamiliar to all the children both in the Constructivist Group and in the Comparison Group. None of these third graders in either group had worked with chips as an aid for understanding computational procedures.

As can be seen in Table 13.3, all the children in both groups wrote the correct answer of 52. Almost all the children (97%) in the Comparison Group used the algorithm, while none in the Constructivist Group did. The procedures of the Constructivist Group were distributed as follows:

FIGURE 13.3 The chips shown by some children to explain (a) 4 × 3 and
(b) 4 × 1.

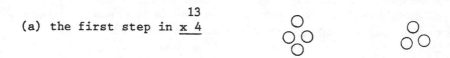

```
                        13
(a) the first step in  x 4
```

```
                       13
(b) the next step in  x 4
```

40 (written by seven children)
+12
52

13 (written by two children)
13
13
+13
52

26 (written by two children)
+26
52

39 (written by one child)
+13
52

One child wrote the first three of the preceding procedures.

The proportion who adequately explained all the steps of their written computation was 92% for the Constructivist Group and only 5% for the Comparison
Group ($p < .001$). The inability of the Comparison Group to explain the algorithm they had used correctly was due mostly to their poor knowledge of place
value. Forty-seven percent of this group "carried" only one chip when they carried the 1 of 12. Eighty-seven percent interpreted the 1 of 13 as a one and
showed only four chips (oooo) to explain the 4 × 1 part (see Figure 13.3b). It
was truly amazing that when asked whether or not all 52 of the chips had to be

TABLE 13.3 Percentages in the Constructivist and Comparison groups
explaining how they got the answer to $\times 4$ $\frac{13}{}$

	Constructivist group ($\underline{N}$=13)	Comparison group ($\underline{N}$=39)	Difference	Significance (2-tailed)
Correct answer (52)	100	100	0	
Use of algorithm	0	97	97	.001
Adequate explanation of all the steps	92	5	87	.001
Interpreting the "1" of "13" as a one	0	87	87	.001

used to explain the algorithm, these third graders said that it was not necessary to use all of them.

It can be concluded that the children in the Constructivist Group used a variety of procedures they had invented and could explain their own reasoning. By contrast, those in the Comparison Group could get the correct answer by using the algorithm that had been taught but could not explain the conventional algorithm.

It is significant that one of the 39 children in the Comparison Group immediately wrote the answer of 52, without writing anything else. After explaining that 10 four times made 40, and that 3 four times made 12, she took 10 chips from each of the four piles of 13 to show where the 40 came from and then pushed together the four groups of 3 each that remained on the table, saying "Four 3s is 12." This child attests to the fact that alert, bright, and autonomous children can invent their own procedures *in spite of* the instruction they receive.

Interview About an Easy Subtraction Problem

Procedure. The procedure for the second question was as follows:

1. On the other side of the paper the interviewer wrote

$$\frac{32}{-18}$$

as she said, "Thirty-two minus 18." She asked the child to "work this problem," offering her pen to the child.
2. When the child finished writing the answer, the interviewer put all the chips in front of the child and said, "I'd like you to explain with these chips how all

FIGURE 13.4 The chips shown by some children to explain regrouping

(borrowing) in $\begin{array}{r} 32 \\ -18 \\ \hline \end{array}$

(a) The $'2$ in $\cancel{3}'2$ O   ⅋O

(b) The $\cancel{3}$ in $\cancel{3}'2$ °O

this works that you wrote. Let's count out 32 chips for this number that you had before taking 18 away [pointing to the 32 on the paper]."

3. When the child was satisfied that there were 32 chips, the interviewer asked for an explanation of each step in the written procedure. If the child did not seem to know what to do, the interviewer focused on the child's sequence of writing by saying, for example, "I noticed the first thing you did was to cross this out [pointing to the slashed 3 in 32], and then you wrote this [pointing to the 2 written above the slashed 3]. Could you show me with the chips what this mark means [pointing to the slash across the 3] and what this number means [pointing to the 2 above the slashed 3]?"

4. The interviewer asked for an explanation of every subsequent step (changing the 2 to 12, subtracting 8 from 12, writing "4," subtracting 10 from 20, and writing "1").

5. If the child showed only one chip next to two chips (o   oo) to explain what 12 meant (see Figure 13.4a) and/or only two chips (oo) to explain what the 2 above the slashed 3 meant (see Figure 13.4b), the interviewer pointed out, "You used all of these chips [pointing to the chips used to explain borrowing and subtracting] to explain what you wrote but not any of these [pointing to the unused chips]. Are you supposed to use all the chips, or don't you need to use all of them?" The purpose of this probe was to offer to the child a chance to correct himself or herself.

Findings. As can be seen in Table 13.4, 97% of the Comparison Group got the correct answer of 14 by using the algorithm, and 85% of the Constructivist

TABLE 13.4 Percentages in the Constructivist and Comparison groups explaining how they got the answer to $\frac{32}{-18}$

	Constructivist group ($\underline{N}$=13)	Comparison group ($\underline{N}$=39)	Difference	Significance (2-tailed)
Correct answer (14)	85	97	12	n.s.
Use of algorithm	0	100	100	.001
Adequate explanation of all the steps (percentages only of those who got the correct answer)	100	21	79	.001
Interpreting the tens as ones	0	87	87	.001

Group got this answer. In the Constructivist Group, 10 of the 11 children who got the correct answer used one of the following two procedures:

$$30 - 10 = 20 \qquad 2 - 8 = \text{negative } 6$$
$$2 - 8 = \text{negative } 6 \qquad 30 - 10 = 20$$
$$20 - 6 = 14 \qquad 20 - 6 = 14$$

The eleventh child's way was the following:

I need 2 to get to 20, and from 20 to 32 is 12.
So the answer is $12 + 2 = 14$.

In the Constructivist Group, those who got the correct answer could all explain how they got it. By contrast, only 21% of those in the Comparison Group who got the correct answer could explain the algorithm they were using ($p <$ .001). The difficulty of the Comparison Group was again due mostly to poor knowledge of place value. Seventy-two percent of the Comparison Group showed 2 chips instead of 20 to explain the last step of the conventional algorithm ($20 - 10$). By contrast, those in the Constructivist Group all interpreted the tens as tens ($p <$ .001). The children in the Comparison Group who could not explain the algorithm all said that it was not necessary to use all 32 chips to explain their written procedure.

It can be concluded that while almost all the children in the Comparison Group produced the correct answer to $32 - 18$ written vertically, only a small proportion (21%) could explain how they got the correct answer. By contrast, in the Constructivist Group, the proportion producing the correct answer was smaller (85%), but these children could all explain how they got their answer.

TABLE 13.5 Percentages in ths Constructivist and Comparison groups giving correct answers to computational problems

	Constructivist group ($\underline{N}$=13)	Comparison group ($\underline{N}$=39)	Difference	Significance (2-tailed)
195 + 65	100	41	59	.001
299 + 301	92	54	38	.05
612 - 513	92	38	54	.001
642 -368	69	46	23	n.s.
99 x 7	62	5	57	.001
Simplifying problem to: (700 - 7)	38	0	38	.001
13 x 11	31	13	18	n.s.
504 -306	77	49	28	n.s.
6 + 53 + 185	77	26	51	.001

ASSESSING NUMERICAL REASONING USING COMPUTATIONAL PROBLEMS

Correct and Incorrect Answers

The problems shown in Table 13.5 were photocopied on one sheet and presented to each child in individual interviews. The child was first asked to give the answer to the first question, and if he or she requested a pencil, the interviewer said, "I know you can do it with a pencil, and I want to know what you do with just your head." After writing the first answer down and circling it, the interviewer asked, "How did you get [the answer]?" and recorded the procedure explained by the child. This procedure of recording the answer and the method used to get it was repeated for every subsequent item. When necessary, questions were asked for clarification.

As can be seen in Table 13.5, the Constructivist Group gave higher percentages of correct answers for all the items. The difference was not always statistically significant, but the pattern was consistent. The significant differences, however, lay not in correct answers but in the methods used to get the answers and in the number sense revealed by the magnitude of wrong answers.

It can be seen in Table 13.6 that almost all the children in the Comparison Group used algorithms for problems that could have been solved more easily

TABLE 13.6 Percentages in the Constructivist and Comparison groups using algorithms

	Constructivist group (N=13)	Comparison group (N=39)
195 + 65	8	90
299 + 301	8	87
612 - 513	8	95
504 -306	8	100

with other methods. By contrast, the children in the Constructivist Group used the following variety of methods to tackle the first problem, 195 + 65:

195 + 5 + 60	four children
90 + 60 + 10 + 100	four children
90 + 60 + 100 + 10	two children
100 + 150 + 10	one child
95 + 60 + 5 + 100	one child
The algorithm of carrying	one child

The last child in the preceding list was the only child in the Constructivist Group who was regularly taught algorithms at home. She was a slow developer, and this combination of slow development and algorithms often produced the 8% of poor performance in the Constructivist Group.

The magnitude of wrong answers given by the Comparison Group revealed the poor number sense resulting from the teaching of algorithms. The Comparison Group gave the following incorrect answers to 195 + 65, many of which were outlandish: 1,160, 578, 280, 270, 270, 270, 265, 261, 250, 250, 250, 250, 250, 250, 230, 228, 225, 215, 200, 200, 170, and 150. (One child said, "I want to skip it.")

With respect to the subtraction problem of 612 − 513, a similar point can be made. The methods used by the Constructivist Group were the following five:

600 − 500 = 100	
12 − 13 = negative 1	
100 − 1 = 99	six children

600 − 500 = 100	
10 − 10 = 0	
2 − 3 = negative 1	
100 − 1 = 99	four children

$$600 - 500 + 12 - 13 = 99 \qquad \text{one child}$$

$$513 + 100 = 613$$
$$\text{So } 513 + 99 = 612 \qquad \text{one child}$$

The algorithm of borrowing   one child

As for the incorrect answers obtained, one child in the Constructivist Group "subtracted up" and got 101. In the Comparison Group, by contrast, poor number sense was manifested in many of the following answers: 901, 410, 199, 199, 196, 191, 190, 135, 119, 116, 109, 109, 109, 109, 103, 101, 101, 91, 19, 10, 9, and 1. (Two children claimed to need a pencil.)

The preceding pattern remained the same when the other subtraction problem in Table 13.6, 504 − 306, was presented in vertical form. While 100% of the Comparison Group used the algorithm, the Constructivist Group used the following three procedures:

$$500 - 300 = 200$$
$$200 - 2 = 198 \qquad \text{eleven children (one of whom got the}$$
$$\text{answer of 180)}$$

$$200 + 300 = 500 \qquad \text{one child}$$
$$4 - 6 \ldots, \text{I'm stuck.}$$

The algorithm of borrowing   one child

The incorrect answers in the Constructivist Group were 205, 202, and 180. By contrast, those in the Comparison Group were the following, most of which were unreasonable: 892, 891, 891, 801, 801, 398, 308, 299, 298, 208, 207, 202, 202, 196, 108, 108, 108, 108, 108, and 107.

The pattern for another subtraction problem, 642 − 368 written vertically (refer to Table 13.5), was less extreme but similar. The children in the Constructivist Group used a variety of procedures, and the incorrect answers they got were 317, 273, 226, and 224. The Comparison Group, by contrast, all used the algorithm of borrowing and got wrong answers, many of which deviated much more from the right one, namely, 724, 574, 492, 472, 472, 472, 374, 374, 364, 326, 286, 284, 284, 284, 284, 283, 244, 226, 174, and 74. (One child did not want to even try.)

One of the multiplication problems, 99 × 7, was given to find out how many children thought of simplifying it to something like 700 − 7. Most of the children in the Constructivist Group, 62%, got the correct answer, 38% by changing the problem to 700 − 7. An example of a different way is the following:

90 plus 90 = 180, plus 90 is 270, plus 270 is 540, plus 99 is 639.
9 plus 9 = 18, plus 18 is 36, plus 18 is 54.
I added 54 to 639 and got 693.

By contrast, all the children in the Comparison Group used only one approach, the conventional algorithm, and only 5% got the correct answer. (The wrong answers obtained cannot be compared, as we let children give up when they seemed frustrated.)

The other problems in Table 13.5 are not discussed, but the pattern was always the same. The Constructivist Group used a variety of procedures, got more correct answers, and made more reasonable errors when they got incorrect answers. The Comparison Group by and large had only one way of approaching each problem—the conventional algorithm—and tended to get incorrect answers that revealed poor number sense.

Reasoning, Independent of Correctness of Answers

We wanted to know how the children *reasoned* about certain computational problems, independent of the correctness of the answers. To study reasoning, we devised two methods.

Questions About the Logic of Multiplication. The following problems were photocopied, and the children were asked to solve each of them by using the work below it that another student had already begun. These questions were presented in individual interviews to make sure that the respondent used the work already done by "another student."

$$34 \times 6 = \underline{}$$

$$\begin{array}{r} 34 \\ 34 \\ +34 \\ \hline 102 \end{array}$$

$$14 \times 12 = \underline{}$$

$$14 \times 10 = 140$$

$$22 \times 15 = \underline{}$$

$$22 \times 10 = 220$$

This was an unfamiliar type of problem for both groups of children, but the students who invented their own procedures for multiplication clearly had the advantage. As can be seen in Table 13.7, many children answered the first ques-

TABLE 13.7 Percentages in the Constructivist and Comparison groups giving correct answers to computational problems by completing another student's work

	Constructivist group ($\underline{N}$=13)	Comparison group ($\underline{N}$=39)	Difference	Significance (2-tailed)
34 x 6 = _____ 34 34 +34 102	92	79	13	n.s.
14 x 12 = _____ 14 x 10 = 140	92	41	51	.01
22 x 15 = _____ 22 x 10 = 220	85	33	52	.001

tion correctly both in the Constructivist Group (92%) and in the Comparison Group (79%). However, when repeated addition was not explicitly written in the second question, 14×12, and the multiplicand increased from 6 to 12, the percentage in the Comparison Group decreased sharply (from 79% to 41%), while it remained unchanged (92%) in the Constructivist Group. In the third question, 22×15, the percentages fell slightly in both groups.

An analysis of the procedures used by the Comparison Group to answer the second question, 14×12, revealed their lack of understanding of multiplication. Following is a list of procedures they used:

$14 \times 12 = 140 + 2$	(seven children)
$14 \times 12 = 140 + (2 \times 12)$	(two children)
$14 \times 12 = 140 + (2 \times 10)$	(two children)
$14 \times 12 = 140 \times 2$	(two children)
$14 \times 12 = 140 + (2 \times 4)$	(one child)
I don't know	(nine children)

More than half of the children in the Comparison Group thus demonstrated their inadequate understanding of 14×12.

A Question Requiring No Computation. Finally, we asked the following word problem: "I am planning a big party for 98 people and want 4 cookies for each person. Cookies come in boxes of 100. How many boxes should I buy?" This question was photocopied, and the interviewer presented it to each child by asking, "Shall I read it aloud, or would *you* like to read it?"

As can be seen in Table 13.8, the percentage getting the obvious answer of

TABLE 13.8 Percentages in the Constructivist and Comparison groups giving the correct answer with and without computation

	Constructivist group ($\underline{N}$=13)	Comparison group ($\underline{N}$=39)	Difference	Significance (2-tailed)
Without computation	69	15	54	.001
With computation	8	5	3	n.s.

four boxes without computation was 69 for the Constructivist Group and only 15 for the Comparison Group ($p < .001$). The other children in both groups tried to compute 4×98 with much difficulty and to divide the result by 100. Only 8% and 5%, respectively, got the correct answer by computing it.

It must be pointed out that the children in the Constructivist Group had been given this type of problem in class two or three times during the year but that the Comparison Group probably had not. If the Comparison Group did not get this kind of problem in class, as well as a variety of other nonroutine problems, the absence of such nonroutine problems was one of the weaknesses of traditional instruction.

CONCLUSION

It can be concluded from the preceding analyses that the children who had three years of constructivist arithmetic generally did better than the traditionally instructed children both in logical and in numerical reasoning. The data show that children become better thinkers when they are encouraged to do their own thinking.

For those who are skeptical about basing an evaluation on a sample of 13, I now focus on the Comparison Group, which represented a socioeconomically advantaged segment of third graders in general. As far as their qualitative reasoning in word problems was concerned, their logic was often poor (Table 13.2). The traditionally instructed children also tried to compute an answer when computation was superfluous (Table 13.8). With respect to numerical reasoning, traditionally taught children had only one way to approach each operation and used the conventional algorithm even for problems such as $195 + 65$ and $612 - 513$ (Table 13.6). When asked to explain the algorithms they were using, most of the traditionally instructed children could not explain them (Tables 13.3 and 13.4). Their number sense was generally poor because their knowledge of place value was shaky. This point was also made with larger samples in Chapter 3.

Telling children how to add, subtract, multiply, and divide and how to apply each algorithm to word problems hampers their development of logico-mathematical knowledge. Arithmetic has long been taught as if it were social (conventional) knowledge, and we urgently need to teach it as logico-mathematical knowledge.

The program can also be evaluated from another point of view. Among the characteristics of a scientific endeavor mentioned by Piaget are meticulous observation, interpretation of observation in relation to deep theoretical principles, and the necessity of discussion and verification among the participants in the enterprise.

We have reported many children's ways of solving problems without using conventional algorithms. We have analyzed what they did and how they explained their reasoning, linking these observations to deep principles of Piaget's constructivism. As a team of theorist (CK) and teacher (SL), we exchanged points of view all along about children's progress and difficulties. Equally important is the fact that the children were encouraged to exchange ideas among themselves and to elaborate their own theory of what addition, subtraction, multiplication, and division are all about.

We hope that the reader will recognize the scientific theory building both on the part of the adults about education and on the part of the children about mathematics. Only through discussion and verification can we hope to construct an adequate theory about the teaching of mathematics.

APPENDIX

RESOURCES

COMMERCIALLY MADE GAMES

Readers are referred to the next section for the catalogs mentioned here.

The Allowance Game. (1984). Carson, CA: Lakeshore Curriculum Materials. (Listed in Toys to Grow On catalog.)

Fish. (1975). Racine, WI: Western Publishing Co.

Lotto Calcul. (1984). Germany: Ravensburger. (Discontinued)

Mille Bornes. (1982). Beverly, MA: Parker Brothers.

Multiplication Dominoes. (1981). Leicester, England: Taskmaster Limited. (Listed in Didax catalog.)

Number Rings. (1976). P. M. Merom Hagalil, Israel: Orda Industries, Ltd. (Also called *Ring-A-Round*)

Numbers Challenge. (1990). Taiwan: Kaidy International, Inc. (Listed in Nasco catalog)

1 × 1 Bingo. (1984). Germany: Ravensburger. (Discontinued)

101. (1978). Hanover Park, IL: Gerry Products Co. (Discontinued)

O'N099. (1982). Joliet, IL: International Games, Inc.

Quad-Ominos. (1978). New York: Pressman Toy Corp.

Ring-A-Round. (1976). P. M. Merom Hagalil, Israel: Orda Industries, Ltd. (Also called *Number Rings*)

Ring Toss. (n.d.) (Listed in World Wide Games catalog)

Rummikub. (1985). New York: Pressman Toy Corp.

Safe Dart Game. (Listed from time to time in Paragon catalog)

Shoot the Moon. (n.d.). Grand Rapids, MI: Wm. F. Drueke & Sons. (Listed in World Wide Games catalog)

Snap. (n.d.) Racine, WI: Western Publishing Co.

'Smath. (1984). New York: Pressman Toy Corp. (Listed in ETA catalog)

Tabby Cats. (1983). Leicester, England: Taskmaster Limited.

Table Shapes. (1979). Leicester, England: Taskmaster Limited. (Listed in Didax and Nasco catalogs)

Tribulations. (1981). Racine, WI: Western Publishing Co. (Discontinued)

Twenty-Four. (1989). Easton, PA: Suntex International, Inc. (Listed in Creative Publications, ETA, and Nasco catalogs)

Vantage. (1985). Joliet, IL: International Games, Inc.

X from Outer Space. (1985). Pleasant Hill, CA: Discovery Toys. (Discontinued)

Yahtzee. (1956). Springfield, MA: Milton Bradley Co.

COMPANIES WITH MAIL-ORDER CATALOGS

The list of firms given here is intended to assist teachers in ordering some of the commercially made games and game equipment described in Chapter 8. The information presented was current when this book went to press.

Creative Publications, 5040 West 111th St., Oak Lawn, IL 60453
Cuisenaire Co. of America, P. O. Box 5026, White Plains, NY 10602-5026
Didax Educational Resources, 395 Main St., Rowley, MA 01969
ETA, 620 Lakeview Parkway, Vernon Hills, IL 60061
Hearth Song, P. O. Box B, Sebastopol, CA 95473-0601
Nasco, P. O. Box 901, Fort Atkinson, WI 53538-0901
Norm Thompson, P. O. Box 3999, Portland, OR 97208
The Paragon, 89 Tom Harvey Road, Westerly, RI 02891
Toys to Grow On, P. O. Box 17, Long Beach, CA 90801
World Wide Games, P. O. Box 517, Colchester, CT 06415-0517

References

Bennedbek, B. (1981). Is self-taught well taught? *Mathematics Teaching*, No. 95 (June), 11–13.

Bickerton-Ross, L. (1988). A practical experience in problem solving: A "10 000" display. *Arithmetic Teacher, 36,* 14–15.

Broadbent, F. W. (1975). "Contig": A game to practice and sharpen skills and facts in the four fundamental operations. In S. E. Smith, Jr., & C. A. Backman (Eds.), *Games and puzzles for elementary and middle school mathematics* (pp. 58–60). Reston, VA: National Council of Teachers of Mathematics.

Burns, M. (1987). *A collection of math lessons from grades 3 through 6.* Sausalito, CA: Marilyn Burns Education Associates.

Burns, M. (1992a). *About teaching mathematics: A K–8 resource.* Sausalito, CA: Marilyn Burns Education Associates.

Burns, M. (1992b). *Math and literature (K–3).* Sausalito, CA: Marilyn Burns Education Associates.

Burns, M. (1992/93). A focus issue—Arithmetic. *Newsletter for Math Solutions Participants,* No. 14. (Available from Marilyn Burns Education Associates, 150 Gate 5 Road, Suite 101, Sausalito, CA 94965)

Carraher, T. N., Carraher, D. W., & Schliemann, A. D. (1987). Written and oral mathematics. *Journal for Research in Mathematics Education, 18,* 83–97.

Carraher, T. N., & Schliemann, A. D. (1985). Computation routines prescribed by schools: Help or hindrance? *Journal for Research in Mathematics Education, 16,* 37–44.

Clark, F. B. (1993). *Identification of multiplicative thinking in children in grades 1–5.* Unpublished doctoral dissertation, University of Alabama at Birmingham.

Cobb, P., & Merkel, G. (1989). Thinking strategies as an example of teaching arithmetic through problem solving. In P. Trafton (Ed.), *1989 Yearbook of the National Council of Teachers of Mathematics* (pp. 70–81). Reston, VA: National Council of Teachers of Mathematics.

Cobb, P., Wood, T., Yackel, E. Nicholls, J., Wheatley, G., Trigatti, B., & Perlwitz, M. (1991). Assessment of a problem-centered second-grade mathematics project. *Journal for Research in Mathematics Education, 22*(1), 3–29.

Doise, W., & Mugny, G. (1984). *The social development of the intellect.* New York: Pergamon. (Original work published 1981)

Duckworth, E. (1987). *"The having of wonderful ideas" and other essays on teaching and learning.* New York: Teachers College Press.

Golick, M. (1973). *Deal me in.* New York: Jeffrey Norton Publishers.

Gréco, P., Grize, J. B., Papert, S., & Piaget, J. (1960). *Problèmes de la construction du nombre.* Paris: Presses Universitaires de France.

Groza, V. S. (1968). *A survey of mathematics: Elementary concepts and their historical development*. New York: Holt, Rinehart and Winston.

Heege, H. ter. (1985). The acquisition of basic multiplication skills. *Educational Studies in Mathematics, 16*, 375–388.

Inhelder, B., & Piaget, J. (1958). *The growth of logical thinking from childhood to adolescence*. New York: Basic Books. (Original work published 1955)

Inhelder, B., & Piaget, J. (1963). De L'Itération des actions à la récurrence élémentaire. In P. Gréco, B. Inhelder, B. Matalon, & J. Piaget (Eds.), *La Formation des raisonnement récurrentiels* (pp. 47–120). Paris: Presses Universitaires de France.

Inhelder, B., & Piaget, J. (1964). *The early growth of logic in the child*. New York: Harper & Row. (Original work published 1959)

Inhelder, B., Sinclair, H., & Bovet, M. (1974). *Learning and the development of cognition*. Cambridge, MA: Harvard University Press.

Jones, D. A. (1975). Don't just mark the answer—Have a look at the method! *Mathematics in School, 4*(3), 29–31.

Kamii, C. (1982). *Number in preschool and kindergarten*. Washington, DC: National Association for the Education of Young Children.

Kamii, C. (1985). *Young children reinvent arithmetic*. New York: Teachers College Press.

Kamii, C. (1989a). *Young children continue to reinvent arithmetic, 2nd grade*. New York: Teachers College Press.

Kamii, C. (1989b). *Double-column addition: A teacher uses Piaget's theory* (videotape). New York: Teachers College Press.

Kamii, C. (1990a). *Multiplication of two-digit numbers: Two teachers using Piaget's theory*. New York: Teachers College Press.

Kamii, C. (1990b). *Multidigit division: Two teachers using Piaget's theory*. New York: Teachers College Press.

Kamii, C., & DeVries, R. (1980). *Group games in early education*. Washington, DC: National Association for the Education of Young Children.

Lankford, F. G. (1974). What can a teacher learn about a pupil's thinking through oral interviews? *Arithmetic Teacher, 21*(1), 26–32.

Lindquist, M. M. (Ed.) (1989). *Results from the Fourth Mathematics Assessment of the National Assessment of Educational Progress*. Reston, VA: National Council of Teachers of Mathematics.

Madell, R. (1985). Children's natural processes. *Arithmetic Teacher, 32*(7), 20–22.

Murray, H., & Olivier, A. (1989). A model of understanding two-digit numeration and computation. In G. Vergnaud, J. Rogalski, & M. Artigue (Eds.), *Proceedings of the Thirteenth International Conference, International Group for the Psychology of Mathematics Education* (pp. 3–10). Paris: Centre National de Recherches Scientifiques.

Murray, H., Olivier, A., & Human, P. (1992). The development of young students' division strategies. In *Proceedings of the Sixteenth International Conference, International Group for the Psychology of Mathematics Education* (Vol. 2; pp. 152–159). Durham: University of New Hampshire.

National Council of Teachers of Mathematics. (1989). *Curriculum and evaluation standards for school mathematics*. Reston, VA: National Council of Teachers of Mathematics.

Olivier, A., Murray, H., & Human, P. (1990). Building on young children's informal mathematical knowledge. In G. Booker, P. Cobb, & T. N. Mendicuti (Eds.), *Proceedings of the Fourteenth International Conference, International Group for the Psychology of Mathematics Education* (Vol. 3; pp. 297–304). Oaxtepec, Mexico.

Olivier, A., Murray, H., & Human, P. (1991). Children's solution strategies for division problems. In R. G. Underhill (Ed.), *Proceedings of the Thirteenth Annual Meeting, North American Chapter of the International Group for the Psychology of Mathematics Education* (Vol. 2; pp. 15–21). Blacksburg, VA: Virginia Polytechnic Institute and State University.

Pearson, E. S. (1986). Summing it all up: Pre-1900 algorithms. *Arithmetic Teacher, 33*(7), 38–41.

Perret-Clermont, A.-N. (1980). *Social interaction and cognitive development in children*. New York: Academic Press. (Original work published 1979)

Piaget, J. (1928). *Judgment and reasoning in the child*. London: Kegan Paul Trench Trubner. (Original work published 1924)

Piaget, J. (1929). *The child's conception of the world*. London: Routledge & Kegan Paul. (Original work published 1926)

Piaget, J. (1948). *Le Langage et la pensée chez l'enfant* (3rd ed.). Neuchâtel (Switzerland): Delachaux & Niestlé. (Original work published 1923)

Piaget, J. (1950a). *Introduction à l'épistémologie génétique: Vol. 1. La pensée mathématique*. Paris: Presses Universitaires de France.

Piaget, J. (1950b). *Introduction à l'épistémologie génétique: Vol. 2. La pensée physique*. Paris: Presses Universitaires de France.

Piaget, J. (1950c). *Introduction à l'éspitémologie génétique: Vol. 3. La pensée scientifique en biologie, en psychologie et en sociologie*. Paris: Presses Universitaire de France.

Piaget, J. (1952). *The origins of intelligence in children*. New York: International University Press. (Original work published 1936)

Piaget, J. (1954). *The construction of reality in the child*. New York: Basic Books. (Original work published 1937)

Piaget, J. (1962). *Play, dreams, and imitation in childhood*. New York: Norton. (Original work published 1945)

Piaget, J. (1963). *The psychology of intelligence*. Paterson, NJ: Littlefield, Adams & Co. (Original work published 1947)

Piaget, J. (1965a). *Etudes sociologiques*. Geneva, Switzerland: Librairie Droz.

Piaget, J. (1965b). *The moral judgment of the child*. New York: Free Press. (Original work published 1932)

Piaget, J. (Ed.). (1967). *Logique et connaissance scientifique*. Paris: Gallimard.

Piaget, J. (1971). *Biology and knowledge*. Chicago: University of Chicago Press. (Original work published 1967)

Piaget, J. (1973). *To understand is to invent*. New York: Viking. (Original work published 1948)

Piaget, J. (1976). Ecrits sociologiques. *Revue Européenne des Sciences Sociales, 14,* 44–123.

Piaget, J. (1981). *Experiments in contradiction*. Chicago: University of Chicago Press. (Original work published 1974)

Piaget, J. (1987). *Possibility and necessity*. Minneapolis: University of Minnesota Press. (Original work published 1983)

Piaget, J., & Garcia, R. (1974). *Understanding causality*. New York: Norton. (Original work published 1971)

Piaget, J., & Garcia, R. (1989). *Psychogenesis and the history of science*. New York: Columbia University Press. (Original work published 1983)

Piaget, J., & Inhelder, B. (1969). *The psychology of the child*. New York: Basic Books. (Original work published 1966)

Piaget, J., Inhelder, B., & Szeminska, A. (1960). *The child's conception of geometry*. London: Routledge & Kegan Paul. (Original work published 1948)

Plunkett, S. (1979). Decomposition and all that rot. *Mathematics in School, 8*(3), 2–7.

Ross, S. H. (1986, April). *The development of children's place-value numeration concepts in grades two through five*. Paper presented at the annual meeting of the American Educational Research Association, San Francisco. (ERIC Document Reproduction Service No. ED 273 482)

Ross, S. H. (1990). Children's acquisition of place-value numeration concepts: The roles of cognitive development and instruction. *Focus on Learning Problems in Mathematics, 12*(1), 1–17.

Schwartz, D. M. (1985). *How much is a million?* New York: Lothrop, Lee & Shepard Books.

Slavin, R. E. (1990). *Cooperative learning: Theory, research, and practice*. Englewood Cliffs, NJ: Prentice-Hall.

Smith, D. E. (1925). *History of mathematics* (Vol. 2). Boston: Ginn and Co.

Szeminska, A., & Piaget, J. (1977). From coproperties to covariations: The equalization and estimation of inequalities. In J. Piaget, J.-B. Grize, A. Szeminska, & V. Bang (Eds.), *Epistemology and psychology of functions*. Boston: D. Reidel. (Original work published 1968)

Taylor, F. S. (1949). *A short history of scientific thought*. New York: Norton.

Thornton, C. A., & Noxon, C. (1977). *Look into the facts: Multiplication and division*. Palo Alto, CA: Creative Publications.

Treffers, A. (1987). Integrated column arithmetic according to progressive schematisation. *Educational Studies in Mathematics, 18*, 125–145.

U.S. Department of Education. (1991). *America 2000: An education strategy*. Washington, DC: U.S. Government Printing Office.

Index

About the Author

Constance Kamii is Professor in the School of Education at the University of Alabama at Birmingham. She previously held a joint appointment in the College of Education, University of Illinois at Chicago and in the Faculty of Psychology and Sciences of Education, University of Geneva, Switzerland. Following receipt of her Ph.D. from the University of Michigan in 1965, she was a research fellow under Jean Piaget at the International Center of Genetic Epistemology and the University of Geneva.

44